MW01247331

Growing Up Superheroes
The Extraordinary Adventures of Deihlia Nye

by Diane Fraser

Author's note: This is a memoir. The stories in this book are based on true stories and memories, but may not be entirely factual. Other than family members, all the characters and some places have fictitious names, in order to protect their privacy. Some stories are composite renderings, taken from a variety of sources.

Library of Congress Cataloging-in-Publication data

Fraser, Diane

Growing Up Superheroes / by Diane Fraser

ISBN: 9780692288924 (paperback)

1. Diane Fraser – Memoir

Published under Diane Fraser's imprint The Cosmic Thread

Book design by Chelsea Nye/ Blinkofanye.com

Inside illustrations by Paul Gould

For photos and to learn more visit: growingupsuperheroes.com

For Deihlia,

and everyone who loves her.

Chapters

Chapters (continued)

Chapters (continued)

"According to Australian Aborigines, the story owns the storyteller. The big stories are hunting the right people to tell them."

- Robert Moss

Perhaps the big stories hunt the right people to live them.

On the Fence, 1983

My sister's baby crashed into the world three weeks early, on December 17, 1983. Our mom arrived at the hospital just in time to see her newborn granddaughter before they took her away for emergency surgery. "Her fists were pumping, she was screaming, her heart and lungs are good. She's a fighter," Mom said. But Deihlia was born with spina bifida. She had a lump of tissue on her lower back where the nerve endings of her spinal cord tangled together abruptly. That wasn't all - her abdomen was wide open. Organs were on the outside of her body, she had one tenth of the intestines she should have, and she had no bladder. In the midst of the turmoil, my sister Donna's husband Linc named her Deihlia, an old family name from deep in his family's past.

Deihlia required immediate surgery, and the best surgeon was seventy-five miles north, in Boston. Donna's doctor was apologetic, distraught, and deeply upset. We'd had a feeling something was wrong during her pregnancy, and when she talked to him about it, he assured her everything was ok. No tests, no worries. Shock, confusion, chaos. Welcome to the world, little star.

My sister Donna was nineteen, two years younger than me. She'd gotten married at seventeen, moved to Cape Cod with her husband Linc, who was twenty-seven, and less than a year later she became pregnant with Deihlia. As the baby grew inside her, we became closer. My mother and I gathered around her to build bridges for her and the child she was bringing into our family. A new life was entering ours. Donna was so young and going through something very adult - carrying a child for almost nine months then having her taken away almost immediately, after a brief and tumultuous hello.

We learned that spina bifida is a condition that begins in utero, with abnormal growth of the spinal column. Sometimes it affects not just the child's body, but also their brain. The condition has a range of expressions, from mild to severe. Deihlia had the most severe form since her spinal cord ended in a lump on her lower back, leading to paralysis. It wasn't yet clear if it had affected her brain. The condition had many other possible complications, including one in which the brainstem and cerebellum extend down into the neck, causing multiple problems, such as choking, breathing problems, and swallowing issues. We were also told that the reverse can happen - the

1

brainstem can push up into the brain and cause brain damage. It was too soon to know how it would affect Deihlia.

How did this happen? Donna's pediatrician told us that only one half of one percent of babies born each year are born with spina bifida. It could be genetic, environmental, or due to lack of folic acid in the mother. There was no way to know for sure *why* it happened, but we had to prepare ourselves, as much as we could, for whatever else was *going* to happen.

I felt like a coward. I was afraid to meet her, knowing I'd fall for her, afraid to love her then lose her. There was no time to waver. No time to adjust, to think, to plan, to recover, to pray, to be held, to hold, to connect. There was no time. She wasn't going to make it. They had to bring her to Suffolk Universal Hospital in Boston. The ambulance was waiting. Surgery the next day lasted seventeen hours. We were all there: Donna, Linc, our mother, and me. It was the longest day of our lives. All the surgeon could do was get in there and figure it out as she went along. She couldn't explain everything she had to do.

Deihlia died once that day in surgery. She was clinically dead according to the surgeon in charge and they brought her back. She was a strong heart in a small, unfinished body. The next day came and it was the same thing: another seventeen hours in surgery and another death. But the surgical team did it again, pulling her back into a body that wasn't equipped to hold her.

We sat in the waiting room. Metal chairs with faded light blue cushions were crowded together in a small, windowless area off the main hallway. Tattered magazines that had been read and re-read lay in loose, shiny piles on the small tables, their seams worn and coming undone, pages slipping out. The dry air felt like it contained the held breath of the hundreds of parents who'd waited in the small, cramped space for their children to get through surgery. We were the only people in there that day, and we were tense, scared, and overwhelmed. Lightning had struck our lives, and we had no idea how completely our world had changed.

Linc was restless. He had a hard time sitting still before this happened, but this put him over the edge: his daughter on an operating table, the small waiting room, his young wife distraught and overwhelmed, and the helplessness. More than anything, it was the helplessness. "I need to go for a walk," he said, his wiry body jumping up suddenly. He ran his hand through his short, light-brown hair as if he could pull the situation out of it. "You stay here. I'll be back in a bit," he said. Donna looked up at him and nodded, her large cheekbones stood out against her dark, wavy, shoulder length hair. Her face was still pink from giving birth the day before. Linc grabbed his brown leather bomber jacket off the back of the chair and shoved one arm into a sleeve as he left the room.

As we sat and waited, something appeared in the doorway like a mist. Like static or a light shadow, it came towards us, becoming more solid the closer it got. Then he was there - a kindly looking old guy in a light blue bus-driver's uniform. My sister didn't notice him. She continued to thumb through the magazines she held in her lap. He sat down across from me in the small space, resting his elbows on his knees. He looked directly at me, keeping his eyes on mine. Was he trying to tell me something? Who was he? What was he doing here? He nodded his head slightly, as if we'd just been introduced.

Then I understood. He wasn't the ghoulish skull-faced creature from movies, this Death. He was more like a regular working guy doing his job, keeping watch over a possibility. I kept my eyes on him, it seemed important to acknowledge his presence. Was he going to carry Deihlia out of the hospital that day? I memorized his uniform: the breast pocket, the crease down the center of his slacks, the sturdy no-nonsense black shoes. I looked over at my sister, getting ready to say something to her. He shook his head no.

A little while later, Deihlia's surgeon Dr. Zee stepped purposefully into the room, her face grave. A tall, hearty woman with short black hair peppered with gray, she started to speak with her hands out, stretching them away from each other like an invisible game of cat's cradle. Then she paused, keeping her fingers wide and open like something fragile rested between them. "She won't live the week," she said, looking first at my sister, then at her husband Linc. "You need to make a decision. If she dies a third time in surgery, should we resuscitate her again, or let her go?" We stared at each other with hollowed-out faces, the precarious enormity of Deihlia's life was something we couldn't grasp, let go, or hold.

Deihlia. Would she know more than these two days of life?

Hello, I Love You

Even if Deihlia was only going to be with us for a short while, I wanted to know her. I'd never been in a neonatal intensive care unit before. Walking by the cribs where each critical infant lay, hooked up to monitors, with liquids hanging in IV drips, tubes for input and output, dressings, nurses checking and adjusting them made me hold my breath - beeps, the hush of controlled air, sedation. With half of her body in a cast, she was like a cute little bug with tubes and wires here, there, and everywhere. Delicate and strong. Donna and I stood next to her crib. We could touch her arms, her face, her hands.

We wanted her here, on Earth. It was a lot to ask of her.

Looking down at her in the crib, the axis of my world shifted. Some things dropped away, and others rose up out of the darkness. Here was Deihlia - a tiny little being, a fighter, part of my family, part of us. What was she doing here, coming in like that? Whatever it was, we now had a team. Team Deihlia. How long would we have with her? Her surgeon said that if she survived she'd require many, many surgeries. We had to prepare for her probable death. There was nothing to rest on, there was no false hope. There was today, and more surgery tomorrow. All we could do was be there, stand by her, love her - and pray.

Up until then, babies born with complex conditions such as hers didn't survive. They lived a couple of days, maybe a week. Dr. Zee was advancing pediatric surgery in profound ways, but we didn't know that then. We didn't know anything about her in those first few days, but that's who Deihlia got. Deihlia wasn't born in a country or area with limited medical care. That was the first stroke of luck: she was born near Boston, where we have excellent, world-class medicine. The second stroke of luck was her surgeon, who took not only an interest in her case, but who also had the ambition, skill, and courage to handle it. Soul mates come in many forms. There was only one thing we did know for sure then. We knew that we loved Deihlia and we were in it with her, wherever it was taking us. That was the third stroke of luck: love with commitment. Or maybe that was really the first one, after all.

Christmas came up fast a few days later. Donna and I drove through deserted Boston streets on our way to spend it with Deihlia at the hospital. The brownstones on Commonwealth Ave were sleepy, blinking at us as we drove by and disturbed their holiday slumber. On

Boston Common, lights strung on trees blew in the winter wind like party decorations someone forgot to take down. There was no one on the sidewalks, no cars in the streets. We had Boston all to ourselves as we made our way to the hospital. Silver garland hung in the halls on the ward. There, we stood by Deihlia's crib, holding her small hand and looking at her. Saying a few words here and there, telling her about us, telling her her name - Deihlia - trying to conjure a future outside of the hospital walls. Saying I love you.

The Center

The winter and spring after Deihlia's birth went by in a chaotic blur. Deihlia's prognosis wasn't good. "Have another child," the doctors told Donna and Linc, as if another child would soften the blow of losing Deihlia. She was a part of our family and looked like her Dad, with his blonde hair and small nose; her mischievous grin. She had presence. Some of the surgeries she had to have were so complicated, the recoveries so long and arduous, the potential for her to die was extremely real. I wouldn't see it, couldn't see it, refused, though sometimes the Bus Driver would shimmer into the room, then stand quietly in the corner with his hands in his pockets, joining our vigil.

Deihlia was three weeks premature. She had water on the brain from her spinal condition, so they put a shunt into her head to help it drain. She had seizures. Every day was a rollercoaster ride of medical issues and emergencies. During one of the surgeries, the surgeon had to make a bladder for Deihlia, using pieces of her intestine. They had to take skin from the lump on her back to cover her abdomen. They gave her a colostomy. There was no other way, not with her intestines being too short. Every surgery was critical to her survival. She was so tiny, just a little premature baby. How did they do all of that inside her? There were long periods of not being able to hold her, show her things, rock her to sleep, take her out. More than anything, we wanted her to live, to survive. That was our prayer.

From home to the hospital and back again, my sister Donna went from being a scared, mixed-up nineteen year old to a tenacious mother bear. She did it pretty quickly, getting her driver's license and triumphing over the gnarled Boston streets. It was a lot to navigate – the medical system, the emergencies, Deihlia's unique body, the extensive planning for "maybe." - then always, always having to change plans because of the surgeries and their aftermath.

Deihlia was still with us, the center of our lives. Someone wise and playful looked out of her eyes, but kind of held back. Just checking things out, she was non-committal. I understood why. We all did. We wanted to give her everything we could, with no guarantee for tomorrow. As she passed the eighth month mark, she was tentative, exploring things, opening up slowly. The shunt was removed. The seizures stopped. When her body was healed enough, her mom let her crawl around on the floor. For her, that meant using her arms and elbows to pull the bottom half of her body along. She wanted to explore everything; she was starting to get interested in life. There were adventures to be had in the kitchen, on the porch, over there. She wanted to have fun, she wanted to know. But food was an issue — it was hard getting enough nutrition into her, combined with her medicine and the antibiotics. She had so much streaming through her fragile sewn-together system. She didn't have much of an appetite for food, but she was developing one for life.

People would avert their eyes when they'd watch her crawling and realize that she was paralyzed from the waist down. Some couldn't bear to look. For others, it was simply a politeness - not staring. But Deihlia got the right Mom when she crashed into this world. As a kid, my sister's neighborhood nickname was Chimp. At eight, she climbed a neighbor's chimney barefoot in her shorts, t-shirt, and dark braids, then waved at the teenage boy next door through his second floor bedroom window as she hung on to the chimney stones outside with the other hand. Sitting at his desk doing homework, he jumped when he saw her smiling and waving outside. She was always out riding her bike, climbing, playing games, getting her school dress dirty. I was the bookish artist, holed up in our bedroom drawing, reading, writing stories, and putting together outfits as I wished for magic powers that would turn me into someone with a different life.

Donna was always very physically active and she was going to help Deihlia be physically active, too. She let her scrape and bruise along the floor, her knees thumping and banging behind her. I was more cautious, trying to keep her from harm. Deihlia would grin and look back at me over her shoulder as she scuttled off like a mermaid child across the linoleum, chasing the cat. Donna would tell me to let her go. "Just let her be a kid," she'd say to me, watching as Deihlia went off into the other room. I held my breath, giving her a few paces before I chased after her. My sister was still a kid, only nineteen. We both were. In a way, we were all kids.

It was just the four of us for her first birthday. Miraculously, she was home and not in the hospital. My sister baked a big round cake. Linc came in, waiting for the candles to be lit, and paced around the kitchen. Deihlia only ate a couple of bites, but she wore it, chocolate frosting smeared around her mouth, just like other one year olds. It was her birthday. She'd made it a year, fifty-one weeks longer

7

than they'd given her. I ate a big piece of cake, wide awake, taking her in.

Family Debris

Mental illness and violence had plagued our family for a couple of generations. Growing up, I didn't understand why my Dad was so volatile. I didn't know he had a mental illness so I certainly didn't know his diagnosis. He didn't know it either. All I knew was that I needed to disregard everything he said to me, ignore his mental cruelty, stick to my own experience, and stand up to him physically when he raised his fists. When my mother finally got the strength and courage to divorce him, it initiated a period of loss and upheaval. Even though I was glad I would never have to live with my father again, it was a lot of change.

When Deihlia was born, I was still numb and submerged, digging my way out from the debris of changes. In a short period I'd lost a lot. My parents divorced, my Mom was focused on her new husband, Donna ran away, my violent father was adrift, my grandmother, dog, and cat died, our family home was gone, and my best friend moved away. The trauma and losses accumulated in me.

Donna's marriage at the age of seventeen was her attempt at finding an island in the storm. She ran to a man, to marriage, trying to replace what she thought was lost. Then she became pregnant with Deihlia. Her pregnancy brought us closer together, pulling us into the center from opposite sides of the family boxing ring. Part of my father's illness played out by dividing sisters, and breaking mother-daughter bonds. He was really good at it. His untreated schizophrenia and narcissistic borderline personality disorder caused him to see things in black and white, including us. His mother probably had mental illness too - she was vitriolic and bitter all the time. His father disappeared when he was five and his parents divorced. Whether it was genetic or environmental, his mental disorders added fuel to his violent and cruel nature. His behavior had a devastating impact on each of us. Donna, my mother and I were on slippery, tentative ground with each other when Donna became pregnant, but an unborn child put more roots down between us.

We were all broken, barely finding our way out of the past when Deihlia arrived. What did we have to offer a new family member, when we hadn't even forged a strong connection between us? Not much, but we didn't have time. Deihlia rushed in on a cosmic chariot pulled by the twin horses Life and Death. Her birth was rocky; a shock to our fragile family system. I didn't know it at the time, but

9

she was a jolt that I needed. Maybe we all did. Somewhere in the strands of our DNA and in the constellations of our stars in the sky, other potentials lay dormant inside each of us, deeply invisible. Deihlia's arrival activated them, setting off sparks in each of our soul's trajectories, and whether we were ready or not, they were lighting our way.

Crawling

Witnessing and supporting Deihlia through the multitude of surgeries she had in her first few years of life woke me up to a broader reality, and helped me realize the world was much bigger and more diverse than my own limited experience had shown me. I was still undoing the damage that I'd experienced when I was younger, and other parts of me that were more subtle were coming back to life. Part of it was Deihlia. She was the vessel for all the love I had inside me. That kind of love heals, especially when it is returned. Bearing witness to the extreme precariousness of her mortality and the medical procedures she had just to survive made me wonder about what each of us was doing here.

Deihlia's life made ripples in the world almost immediately. Not just in our family, but through her surgeon. No one likes to think about how medical procedures come to be, but they are born out of necessity and real human need. They come from experimentation, from trial and error. Dr. Zee had considerable skill and experience, but somehow it was Deihlia who became her success. The enormity of what she had to go through was overwhelming, and it felt so much bigger than us. It was bigger than us. I'd say it was bigger than Deihlia, but somehow she had the capacity to meet her ordeal. Many times she'd come close to death, and every time she came back. Where did she come from? How did she do it? Certainly medical care at one of the best hospitals in the country played a part, but so did our prayers, our love, and more than those - Deihlia's own will.

As I got to know her, the universe became more tangible; a real presence. Sometimes it showed up as a mantle of stars draped around her neck as she lay in the hospital bed recovering, and other times it was the blue cape that dragged behind her as she crawled around by her elbows on the kitchen floor. Being with Deihlia opened a window I'd never noticed before - one that gave me glimpses into the power and majesty of an intelligent universe. Most days, it made me feel small and undeveloped. But we were all growing and learning together.

Double Trouble

Donna and Linc listened to the doctors, who gave them permission to have another child, to try again, to be parents to a child who didn't have medical issues. Deihlia's prognosis was still death, sometime soon. This time, the pediatrician kept a much closer eye on Donna's pregnancy, testing her amniotic fluid to make sure that the fetus growing inside her didn't have the same issue. The thing is, my sister was tough and resilient even then. She was ready for whatever was going to happen next. Part of it was her youth, but it was something else, too. I'd known my sister my whole life, but in those few years, her steel spine surprised me. I know Deihlia helped to forge it, like she did with mine. When Deihlia was born our bones changed.

Sixteen months after Deihlia's birth, Chelsea arrived. My second niece got the name I'd originally chosen for Deihlia. I felt lucky to name one of my sister's kids. Deihlia Mae, and Chelsea Rose: modern and old-fashioned all at the same time. Not like Diane and Donna, the common names that my sister and I were given. We hadn't been close growing up, which had hurt. But the day of Deihlia's first seventeen hour surgery, as my sister and I sat tensely together in the hospital waiting room, each of our stars slid over into another spot in the sky, forming a new constellation.

Chelsea was a physical counterpoint to Deihlia. Deihlia was spindly, it was hard to put weight on her, her unusable legs were little twigs. Chelsea was hearty. I looked at her round cherubic face and fell for her instantly too. Chelsea was born without any physical issues, her birth went normally. Donna and Linc brought her home from the hospital. Nana had stayed with Deihlia while Donna gave birth, so she and Deihlia were waiting. Donna walked into the house holding Chelsea swaddled in her arms.

Nana held Deihlia in her arms so she could look at her new sister's face.

"Who is that?" Deihlia asked, looking at the baby in her mother's arms, then up at her Mom's face, searching.

"This is your sister, Chelsea. You're a big sister now," her mother said.

Deihlia reached over and smacked Chelsea on the head, just like I hit Donna on the head when she was brought home from the hospital. Sisters!

We all breathed a sigh of relief that Chelsea was born whole. It was already a lot for my sister as it was - two kids under the age of two, one of them medically fragile and diagnosed as terminal. My Mom and I were doing everything we could to help, to provide support, to be involved. Two babies with medical issues would have tipped the scales in the wrong direction, depleting everyone.

There was my sister with a baby in each arm, her face still red and swollen from pregnancy. Deihlia wasn't too happy about it at first. Chelsea was another force to be reckoned with. She wasn't some quiet, mild-mannered baby girl. The name was right for her: it had city edge, a little bit of tomboy, some ferocity, and cuteness.

Deihlia watched Chelsea grow and saw her start to do things very early, things she couldn't do. Chelsea did everything early - crawling, eating real food, potty-training. She had to. She had to be independent because Deihlia required so much extra care. Chelsea loved food and would always have a ring around her mouth from eating something, while Deihlia picked and barely ate, needing a G-tube put into her stomach so she could receive fluid nutrition and not perish. My sister kept cans of pediatric ensure in the kitchen cabinet. When Deihlia wouldn't eat, which was most of the time, she had to lift Deihlia's shirt and pop the snap-cap of the g-tube open. Then she'd administer the liquid via a large plastic syringe, pulling the liquid up into the syringe then pushing a little at a time into Deihlia's g-tube. Deihlia would continue with whatever she was doing, ignoring the procedure, playing with whatever she had in her hands.

Small Circles

I started to notice synchronicities here and there. Things I shouldn't ignore. I'd been seeing a therapist for a couple of years to help me recover from the family trauma. My therapist recommended a psychic named Maria to help me get deeper insight into what was going on in my life. She lived in a Victorian gingerbread house in an outlying neighborhood of Boston. The pink and white exterior sat in the middle of a cluster of old homes and newer split-level houses that were squished next to each other at the end of a small cul-de-sac. When I arrived, Maria opened the door wearing a red and white gingham apron over her old jeans and a purple blouse. Her round, wrinkled face was framed in light brown curls that bounced when she moved. I didn't know what to think.

She brought me into a small porch off of the kitchen that looked out into a surprisingly large backyard where birds flitted around a hanging feeder. She smiled warmly, asking me to sit across from her, then brushed her curly hair off of the side of her face as she sat down. I told her I was looking for more insight and information about my life, and later we talked about Deihlia. When I explained to her what Deihlia was dealing with, Maria furrowed her brows and stopped for a moment.

"One of my colleagues is a Reiki practitioner, and he's been having dreams about helping a little girl. He just told me about them the other day. He feels a strong calling to do it, that it is important for him to help her," she said, putting her palm flat on the table between us.

I listened. I didn't know what "Reiki" was. She told me it was a form of energetic healing from Japan.

She turned her head to her right, as if there were someone there she was conversing with. Then she turned back to me. "I believe your niece is that girl. I'm going to give you his number and you can call him and talk to him about it. I urge you to call him." She took a piece of paper from the small pad next to her, and scribbled his name and number down.

Donna called Mike a few days later. He explained that he was a Reiki practitioner, and had indeed been having dreams about helping a little girl - there was an urgency to the dreams, the girl needed assistance now. "This is something I am supposed to do," Mike said.

"I understand that you can't afford any more medical costs. If you can get to my office, I'll be happy to do this without charging you."

A few weeks later, Donna, Deihlia and I made our way from my apartment to his office in Brighton. Nana was babysitting Chelsea at home. We drove along Harvard Street through Brookline, then Allston, in thick Saturday afternoon traffic. Donna parked on the street in a metered spot near the large old house where the office was. We rang the doorbell and Mike let us in. The old house had been converted into therapist's offices a long time ago. The waiting area used to be a living room, the sealed fireplace had a bouquet of silk flowers sitting in front of it. We didn't have to wait. Mike led us into his practice room. The lavender walls were bare, and only a candle flickering on a small shelf in one corner offered any adornment. The massage table took up the center of the room. Mike had two chairs set up against the wall so we could sit. He was a genial man in his thirties, soft spoken and kind. A smiley face peeked out on the t-shirt he wore under his open long sleeve shirt. I hadn't seen one of those in a long time. "Deihlia should be over here," he said, touching his table lightly. Donna put Deihlia on the table, resting her on her back. She and I sat down. Deihlia looked up at Mike from the table, then over at us. She smiled, as if to reassure us. My sister and I exchanged glances.

After dimming the light, Mike stood next to the table, facing us. "Deihlia, I'm going to put my hands above your body. I won't touch you. Just tell me if anything is bothering you."

Deihlia looked up at him, nodding.

A small glow lit the corner of the room. Mike closed his eyes and put his hands above her. They hovered and moved up and down her body, then came to rest at her abdomen. Donna and I looked at each other, unsure of what was happening. Deihlia's eyes fluttered, opening and closing, then she fell asleep. The room felt peaceful. Mike stood over Deihlia, his hands in one place, for about twenty-five minutes.

The room was still. It was hard to keep our own eyes open, but we sat quietly, watching. Mike pulled his hands back to his sides, and opened his eyes. "I helped to get her energy moving again," he whispered to us. Deihlia was still asleep on the table. "The trauma of surgeries can really linger in the body and energy field. I want to help her with this. She's strong but this will help her be stronger, help keep her energy together."

15

Donna nodded. I went over to the table and touched Deihlia lightly on the arm. She opened her eyes and looked up at me, then looked around. "All done Deihl," I said, lifting her up and holding her in my arms.

"Ok," Deihlia said.

"Thank you Mike," Donna said, shaking his hand, "Let's make another appointment."

As we drove away, Donna looked back through the rearview mirror at Deihlia seated in her car seat. "I didn't know about the energy field, did you?" she asked.

I shook my head. "No, but I guess it makes sense," I replied. There seemed to be a link between what was going on in our bodies and what was going at the spirit level. I started to get a picture of it in my head but the picture still had a lot of holes in it.

"How do you feel Deihlia?" I asked, turning my head to look at her.

She looked up from the small stuffed dolphin she held in her hand. "I'm hungry."

I smiled back at her, reaching into the back seat to touch her arm. "I'm glad, Bug. We're going home."

I turned around to face forward, and Donna put her foot on the gas as the light turned green. "She's never said she was hungry before. Ever," she said as the traffic began to move, red tail lights going off in one car then another.

Deihlia listened from the back seat, her antennae up. She looked at her mother, then over at me. Holding the toy dolphin in her right hand, she made it fly above her in the air, then arced it back down to her lap and up again, in small circles.

Keeping Up, Franklin, 1986

It was October, plants and flowers that had hung on past September were now just skeletons, with a few red or shriveled leaves clinging to them. It was a warm dry day, unseasonably warm - no jacket required. Donna, our mother (whom the girls called Nana), and the girls were out in the backyard. Chelsea and Deihlia crawled around on the grass while Donna worked in her garden, cleaning it out to prepare for winter. Nana stood by watching the kids. She was tall, her short dark hair was the same color as Donna's. She wore jeans and a sweatshirt with a cat-face on it, the cat's eyes glittered with sequins. Deihlia was two and a half, Chelsea was one. They both crawled around on the grass, picking up stones or leaves, getting dirty and looking at things.

Chelsea crawled over to the bulkhead, the angled metal basement doors that jutted out of the back of the house, and proceeded to climb up on her hands and knees. When she got to the top, she turned around and slid down, landing on her bottom on the small patch of concrete. Then she turned around and went up and did it again. "Chelsea come down here with Nana and Deihlia," Nana said, still on the grass a few feet away, unable to be in two places at once. Chelsea grinned, her cheeks rosy, and crawled back up to the top of the bulkhead, sliding down once more.

Deihlia watched her from the grass, then got down on her elbows and pulled herself over to the bulkhead. "Deihlia, don't you get up there too. Come on Chelsea, come down now!" Nana said. Chelsea slid down, giggling. Deihlia put one hand on the rim of the bulkhead door, and started pulling herself up. "Deihlia!" Nana said, trying to grab Chelsea before she began to climb again. She wanted them both to get off the bulkhead. Deihlia was going to get hurt.

Donna heard her mother in the backyard, and came back around the side of the house, her hands dirty from the garden. "What's going on?" she asked.

Chelsea was pulling away from Nana's hand and struggling to get free. Deihlia was a third of the way up the bulkhead, inching her way towards the top, pulling herself up using only her hands. "Deihlia shouldn't go down the bulkhead, she's going to hurt herself!" she said shortly, exasperated that she had to explain it. Wasn't it obvious what was going on?

17

Donna looked at Deihlia, and Chelsea broke free, crawling back up the bulkhead ahead of her sister. "Just let her be a kid, Mom. She's not going to get hurt."

Deihlia looked back over her shoulder at her Mother and Nana, and continued up the bulkhead, one hand over the other on the edge of the door. Chelsea slid down the other side past her, landing on her feet then toppling over on to her hands. Chelsea was on her way up again when Deihlia reached the top, turned herself around on her back, then let go, her hands in the air. She slid down the bulkhead door. Nana reached out and caught her before she hit the ground. Nana pulled her close, unable to hide her concern.

Deihlia looked up at her with a smile. "See Nana, I can do it too!"

Donna nodded, and went back to her gardening. Nana hugged Deihlia close. "Of course you can do it too sweetie. Of course," she said, watching as Chelsea turned around and crawled back up. "Just let Nana catch you, ok?"

This game went on for thirty minutes, up and down, Chelsea sliding down three times to Deihlia's one. Then their black cat Mugsy sauntered out past them. She ignored them and stood in the middle of the yard, her tail twitching as she contemplated her next move. Chelsea crawled away from the bulkhead, making her way to the cat, who gazed out at the trees. Nana caught Deihlia one more time, then turned to watch Chelsea. Deihlia turned her head to watch too.

In the middle of the back yard, Chelsea stopped crawling and got on her feet, teetering halfway between crawling and standing, then straightened up and walked several steps towards the cat, who ran off as she approached. She stood shaky and uncertain on her feet, then dropped back to the ground.

Nana smiled, and started walking towards her. "Wow Chelsea! You were walking there for a minute," she said. Chelsea looked up and grinned and continued to crawl after the cat, who jumped on to a low limb in the pine tree bordering the neighbor's yard.

Deihlia watched her sister then turned her face back to her Nana, looking her in the eyes. "Nana, why can't I walk?" she asked.

Nana stopped in mid-step, searching the trees for an answer, unprepared for the question. Deihlia looked up at her, waiting. Nana couldn't go any further. The question was so big, it overwhelmed her. She sat down on the grass where she was, unmoored by the question.

18

"I don't know why God doesn't want you to walk, but I guess he doesn't," Nana said, biting back tears. "I don't know why. I'm sorry that he doesn't, Deihlia. I wish you could walk. God made you a special girl for a reason but I don't know why." Tears rimmed her eyes, then spilled over.

Deihlia began to cry. "I want to walk like Chelsea," she said, her mouth a wailing frown, tears rolling quickly down over her pale cheeks.

From the side yard, Donna saw them sitting on the ground, and saw that Deihlia was crying. She dropped her garden gloves, walking quickly over to them. "What's the matter? What happened?"

"I want to walk like Chelsea! Why can't I walk?"

Donna looked at Nana as she bent down to take Deihlia. Chelsea saw them all together and began to crawl towards them. "Deihlia, it's ok sweetie. You can't walk like Chelsea but I promise you'll do lots of other things. I promise." She said.

Deihlia kept crying, tears made small rivers down her cheeks. She was bawling. Nana got up and picked Chelsea up off of the ground, holding her close, hugging her. Chelsea smiled at her Nana, then she looked over at Deihlia. Her smile disappeared as she reached out her arms towards her sister.

"Chelsea walked for a few minutes today," Nana said.

Donna nodded, kissing Deihlia on the forehead as she rocked her back and forth in her arms.

Two Worlds

Chelsea stood beside her mother at the edge of the plain yard, her chestnut-brown ringlets falling over one eye. They'd moved into the new neighborhood a few months ago. Deihlia was in the hospital, recovering from surgery. Everything was new to Chelsea, and she wasn't sure if she liked it.

"We wanted to introduce ourselves and say 'hello,'" the young mother said, handing Donna a loaf of pumpkin bread. "I'm Elsa, I live across the street. This is my son, Sean." Elsa was in her late twenties, her dirty blonde hair was permed into a popular "big hair" style. Her round, clear face and brown eyes were warm and open.

Sean stood across from Chelsea, looking at her through squinted eyes. They were the same age and height, and stood a foot away from each other, staring. Sean's blonde hair was buoyant on top and cut short around his neck. Freckles dotted his nose. He wore baggy, red pants and a grey sweatshirt.

"Oh, thank you. Nice to meet you, I'm Donna, and this is my daughter Chelsea."

Chelsea didn't like the look on Sean's face, how he just stood there scowling at her, so she stuck her tongue out at him - a quick little gesture that no one saw but him.

Donna took the pumpkin bread.

"Where did you move here from?" Elsa asked.

"We lived on the Cape." Donna briefly pictured the small house they'd just left in Hyannis, halfway down off of Route 6 on Cape Cod. It was too far from Boston, and the summer traffic, which was heavy with tourists and vacationers, made it nearly impossible to go back and forth as often as they had to, so they'd moved to Franklin.

"Nice," Elsa said, looking down at Chelsea. "Chelsea, maybe you and Sean can play together sometime."

Chelsea looked up at Elsa. Sean saw his moment and put out his hands and pushed her. Chelsea fell to the ground on her behind, then jumped back up quickly and put her face into Sean's face. "Ha!" she said.

"I guess their version of hello is a little more primitive. Sean, apologize to Chelsea right now!"

Sean pushed his bottom lip out once more and turned around and ran back across the street, slamming the door behind him as he ran into his house.

Donna was grateful for the distraction. She didn't know how to tell strangers that she had another daughter, one who was in the hospital. That Deihlia was recovering from surgery for...what could she tell them? It was so complicated and it wasn't easy to say while someone was handing you pumpkin bread on the street. It was a longer conversation, and so personal. Elsa seemed nice but she was still just a stranger.

"Chelsea can play with Sean sometime," she said instead.

Chelsea looked up at her mother, her lips pursed. She would rather play with Deihlia. But Deihlia was away.

"It was so nice to meet you, Donna and Chelsea. We'll see you soon. Please come by if you need anything," Elsa said as she turned and followed Sean home. She seemed good humored, walking quickly back to her own house after her son.

Donna watched them go, then turned back to her new house. "Come on Chels, let's go back inside." Chelsea turned and ran back up the stairs, into the kitchen. Donna looked at her watch, and wondered how Deihlia was doing. The days when she couldn't get into Boston to see her daughter stretched long and thin. Was anyone talking to her? How was she feeling? The nurses were like family, but they weren't family. At least here they were closer to Boston.

I arrived at the hospital after my creative writing class, taking the subway directly from school in Boston. I knew my sister couldn't get into the hospital that day, and wanted to see Deihlia. If she was in the hospital, visiting her was a priority. She was almost three years old. The elevator let me out on Starfish Five, the ward where Deihlia lived when she wasn't at home. Jess and I said "hello." She worked the desk on the 7 a.m. to 3 p.m. shift. She waved as she continued talking on the phone, and I turned left down the beige and grey corridor. Visiting Deihlia on Starfish Five was like going back in time to the 1950's. The ward was probably built earlier than that, and hadn't been updated since. I went into the room that she shared with another girl.

"Hey Deihl," I said, smiling at her.

She looked over at me. She was lying in bed with the bed raised slightly. The TV was on PBS. "Hi Auntie," she said.

I leaned over and gave her a kiss. "What are you watching, Bug?"

"Sesame Street." She replied, taking her eyes off the screen to look at me.

"How are you feeling today?" I asked.

"Ok," she said. "Where's Mom?"

"She couldn't come in today sweetie. She'll be in tomorrow. Do you want to read a book?"

She shook her head. "I like Snuffy. I want to see if he's here today."

We sat and watched the rest of the episode together, waiting for Snuffy to appear. The girl in the bed next to Deihlia had a cast on her lower half. Her mother sat next to her bed, both of them watching the TV with us. A nurse walked by, poking her head into the room. "I'll be in to change Deihlia's dressing in just a minute," she said.

I nodded. Deihlia looked over at her then back at the TV. Then she turned to me. "Will you stay while she does it, Auntie? Will you stay?"

"Of course Bug, of course." I said, touching her face lightly, smoothing her hair.

It was an afternoon like countless other afternoons. Outside, the sun was shining. Bright orange leaves fluttered to the ground one at a time. Ambulances drove in, pulling up to the entrance, some in a hurry, some not. The subway rumbled in the distance. Kids were getting out of school, their heavy backpacks weighing them down as they boarded the school bus or walked towards the subway station, in Boston called "the T." Nurses were getting ready to change shifts. As a family, we had to take shifts. Deihlia was going to be in the hospital for several weeks, maybe longer. It was impossible for her mother to be there every day.

The nurse came in, pulling the curtain closed between Deihlia and her roommate. "You're doing good today, aren't you Deihlia?" she said, pulling back the thin blanket that covered Deihlia's body.

Deihlia nodded. The curtain blocked her view of the TV. She turned to me, reaching out her hand. I put my two fingers in her palm, and wrapped the rest of my hand around hers. I smiled at her again, looking in her eyes. "Just a few minutes Bug, then you can have dinner. I can read a book while you're eating if you'd like."

22

She kept looking at me, not wanting to watch the nurse work on her, remove the dressing, clean her. It happened a few times a day, but she didn't want to watch it. "Ok Auntie, let's read a book. *Hop on Pop!*"

Back in Franklin, Donna picked up the phone and called the hospital, unable to wait any longer. She wanted to know how her daughter was doing. The nurse slid the curtain back open and left the room. Jess popped her head in, leaning around the doorway. "Donna's on the phone. Can you pick it up when I transfer in?"

The phone on the wall near Deihlia's bed buzzed and I lifted the receiver. "Hey," I said. "Deihlia's doing ok. Do you want to talk to her?"

Deihlia took the phone. "Mom! When are you coming in?"

I could hear Donna talking to her through the receiver. Deihlia nodded slowly, her eyes tearing up. They spoke a little longer, then she suddenly pushed the phone back at me.

"It's me again."

"What happened?" Donna asked.

"I guess she's done talking for now, I don't know," I said. Deihlia was back to watching TV, her eyes dry. "I'll stay until bedtime. It's gonna be ok. You'll be in tomorrow afternoon."

Just Another Day at Preschool

Deihlia was in her car seat in the back of the silver Thunderbird. At four years old, she went to the preschool at the Mass Hospital School, the state school for children with multiple and severe disabilities. Donna had just picked her up. It was early December, and the sky was already dark. It felt like midnight.

"How was school today?"

Deihlia nodded her head. "Good, Mom."

"Anything special happen today?"

"Not really." Deihlia shook her head.

Donna looked back at her in the rearview mirror. She knew that Deihlia's class had gone to the State House that day to help decorate Governor Dukakis's Christmas tree. She'd dressed Deihlia up in her white and lavender jumper for the occasion, and Deihlia had been excited on the way to school that morning.

"Deihlia! Come on! You know you went to the State House today."

Deihlia looked out the car window. "Oh yeah," she said, rummaging around under her butt. She pulled out her GI Joe, and began moving his arms this way and that.

"Was the governor nice?" Donna asked. They sat in traffic at a red light. She could see a kid bouncing up and down in the back seat of the car in front of her.

Deihlia nodded. "Uh-huh. Mike was nice. We hung some Christmas balls on the tree and he gave us cookies. I told him that he looked like one of my GI Joe's, the one with the black hair."

"Mike?" Donna laughed. "Did you call the governor 'Mike' and tell him he looked like one of your action figures?"

Deihlia made her GI Joe walk across her car seat, then up the side towards her shoulder. "Uh-huh. Mom I did my ABCs today on the bus ride!"

"Wow! I'm so proud of you Deihl," Donna shook her head, amused by her daughter's personality.

Later, she called Deihlia's teacher, Carol. In addition to teaching the kids at the Hospital School their ABCs, numbers, colors, and how to play nice with other children, Carol also worked with them to help them learn how to use their differently functioning bodies, their wheelchairs, their braces, and their prosthetics. She also taught the parents how to help their children manage themselves. She

24

was in her mid-thirties, her long, wavy, light-brown hair went halfway down her back. It was sometimes a liability with the youngest kids, but she'd always worn her hair like that and she wasn't going to change it. It was part of her. She'd been busy when Donna picked up Deihlia that day and they hadn't spoken.

"Carol, how did it go today? I'm dying to hear about it. How did Deihlia do?"

"Oh, she was a superstar like she always is. She chatted up the Governor, and tagged along with Mickey, the older boy she adores. It was really a special day. The kids had such a nice time."

"Deihlia called the governor 'Mike' in the car. Did she do that with him too?"

Carol chuckled. "That Deihlia! She sure did. I introduced him to the kids as Governor Michael Dukakis, but Deihlia just called him 'Mike' the rest of the visit. He just laughed about it."

"That kid!"

"We're having a family swim next week, do you think you'll make it?"

Donna looked at the front of her refrigerator, scanning it to see if they had any doctor's appointments lined up. "I think so. I'll have to get a sitter for Chelsea, but I want to be there."

Carol sighed on the other end of the phone. "Donna, family swim is so important. All you parents need to get out of your comfort zone and get in the water with your kids. It's a time to connect in their school environment. They are all such troopers, I tell ya. These kids are so amazing."

Donna listened as Chelsea walked into the room, shaking her sippy cup. The bottom of her pajama feet made a scratchy noise on the floor. Chelsea reached up to hand her mother the empty cup and the zipper on her pink one-piece PJs split open at the top, unzipping down to her chest.

"Carol, you're the best. I've gotta go. I'll see you tomorrow." Donna hung up the phone, reaching down to take the empty cup out of Chelsea's hand then pulled the zipper up. "Is your sister thirsty too?" she asked, noting that Chelsea was already outgrowing her pajamas.

Chelsea turned and ran back into the living room on her tiptoes, where her sister sat on the floor playing. "Deihl, do you want some milk?"

Deihlia kept playing and didn't look up. "No."

Chelsea ran back into the kitchen. "No milk for Deihl!" she said, grabbing the full cup out of her mother's hand.

Donna walked into the living room with Chelsea. She didn't know how Carol did it. Each kid had very different medical conditions and needs, and she was personally involved with each one of them. But she was thankful that Carol was so good at what she did. She made it seem so much easier than it really was.

Outside the small bay window, everything was dark. It was only 7:00 p.m. but Donna was tired. Linc was barely ever home, and when he was, he was tired and distracted. His plumbing business was down on the Cape, an hour and a half away, and he usually got home late. She knew he worked really hard, but it wasn't just that. He'd been really distant lately, too - preoccupied and hardly ever home. He was always going somewhere to meet someone, or to work. Donna knew that he was still having a hard time with Deihlia's medical issues and prognosis, but she felt like he was far away in every way. GI Joes and Barbie's were scattered on the floor. Their dog, Spike, a rescue with long ears, was stretched out sideways next to the empty brick fireplace, one eye open watching Donna and the kids. Donna sat down on the floor with her two girls. "Time for bed, let's start picking up."

Chelsea knew her mom could only put one of them to bed at a time, so she sat down on the rug and picked up her doll, hugging it close.

The Prototype, Boston, 1987

Donna was nervous, but she didn't want Deihlia to know it. She pushed Deihlia in her stroller along the sidewalk towards the Suffolk Universal entrance. It felt like so many other days, bringing Deihlia into the hospital. Her daughter spent the better part of her four years of life there. Surgery, long recovery periods, home for a month or two then back to the hospital for another round. Four years. Donna was tired of the surgeries for her daughter. Deihlia would just get going at school with something and she'd have to go back. She was also weary of driving in and out of Boston so much, but there was nothing she could do about it.

Once inside they went past the front desk, aiming for the main hallway. She thought she knew where she was going, even though she'd never been there before. Deihlia looked at the nurses and doctors walking purposefully past them. She'd been coming to this place ever since she could remember. Her Mom brought her around to different parts of the hospital sometimes, but coming here meant something was going to happen to her. It always did. Even though she and her Mom had talked about this visit, Deihlia was going to wait and see before she believed it. Coming here always meant doctors looking at her, checking her, doing things.

"We're almost there," Donna said, pushing Deihlia down a dark hallway she'd never been down before. The walls were brick, the hall narrow. This section of the hospital was particularly old.

Deihlia put her hand up to her face and began to bite the nail on her index finger.

They came to a halt near a door that was closed, and waited for a few moments until a young man opened it and came out. "Mrs. Nye, Deihlia," he said, looking down at Deihlia to speak to her directly.

"Hi," Donna said.

"Doctor Zee is almost ready for you, it will just be a couple more minutes."

Deihlia looked up at him, then craned her head to look at her Mom. She needed to see the look on her mom's face to know what was really going on, and her mom's face was kind of frozen. She had gotten dressed up and put on makeup before they left, dressing Deihlia in one of the Polly Flinders dresses she put her in when they were going somewhere fancy.

27

Donna looked down at her. "Are you ready to speak to these people like we talked about?" she asked.

Deihlia looked up at her and didn't answer, still chewing on her fingertip.

The young man said, "We can go in now," holding the door open for them. He saw a bit of loose bright blue fabric falling out around the edges of Deihlia's stroller. She had a light-pink winter coat on, and corduroy pants with soft knit booties on her feet. *Where are those blue triangles coming from?*, he wondered, then looked up as he ushered them into the room.

Donna got behind Deihlia again, bending over slightly to push her daughter's stroller into the room.

Dr. Zee stood behind a podium in the front of the amphitheater, putting down the paper in her hand.

Deihlia hardly saw her. She was looking around the semi-circular room at all the people in the seats. There were a lot of them - every seat was full and they were all looking down at her. Her mother wheeled her over next to Dr. Zee.

Dr. Zee turned to her, smiling. She bent down, getting closer to Deihlia's height, saying, "Remember we talked about you visiting my class. They're all eager to see you and to know how you're doing."

Deihlia nodded, putting her hands in her lap, suddenly self-conscious about having her finger at her mouth.

Dr. Zee stood up and looked Donna in the eyes. "Every surgeon in this room is here because they want to learn how to help babies like Deihlia. I appreciate you bringing her in."

Donna nodded.

Dr. Zee gestured to Donna to sit in the chair the young man had put next to her daughter. Donna sat down then began looking around at the room filled with surgeons. Dr. Zee had told her that she was holding a symposium for surgeons from around the world, to teach them how to help babies born with some of the problems that Deihlia was born with. The amphitheater was full. There must have been a hundred people sitting there. She felt uncomfortable being on display. She looked over at Deihlia then leaned in towards her. "You ready Deihl?"

Deihlia looked at her mom and blinked. This was better than seeing a doctor and being put on the table. But what was she supposed to say to them?

28

Dr. Zee introduced her to the doctors. "Everyone, this is Deihlia, the girl I've been telling you about today. I wanted you to meet her in person so you could see for yourself how successful we've been, and how well she is doing."

Deihlia looked at the faces of the people sitting closest to her. They looked serious, curious. None of them were smiling. She wished one of them would smile at her.

"Deihlia, why don't you say hello to these doctors, tell them a little bit about yourself."

Deihlia was silent.

"Go ahead," Donna said, touching her daughter's arm. "It's ok. They want to hear from you."

Deihlia swallowed once then looked at the person directly across from her. "My name is Deihlia. I'm four and a half. I go to school at Baylies. I have a sister named Chelsea and a dog named Spike."

A few people giggled, someone smiled.

"I have a friend named Sean, and I like Snuffy on Sesame Street," she continued.

Dr. Zee beamed down at her.

Deihlia was quiet for a minute. She tilted her head down, looking at the floor, trying to muster up more courage. She wanted to say something truthful, something real. She was used to talking to doctors, but not to a bunch of them like this.

"I come here a lot," she said finally, her brave face falling to reveal something else. Only her eyes lifted to meet theirs. "I wish I could just stay home."

The room was silent.

Dr. Zee let her smile drop too. "Yes Deihlia, you do come here a lot. That is true," she nodded. "You're a very strong girl."

For a few seconds the room became a blur. Donna blinked, trying to regain her equilibrium as she held on to her daughter. Deihlia was so much more than just a patient, she was a whole person. She hoped they could see that. She bent sideways and put her arm around Deihlia. She wanted to get out of there.

Dreams

"Have a few more bites of chicken," Donna said to Deihlia. We were seated at their dining room table, having dinner. The dining room was a small room off of the kitchen with two windows, one in each outer facing wall. Six chairs fit around the rectangular, blonde-wood table. Spike, their Doberman, sat next to Deihlia on the floor, his eyes focused intently on her plate, drool dripping from his long snout.

Deihlia pushed the food around on her plate, then picked up the tiniest piece of meat she could find. Pushing it on to the end of her fork, she twirled it around in the air and looked at it. A white lace tablecloth covered the table. Candlesticks, dripping wax, glowed in the middle. Patches of pink and red blotted the lace, evidence of its presence during many dinners.

Chelsea's plate was empty. She sat across from Deihlia drinking the last bit of milk in her glass.

"I forgot to tell you about my dream," I said.

Donna looked up from her plate, then her eyes went to Deihlia's fork of twirling chicken, which now stood upright like a flag in her fist. "Oh. What was it?"

"It was Grandma. The blue telephone was ringing so I picked it up. She was on the other end, telling me that she was better. That she was happy now." In my dream, my grandmother called me on the light-blue, square telephone we'd had in our home when I was growing up. The rotary phone had a clear plastic dial. In my dream, the dial glowed until I picked up the handset and heard my grandmother on the other end of the line.

Donna looked at me sharply,. "Really?"

I nodded. "Yeah. I said, 'How can you be better if you're dead?' And you know what she said? She said 'That's why I'm better. It's so much better here.' " I'd felt my grandmother through the phone. It felt like her, only cleaner, without all of her bitterness. Every time I saw her she was angry and accusatory, criticizing everything. In addition to her unknown mental illness, she had an eating disorder and would never join us at the table for dinner. She was one of 13 children, and was sent away as a teenager to live elsewhere. She wouldn't tell us why, but we suspected it was either her mental disorder, which may have created problems for her in a family that large, or it was something worse. There was no way to know for sure.

30

She'd died in the hospital a few years earlier, and she was mad at me when she died and wouldn't talk to me when I came in to say goodbye. I'd called an ambulance when I found her lying on the sofa, spewing blood. It felt awful knowing she was angry at me when she passed, so I was glad to get the call.

Deihlia looked at me sideways, still holding her chicken aloft. Chelsea's face was open, watching and listening across the table. Spike shook nervously, waiting for Deihlia's chicken to drop off the fork and bounce to the floor.

"I had a dream too," Deihlia said, putting her fork back down on the plate, the chicken untouched.

"Really, what happened in your dream?" I asked.

"Things were happening, I was doing stuff and then this guy came along and took my dream away."

Donna and I exchanged glances. "What do you mean, he took it away?"

Deihlia reached her hand up in the air, as if she were pulling a string. "He comes into my dreams and he pulls them away from me. Everything goes black."

"You've seen him more than once?"

She nodded. "Uh-huh. He does it a lot."

Chelsea looked with concern at her sister from across the table. She didn't know anything about having dreams taken away.

"So you have a dream thief," I said. "Your dreams must be extra special if he wants them." I'd never heard of anyone having their dreams taken from them, and I wanted to reassure Deihlia. I could tell that Donna was surprised, too.

"I don't know. I wish he wouldn't do it." She pushed her plate away from her, sliding it towards her sister. Donna reached over and took the chicken off of her plate and put it on her own. Spike whined in protest.

"Can you talk to him the next time he shows up and ask him why he's stealing your dreams? Tell him you need your dreams for yourself."

Deihlia thought about it for a minute, looking off into the distance, over her mother's head into the kitchen. "Maybe," she said. Was it possible to talk back to a dream thief? She wondered.

"Why did your Grandma call you?" Chelsea asked. "I thought she was dead."

31

I smiled at her. "She is dead. But maybe she was calling me from her next life. She didn't say goodbye to me when she left this one."

"Can dead people use the phone?" Chelsea asked, looking confused.

I looked at her, then at Deihlia. They were both staring at me, waiting for an answer.

"I think dead people can do all kinds of things in their next life."

Chelsea pursed her lips, thinking about it, then picked up her plate and fork and got out of her seat, heading for the kitchen.

The Wish, New York City, 1988

"Mrs. Nye?" the voice on the other end of the phone asked.

"Yes, this is Donna," she answered.

"This is the Starlight Foundation. We grant wishes to terminally ill children and their families. Someone suggested your daughter Deihlia to us. We'd like to grant her a wish."

Donna held the phone to her ear. "A wish? What kind of wish?"

"Any kind of wish. A trip or a meeting with someone special, something like that."

Donna looked around her kitchen as she held the phone. Bills and other papers were stacked against the refrigerator, which was covered in marker drawings by Deihlia and Chelsea, photos, and medical appointment reminders. There were dishes in the sink, and the white floor needed washing.

"Mrs. Nye, why don't you speak with Deihlia about it and I'll call you again in a week to find out what kind of wish Deihlia would like."

"Ok, thank you," she said, shutting off the phone and placing it back in the receiver on the wall. *A wish? Deihlia has so many wishes,* Donna thought as she washed the floor. Since she and Linc had split up a few months prior, it was harder to keep the house clean and orderly, and to stay on top of everything. She worked as much as she could, but she couldn't do everything. The truth was, she was overwhelmed.

"The Starlight Foundation wants to grant Deihlia a wish," Donna told me later that evening on the phone.

"I've heard of them, they grant wishes to terminally ill children. The hospital must have suggested Deihlia to them. What's Deihlia's wish?" I asked.

Two months later, the four of us boarded a Trump Airlines plane for New York City. Deihlia had asked to go to Sesame Street to meet Snuffy.

As we made our way through the airport arrivals section, heading to ground transportation, a man in a livery uniform approached us with a "Nye" sign. He took our luggage and we followed him to the limousine that was parked outside. We sat in the expansive back seat, looking out the windows as we made our way into Manhattan. Large brick buildings loomed over bustling storefronts while countless people and cars moved in every direction. Chelsea sat with her face pressed against the back window, looking out. Deihlia was in her mother's lap, one seat belt strapped across both of them.

The car pulled up in front of the hotel. A doorman came close and opened the car door, smiling at us. "Welcome to the Plaza, ladies," he said as we stepped out of the car. Deihlia looked up at the building, then back at the doorman in his uniform and hat. Chelsea jumped up on to the first step, landing next to a woman in a long, fur coat.

"We're in New York now, girls," Donna said as we proceeded up the stairs into the lobby.

Our plush room had a fruit and treat basket waiting for us, and a folder with an itinerary. We were spending a few days in New York City, living like the storybook girl at the Plaza, with ice-cream sundaes at Serendipities, a private tour of FAO Schwartz before it opened, a carriage ride through Central Park as the sun set, and of course the wish - a visit to the Sesame Street set.

The next day, we took a cab to Broadway, where the studio was located. A young assistant greeted us, ushering us into the large studio. We walked through the large warehouse-like room. Donna pushed Deihlia in a stroller, and Chelsea held my hand. "Look, there's Oscar!" Chelsea shouted, pointing to the ceiling. We all looked up. Oscar, Ernie, Bert, Cookie Monster, Snuffy, and Big Bird hung limp and empty from the ceiling. Their furry yellow, blue, green and brown limbs dangled without moving. Deihlia's eyes widened and she put her hand to her mouth. Chelsea turned white.

"Why are they hanging from the ceiling?" Deihlia asked.

The assistant looked up with us, then smiled at Deihlia and Chelsea. "Those are extra puppet costumes. You'll see the characters come out on set in a little bit."

We pushed forward, pointing to the famous stairs and garbage can, trying to refocus the girls away from the hanging puppet suits. "We're on Sesame Street Deihlia! Isn't this cool?" Donna said, parking the stroller in an aisle of metal folding chairs that were clustered twenty feet from the stage set. There were only a few other people sitting in them. Chelsea let go of my hand and ran up to the set, and began climbing the stairs.

"I want to go up there too!" Deihlia said.

"You can go up there now, but when you hear someone say 'All quiet on the set' you'll have to come back to your seats and be very, very quiet while they film. Do you think you can do that?" The assistant asked, looking down at her.

Deihlia nodded. Donna picked her up out of her stroller and we proceeded to walk up to the stage, where Chelsea was jumping off of the top step of the stoop onto the concrete floor. Donna placed Deihlia on a step. She smiled, looking around at the building façade, at the garbage can, at the other areas of the room. Chelsea kept climbing and jumping, singing a song. Deihlia turned around and pulled herself up to the next step.

A few minutes later a disembodied voice said "All quiet on the set!"

I grabbed Chelsea's hand and told her that meant we needed to sit down because the actors were coming out. Donna picked up Deihlia. Chelsea didn't want to go back to the seats - she wanted to stay on stage. She squirmed and pulled against me as I tried to get her back to the chairs.

"I want to stay here!"

"The puppets and actors won't come out until we sit in our seats. You won't be able to see them until we sit down. Don't you want to see them?"

Chelsea nodded, her lower lip extended in a pout.

"All quiet on the set!"

Donna was in her seat. Deihlia was on her lap, watching me and Chelsea. Deihlia wanted to be up there too. She wished it hard, feeling a powerful urge within herself, around her heart. "I want to go up with Chelsea" she said. Her mother didn't say anything. Deihlia wished for it some more, but she was still seated on her Mom's lap.

I pulled Chelsea squirming back to the seats. Then she got away from me again and ran back up the stoop, her brown curls bobbing as she ran. She stood there, humming. Deihlia watched her, smiling, silently pleased that her sister was doing what she wanted to do - stand on the stoop and be part of Sesame Street.

Finally, the assistant walked over to Chelsea. "I'm sorry but you'll have to get in your seat. We can't film until you do."

Chelsea's rosy face turned back into a pout, this time it was mixed with embarrassment as she trudged down the stairs and back to her seat.

35

Oscar popped his head out of the garbage can and began speaking. Bob walked by, then struck up a conversation with him. They filmed for five or ten minutes, then stopped.

"Do you think we'll see Snuffy?" Deihlia asked.

"I don't know," Donna said, shrugging.

From behind the stage, a man came out, carrying Oscar on his arm. Oscar looked around the room, then spotted us and came over. "What were you throwing in my garbage can?" he asked Deihlia.

Deihlia giggled nervously. "I didn't throw anything in your can."

"Someone did. Was it you?" he asked, turning to Chelsea.

Chelsea shook her head no, staring at his green face.

Deihlia was looking at the man who held Oscar, his arm disappearing inside the green suit. Oscar turned to her once more. "If you're going to throw something in my garbage can, make sure it's something good and stinky!"

Deihlia nodded. "Is Snuffy gonna come out?"

Oscar looked at her and rolled his eyes. "I'm going back into my can. That Snuffleupagus - everybody likes him. I don't know why," he grumbled as he walked away, slipping behind one of the buildings.

Deihlia looked up at her mother, her eyes glittering. Chelsea eyed the stage, contemplating another run for the stoop. "He sure is grouchy, isn't he?" Donna asked.

Chelsea smiled and pointed towards the stage. "Look Deihl!"

Deihlia turned her head and saw him. First his trunk, waving around the corner of the building, then his big eyes, then his large brown body appeared, ambling towards us. Deihlia put her hands together, excited.

Snuffy walked in-between the chairs, pushing them out of the way with his right foot. His trunk dangled, swinging slightly as he walked up to her. "You must be little Deihlia," he said, blinking his big eyelashes.

Deihlia nodded.

"I'm so glad you came to visit Sesame Street today," he said. Deihlia wanted to touch him, she wanted to put her hand on his trunk. *He's real*, she thought to herself. *Snuffy is real*. "Big bird is your best friend, right?" she asked.

36

He nodded. "He is. But I have a lot of good friends. I bet you do too," he said.

Deihlia thought for a moment. She had Chelsea and Sean, some friends at school. "That's my sister, Chelsea," she said.

Snuffy turned and blinked his big lashes at Chelsea. Chelsea continued to look at him, not speaking.

"Sisters are the best friends of all," Snuffy replied.

Chelsea reached out and touched Snuffy's trunk, placing her hand flat against the brown fur.

Deihlia watched her, then reached her hand out and touched him too, petting him as if he were a horse. Donna and I sat quietly.

"Deihlia, I hear you're a brave little girl. Very brave. I need some brave friends. Will you and Chelsea be my friends?" he asked, swinging his trunk back and forth slowly between them.

Deihlia's face glowed. She smiled and nodded yes. *Yes!* "You're my friend too," she blurted out.

Chelsea was also grinning, enchanted by his large, gentle presence.

Snuffy blinked his big eyelashes at Deihlia. "Thank you Deihlia. Yes, I'm your friend too. I need friends like you. I'll see you again around Sesame Street, but I better get back now," he said, turning his large brown body around slowly.

"He's my friend," Deihlia said, turning her head excitedly to look up at her Mom. She lifted her hand and waved at him as he walked away, shuffling on four legs into the space behind the building.

"See girls? Some wishes really do come true," I said.

Chelsea sighed. Deihlia nodded, keeping her eyes on the space where Snuffy disappeared. A minute later she turned around. "Mom, when can we come back to New York?"

Donna and I looked at each other and laughed.

37

Wheelia

I'm not sure what Deihlia's occupational therapists were thinking, pushing for her to wear leg braces. They were heavy, metal things, strapped on and locked to both of her skinny legs, and attached to a molded plastic casing that wrapped around her lower torso. She was five.

A mold was made of her little body and the braces were custom built. She had to use metal crutches to move forward. It was a long procedure strapping her in. Deihlia didn't fight with the therapists or her mother when they put her into them. She was game. She was going to try and make it work, to be able to stand with the other kids and get around. She didn't complain, she just sat there as every buckle was buckled, every strap pulled, the large Velcro straps cinched across her belly.

Her mother had to then get her upright from a lying position, give her the walker or arm crutches, and stand by. Deihlia slipped her arms into the round metal crutches, placing them in front of her. She was paralyzed from the waist down, so moving her legs meant using her arms and upper body to lift and place her lower half. It took her fifteen minutes to get from the living room couch to the kitchen, eight feet away.

What were they thinking? The braces were unwieldy, a worse case than being on the floor and unable to stand up. If she fell, she couldn't get out of them or get up, and falling was very likely.

Chelsea opened the kitchen door to let their dog Spike into the house. As she opened the door he rushed in, running over to Deihlia and putting his nose against her arm as he wagged his tail. Deihlia wanted to pet him, but if she took her arm out of her crutches she knew she'd fall.

"Mom, I can't do anything."

She'd been trying to use the braces and the crutches for months. It was so difficult. "I think it's only going to be the wheelchair from now on, Deihl. Enough is enough. What do you think?" Donna said.

Deihlia looked up at her, then around at the kitchen. She couldn't reach anything on the counters or on the table, she couldn't open the drawers. She wanted to be able to reach things like Chelsea did, she wanted to climb, to open doors. She could see them, she was close to them, but they were completely out of reach. Her braces wouldn't help her do any of those things. She could barely move in them. She shook her head yes, turning to look out the window. She'd wanted to be upright like the other kids, to move around and play with them, to look them in the eyes instead of looking up. But she couldn't move in the leg braces. She was disappointed.

Her small chariot was red, the color of action, of justice, of physicality. It had handles on the back so that people could push it. It was small, like her - made of metal, with a hard little plastic seat. Chelsea affectionately called her sister Wheelia as she held the door open for her.

That Spring, Linc built a deck on the house, off of the kitchen, so she could get in and out more easily in her wheelchair. The ramp he built wasn't quite up to code. The incline was steeper than normal, and shorter. If no one was holding on to her chair, Deihlia was propelled fast down the ramp and spit out into the driveway. She quickly learned how to hold on to the wheels and slow them down a little before the ramp met the pavement. But soaring down the ramp was her favorite thing to do, especially when no one was looking.

Thirteen Days, Boston, 1990

Deihlia was seven years old and for months Dr. Zee had been preparing her and us for another major surgery, a very risky one. Dr. Zee had to move Deihlia's colostomy from one side of her abdomen to the other, because it kept prolapsing - popping out of her body. She had no muscles on that side of her torso to help keep it secure, so they were moving it to the other side, tucking her intestine behind a muscle so it would stay inside of her. They had to open up her abdomen completely. Again. The risk of infection and problems was high. If she made it through the surgery, Deihlia would have to be in a medically induced coma for thirteen days, on a drug that paralyzed the body entirely, so that the body could heal. It wasn't the first time she'd been on it, but she was older now, awake and aware. Deihlia would be on life support for the duration of the coma, her heart and lungs worked by machines. Even with painkillers, she'd still be conscious but unable to move.

We had pits in our stomachs for weeks as the day of the surgery approached. It was something she had to get through to get to the other side. Even with the seriousness of the risks, we were all focused on getting her through it and healing. We never let our minds wander to the possibility of her not making it through, or the surgery going wrong. We knew it was a possibility, just like we knew what winter felt like in our bones. But we kept that possibility over there - on the other side of a river we never wanted to look across.

They needed blood for her surgery. Deihlia and I had the same blood type, AB - the only ones in our family who had it. In fact, it is the rarest blood type of all. It's only shared by 1% of the U.S. population. I went into the hospital a week before and donated. "I really hate needles," I said to the nurse as I sat down.

"Everyone does. People who don't hate them, well, that's a different kind of problem," she said, raising her eyebrows. When she put the needle in my arm, blood spurted out, arcing over her head in a pulse that matched my heartbeat. "Wow, your adrenaline is something else today," she said, trying again. It wasn't the first or last time I would think: *This is nothing compared to what Deihlia goes through. This is nothing. If she can do it, I can too.*

As I lay there, I thought about the people I'd known who'd died of AIDS. Classmates. Friends. I thought of the children born at the same time as Deihlia with medical conditions requiring surgery, and with it, blood transfusions. Some of them became infected with HIV. Deihlia had received a lot of blood, but she'd been lucky once again and hadn't gotten HIV.

The days leading up to her surgery, we used a cassette player and recorded ourselves reading books, so that the nurses could play the tapes for Deihlia while she was in the coma, lying there conscious and unable to move. We couldn't be there all the time, and it was something to help keep her mind occupied and to let her know we were with her when we weren't in the pediatric intensive care unit.

"Do I have to go, Mom?" Deihlia asked the night before she was going into the hospital as she played on the living room floor with her *Teenage Mutant Ninja Turtles* figures. She was focusing on what was within her control - her toys.

Donna looked down at her. Michelangelo flew through the air in Deihlia's right hand, and she kept her eyes on him, bringing him down to land on top of a Barbie, taking her out. "I'll miss school. I don't want to go," she said, the turtles in each of her hands battling it out on top of a stuffed animal.

Donna didn't answer. There was nothing she could say that would make it better, easier, less true, or more palatable. "I know, Deihlia. I know. I wish you didn't have to go, but they need to fix your colostomy," she said, bending down to give her daughter a kiss on the top of the head. Wasn't twenty three major surgeries more than enough? She wondered. Donna didn't want to think any further than this one. It was already too much.

All of us were there that day - Donna, Nana, me, and a few dear friends. Dr. Zee and her nurse came in and put Deihlia on a gurney. Each of us leaned over and kissed her, hugged her, said "I love you" and "we'll be right here waiting for you" as lumps swelled in our throats and our faces took on the flushed look of people trying not to cry. We were trying to be strong for her and for each other, but we were scared. It was going to be a very long day, and an even longer process, and anything could happen.

Morning crept along. We left the hospital in pairs to go for a walk uptown, to look at the pretty historic brick storefronts with the black shutters, to get coffee and muffins, to walk off a little of the fear and anticipation, to try and breathe, to see sky; to see life. One of us always stayed in the waiting room while the others went out for fresh air, anchoring our presence as a family as near to her as we could be.

41

On our forays out we would only get so far, then our concern stopped us, pulling us back to the hospital. That cord would only stretch so far.

In the waiting room, other families came and went. We noticed them across the room from us, reading magazines, fidgeting, tense like we were. Like us, they were there but not there. But their surgeries started, then ended a few hours later. The Bus Driver arrived too. I looked up as he joined us, appearing through an invisible doorway I couldn't see. This time he sat in an empty seat next to me, his legs outstretched and ankles crossed in front of him, arms folded across his chest. He knew us well by then, and nodded at me. I got the feeling that he was rooting for Deihlia too. After all, she'd eluded him several times. Surely having Death on her side was a good thing? Sometimes I'd turn my head and he'd disappeared. I held my breath waiting for the surgeon to come walking through the door, apologetic. Time would pass and I'd breathe normally again, wondering who it was that he'd escorted out. Hospitals shepherd a lot of deaths. But I didn't really want to know. I was simply grateful that it was not our little star.

Sixteen hours later, her nurse walked through the door in green scrubs. Deihlia had made it. She was in the pediatric intensive care unit in a coma. Donna, Nana and I stood up and followed her in. Deihlia lay under a thin white blanket, a tube in her mouth, tubes coming out of her nose, IVs, other things. I hated the way they had to lubricate her eyes then tape them mostly closed. The meager blanket covering her body never seemed like enough.

We stood next to the bed and talked to her quietly. "We're here. You made it. You're going to be ok. Everything is ok. You're doing great. I love you so much." As we stood looking at her, the tension in our shoulders dropped a little, but not all the way. Her mom touched her face lightly, smoothing a wisp of her hair, all the unshed tears of the day welling in her eyes.

Deihlia was in that coma for thirteen days, thirteen being the number associated with death and transformation. This surgery was certainly a major transformation for Deihlia. Each of us visited the hospital as often as we could, eyeing the monitors as we stood by and talked to her. She was still. We knew she was in there, even with the morphine, she was in there somewhere, and we wanted her to know that we were with her. I'd tell her about my day, about Chelsea and

Sean, or I'd read a book to her for a while, knowing that she heard me.

It was hard to see her like that, I can admit it now. We never ever talked about what it was like for us, we never told her how hard it was to let the surgeons do what they needed to do, to stand helplessly by while she was cut open yet again. Our experience was nothing compared to hers, it never would be. We didn't even talk about it with each other. Our focus was her, on being strong and positive for her. At seven she already had to bear more than most people do in a lifetime. She was so much bigger than our fear and sorrow, so much braver than what we had to go through. My strength and ability to soldier on despite how I felt emotionally was not always an asset to me, but when it came to her, it was. Like mother, like daughter, like sister and sister. Like aunt and niece, like grandmother.

The incision was deep and long down the center of her, held together by three giant staples. It needed to heal from the inside out. They were able to transition her off of the life support, but she had to stay in the hospital for a long while so they could be sure she was healing and didn't have an infection. I wondered how she and her body were reconnecting, adjusting to what they had done inside her. Then all of a sudden, she became septic, seriously ill. Her face and body were pale, lighter than white. She looked like a ghost, and she was barely there. Was she going to get through it? She was touch and go. It took a month to recover just from that — the incision took even longer. When I look back, I see us sitting around her bed, streaming love to her; love, love, love. It was the only medicine or magic we had but it was strong and unrelenting.

Was that a point at which Deihlia's soul was rethinking things, deciding if she should stick around? It really seemed to be up to her. Her body had its own storyline, it was the vessel she inhabited, but her will seemed to be the dominant player, the force that her body worked in concert with. Her will was showing me clearly that I had my own will too. What was I doing with it? The universe offers us moments of opportunity every day, in every person, every event, every interaction. Deihlia's unique and profound challenges brought this into sharp relief. Life and death. Growth or stagnation. Awake or asleep. Though there's always a third way, the middle ground - a grey area where both things coexist in relative comfort, the story we were in didn't exist there.

The Playing Field, 1991

The white van pulled into the driveway. Georgia, the driver, got out to open the side door. She was an older woman in her fifties, short but strong. Her grey hair was cropped close to her head, but for the messy bangs that fringed her forehead. Her cheeks were always pink. Georgia liked to talk to Deihlia about her day at school as she drove her home. Opening the van door, she smiled at Deihlia as she released the seat belt from around her chair and rolled her over to the lift.

"Have a good afternoon," Georgia said as she stepped down then lowered the lift to the ground. She studied Deihlia, who was wearing a black jacket and loose, printed pants, her backpack on her lap. Then she looked down the driveway. Deihlia's grandmother's white car was parked in front of the van. Through the window of the kitchen door she could see the kitchen light was on. Georgia reflected for a moment on an odd thing she'd been noticing. Sometimes - it didn't happen today, it never seemed to happen when she was looking for it - there was a light blue color around Deihlia. It wasn't her clothes. One day, as she got back into the van and Deihlia went up the ramp, that light blue fell like a cape off of her shoulders, trailing behind her on the wooden ramp, then was gone as quickly as she saw it.

"Thanks, Georgia. Bye." Deihlia replied, pushing her chair around the front of the van and then up the ramp to her house. Nana opened the door. "There you are. How was school today?"

Deihlia put her backpack on the kitchen table and bent down to pet her black cat, Mugsy.

"Would you like a snack? I brought muffins and apples."

Deihlia continued to pet Mugsy, then lifted the cat onto her lap, holding her there while she ran her hand over Mugsy's back. She kissed the top of her head, rubbing her cheek against the silky black fur.

"You're awfully quiet today, Deihlia. Are you feeling okay?" Deihlia's eyes filled with tears as she continued to look at the cat who purred against her hand, crinkling its claws against her legs.

"What happened?" Nana asked, bending down to put her arm around Deihlia's back. Deihlia shook her head no, then wiped the tears from her cheeks with the sleeve of her shirt. "The kids at school are so mean to me. They call me names. No one will sit with me at

44

lunch or in class. Someone threw a pencil at me today and it hit me in the back of the head! I can't get to the gym and I have to sit in a study hall instead. I hate school, I hate it!" she blurted out.

Nana put both arms around her and hugged her. "I'm so sorry, Deihlia. Children can be so mean. I wish you could go to school with your sister and Sean, but that school doesn't have any ramps. Isn't there anyone in your classes who you like and could sit with?" Deihlia was in a public elementary school in their town.

Deihlia shook her head no. "No one will talk to me, even when I try to talk to them." The white tiled floor blurred beneath her. The cat leapt off of her lap on to the counter. A pile of dirty pans sat next to the sink full of soapy water.

The phone rang. Nana stood up and answered. It was Deihlia's Aunt Cindy, an Aunt on her father's side who lived across town. She had three kids of her own roughly the same ages as Deihlia and Chelsea, and she liked to have them all play together. She asked if Deihlia and Chelsea would like to come over and play with their cousins that afternoon. Nana covered the phone with her hand. "Would you like to go over to your cousins' and play today?"

Deihlia nodded yes, wiping the rest of her tears on to her sleeve. The door opened and Chelsea walked in. It was late spring, the sun was shining brightly outside, turning Chelsea into a silhouette as she entered.

Thirty minutes later, they were in their cousins' backyard. Deihlia was in her new pink wheelchair. Chelsea got behind her and helped to push her over the lumps of grass. Their cousins, LP and Susie, were there. Deihlia had named her younger boy cousin LP, which stood for "Little Paul." His father was big Paul. LP was younger than the girls, but he played well with them. Usually he came over to their house, because his Mom hadn't felt confident about taking care of Deihlia, but she was getting better at it. LP was a petite boy with white blonde hair; the baby in the family. Quiet and reserved, he only spoke when he had something important to say. Otherwise, he tended to hold back. With two older sisters, he had access to a lot of hand me downs, and wore dresses every day. They were comfortable to him, he liked the way they felt - airy and free. His mother tried to encourage him each morning to put on pants, but he stood his ground. "This is what I want to wear," he'd say. That day, Chelsea saw that LP wore a light pink dress over his pants. No one

45

ever said anything about it, and she wasn't going to either. That was just LP.

There were several large cardboard boxes in the backyard, refrigerator boxes their father had brought home for them. The kids put them together and made two tunnels side by side. "First one to get to the end is the winner! But we have to crawl like this," Chelsea said, getting down flat on her stomach. She wanted it to be a fair race for her sister. "No cheating!"

Each of them was down on their stomach at the entrance to one of the boxes, two at each tunnel squished together to fit through it. Deihlia and LP were a team at one, Chelsea and Susie at the other. "Go!" Chelsea said, and the race commenced.

Chelsea and Susie were neck and neck, giggling as they squished against each other, the box warping and bending around them. Deihlia and LP pulled themselves along, smiling at each other. "We can beat them! Come on!" Deihlia said, putting one elbow down and then another, dragging her body behind her. LP used his knees to shimmy his torso up, until one knee caught in his dress. He looked back at Deihlia's legs. They were limp, pulled along by the top part of her body. He'd never noticed that before. Then he looked at her arms, and how she was pulling herself, one elbow at a time. *She can't use her legs*, he thought to himself. *The wheelchair!* He'd never really noticed it before. She was always just Deihlia - his fun cousin. At four years old, the wheelchair had been invisible to him.

"Are you coming?" Deihlia asked, looking back at him over her shoulder.

"Yeah, let's go!" he said, pulling himself up next to her, smiling. He felt close to her. She became something more to him in that moment. He didn't know anyone else like her.

"We win!" Chelsea said, popping her rosy-cheeked face around the end of the box, looking in as Deihlia, then LP reached it.

"Let's do it again. LP was too slow this time. I think we can win the next one," Deihlia said, pulling herself out onto the grass. "I know you can go faster, that dress was in the way," she said as she sat up, looking at LP as he emerged out of the cardboard tunnel.

LP looked down. The front of his dress was smudged with dirt. "My dress matches your elbows Deihlia!"

She laughed. "Can you take it off for the next race?"

LP was already pulling the dress up over his head. He wore a plain green t-shirt underneath. He wanted to win the race with Deihlia and beat his sister.

"Alright, let's win this one," Deihlia said to him, putting her hand on his shoulder. Chelsea and Susie leaned over, getting back on to their stomachs. Deihlia and LP followed. The cardboard tunnels yawned at them, jiggling as they got close.

"Ready?" Chelsea asked.

"Go!" yelled Deihlia.

A Day Like Any Other

Georgia waited until Deihlia was up the ramp and on her deck before she pulled the van out of the driveway. She felt uneasy about dropping Deihlia off after school when no one was home. She knew that Donna worked late sometimes and would be along shortly, but it still made her uncomfortable. She backed the van out of the driveway and glanced back one last time before she drove off. Deihlia was already inside the house.

Deihlia threw her backpack on to the kitchen table and went over to the refrigerator. Leftover broccoli, ham and cheese, a bunch of old apples, and grapes. None of them appealed to her. She couldn't see what was in the cupboards above the counters, and she knew there wasn't anything in the ones below it. She turned around and went back outside, pulling the kitchen door shut tight behind her, closing the dog inside the house so he wouldn't follow her. When she got to the ramp, she lifted her hands off the wheels as soon as she went over the edge of the deck. Her chair rolled quickly down. She leaned back and held on to the sides of her chair as it hit the bottom end of the ramp and thrust her chair into the driveway. Her chair zoomed then slowed as it got close to the street. She put her hands back on the wheels, pushing it across the road.

Sean and Chelsea weren't home from school yet, but Deihlia could see that Sean's mom Elsa was home. She pushed herself into the driveway and parked her chair at the bottom of their kitchen steps, which went into the driveway. She listened to find out if Elsa was vacuuming, and all was quiet.

"Elsa! Elsa!" she shouted.

But nothing happened. "Elsssssaaaa! Elsssssaaaa!" she shouted, for longer this time. Then she wheeled back and looked in the yard to see if she could find a stick long enough to bang on the door. She didn't like to crawl up concrete stairs because she always ended up getting scraped. The grass yielded nothing. *Oh well, up the stairs then*, Deihlia thought as she angled her wheelchair close to the bottom step.

Suddenly the door opened, and Elsa popped her head out. "Deihlia, I thought I heard you out here!"

Deihlia smiled at her. "Hi, Elsa. What are you up to?"

Elsa glanced over at Donna's house and saw that her car wasn't in the driveway. Since the divorce, Donna worked a lot. She couldn't always be home when the girls got home from school. "What a nice surprise

48

to see you before Sean gets home. I was just going to have an afternoon snack. Would you like to join me?"

Deihlia nodded her head yes.

"Do you want to come inside or should we have our snacks out here?"

Deihlia didn't feel like climbing the steps and getting her hands even dirtier. "Can we have them out here?"

"Sure. I have pop tarts, toaster strudels, or homemade apple pie."

"Toaster Strudels please! Two!" Deihlia said. Elsa always had different snacks to choose from. She liked that a lot.

"Of course, give me a few minutes. Would you like a drink? Some milk or water?"

"Milk please," Deihlia replied. She was hungry. She knew Sean and Chelsea would be home from school soon, but she didn't want to wait.

Deihlia sat outside at the bottom of the steps. She turned her chair to face the street and her own house. She could see her dog Spike in the front window, his nose pressed to the glass, watching her, his long ears drooped around his face. "Spike!" she said aloud, waving at him. Spike barked back at her.

Elsa opened the door, carrying a tray, and stepped carefully down the stairs. "Here we are - Toaster Strudels and milk." She placed the tray down on the slab of concrete that served as the base to the stairs, which extended out against the side of the house. Then she sat down on the last step and picked up a napkin.

"I like to put on my own icing," Deihlia said, picking up the packet that came with the Toaster Strudels.

"I know you do, that's why I didn't do it." Elsa said, picking up a glass of water and taking a sip.

"How was school today, Deihlia? Did you learn anything interesting?"

Deihlia had her snack in one hand and the icing packet in another. She began to squeeze the icing over the pastry so that it formed an X over the crust. Then she lifted it to her mouth and took a bite. She shrugged in answer to Elsa's question, looking over at her.

"Well, it's too bad school isn't as fun as running around the neighborhood with your friends."

Deihlia nodded, taking another bite.

49

"What did you do today, Elsa?" Deihlia asked in between bites.

"Oh, you know, cleaned the house, did some grocery shopping, ran a few errands. Nothing too exciting. But I did see a clown today! That was unusual."

Her eyebrows went up. "A clown?" Deihlia asked.

"Yes. Can you believe it? He was in the hardware store buying some window cleaner. He had a white face, a red nose, orange hair, and big orange circles on his cheeks! I asked him why he was in the store, and he said 'I'm buying window cleaner'!"

Deihlia laughed a belly laugh. "I guess he had dirty windows, huh? Or maybe he was part of the cleaning circus. You should've told him to come to our houses."

Elsa giggled. "I could use a cleaning clown."

They turned their heads in unison. They heard the box-on-wheels sound of the bus coming down the street, then it stopped in front of the house. The yellow door swooshed open and Chelsea, then Sean, jumped out.

"Over here, Chelsea," Elsa said, waving, as Chelsea turned her head.

Sean ran up first. "Deihl! What do you wanna do today?"

"Hi Sean," his mother said, standing up.

Chelsea bounced into the driveway behind him. "Hi Elsa! Hi Deihl."

"Would you like a snack?" Elsa asked them.

Chelsea said no, and Sean didn't answer. He walked into the house, dropping his backpack in the driveway before he squeezed past his mother on the step.

"I have homemade apple pie," Elsa said.

Chelsea thought about it for a minute. "That would be nice," she said. Elsa always had something to offer, and it was usually homemade. She wished her mom didn't have to work, and could stay home and clean and bake while they were at school. Since her parents had divorced, her Mom was always working.

Elsa disappeared into the house. They could hear her telling Sean to pick up his shoes, to close the refrigerator door, to shut the bathroom door while he was in there.

Deihlia finished eating her second strudel, then swallowed down the last bit of milk. "The food lady always has good stuff," she said, putting down her glass.

Chelsea laughed. "Yeah, Elsa is the food lady for sure. What time is Mom coming home?"

"I don't know. Wanna play Nintendo for a little while before she gets home?"

Chelsea shook her head no, her ponytail bouncing behind her head.

"I wanna play some Nintendo," Sean said as he pushed the door open and bounced down the stairs. A red ring of juice circled his mouth.

"Cool, let's go," Deihlia said, wheeling towards the end of the driveway.

Elsa came out, a small plate of pie in her left hand. "Here you go, Chels."

"Can I come inside and eat?"

"Of course! Please come in." She looked across the street as Sean and Deihlia made their way up the ramp. Sean was running up the incline, his hands on the back handles of Deihlia's chair.

Chelsea looked over at them too. "They're going to play Nintendo," she said.

"Ok, I guess they can play for a little bit while we visit." Chelsea picked up the tray off the concrete and followed Elsa inside the house. She liked having Elsa all to herself for a few minutes, like she was visiting a fairytale story of how families were supposed to be.

Antennae

Though she only had partial feeling in her body, Deihlia still felt a lot. She saw a lot, she picked up on a lot, she understood a hell of a lot. It was like she had invisible antennae all over her head. Sitting on the floor playing with her Ninja Turtles or Game Boy, she appeared to be engrossed in her play, and she was. But her antennae were always hard at work, picking up information, subtleties, and changes in tone. While her hands and eyes were focused on Super Mario Brothers, her brain was synthesizing other things. She wanted to know what was being discussed in hushed tones on the other side of the door. That's how her antennae grew, sprouting out and sneaking around doorways, stairs, into halls and other rooms.

Her antennae also gave her other skills, like reading people and transmitting their character to her - their points of courage and hidden wounds. She rarely shared what she picked up, she simply used it to connect with someone, finding an easy path around their defenses and sneaking in.

A Big Day

It was Chelsea's first recital. She'd been going to dance class twice a week, practicing at home when she could find a spot. It was her big day, the Spring Fling Dance. Donna was backstage helping the dancers. I brought Deihlia to the dance, and we met up with Nana and Pop, her husband, in front of the middle school. They stood on the sidewalk, Pop in his red t-shirt and jeans, hands in his pockets, wearing bright white sneakers. He kept his dirty-blonde beard trimmed round on his chin. His moustache was so bushy it mostly covered his mouth. With the gray sunglasses on, the only part of his face that was visible were his cheeks.

We walked into the school auditorium, blinking in the darkness after coming in from bright sunlight, and found a row that still had three seats open. Pop, Nana and I slid in. I sat on the end. Deihlia pulled her wheelchair up to the end of the row and parked it beside me. She was sitting out in the aisle like she often did.

All of the seats were filled. Parents and family members of dance students aged four to fourteen murmured, waiting for the show to start. The lights dimmed and the dark blue curtain opened, sliding over to the side of the stage. The youngest dance class trekked out on to the stage, taking their positions. They were only four or five years old, and they had never been on stage before. They wore purple and yellow dance costumes, with feathered tiaras to make them look like birds. The music started and some of them began to spin, raising their arms in the air and moving in circles. One little boy looked out at the audience and stared, unmoving. Another stood in place, yawning. The audience giggled. A few parents were dark silhouettes standing in front of the stage holding their video cameras up. The song was fast, just a little number so the children could experience it, then they walked off stage.

The next group came on, and they were a little better. Their movements had a relationship with the music. One girl jumped up in the middle of the number, twirling around twice. Her classmates looked at her, confused, then resumed the dance.

Chelsea's class was on next. I was proud of her. Donna brought her to this private dance school twice a week and some Saturday mornings, a few towns over. Chelsea stuck with it and had been coming for three years. Her group was markedly better than the last class. Their moves had rhythm, spirit, and personality as they

53

moved to R.E.M.'s song *Shiny Happy People*. Their teacher liked to throw in a new song every few recitals. Chelsea smiled, rosy-lipped, her sequin headband catching in the stage lights. She threw her hips around to the music, jumping in the air. It didn't matter what the other dancers were doing, all I cared about was Chelsea. She was enjoying herself. Her curls bounced as she moved from one side of the stage to the other. I was so proud of her.

I looked over at Deihlia as I smiled at Chelsea's happiness. She sat quietly, still.

The dance ended; everyone clapped. I whistled quickly for Chelsea, calling her name. I looked over at Deihlia again. I could sense that something was wrong. I put my hand on her arm. "What's going on, cutie?" Another group of dancers filled the stage and began to dance.

Deihlia shook her head. I could tell she was trying not to cry.

"It's hard to watch them do things you can't do, isn't it?" I said softly.

She nodded, looking down at the floor as the next set of dancers walked onto the stage. This was just one moment in her life. She'd had, and would have, many, many more of these - every day at school. At home. In the neighborhood. My heart hurt. "Oh Bug, I'm sorry."

Deihlia didn't answer. She sat in her chair in the aisle watching the older kids dance to a New Kids on the Block song. Finally she turned to me. "Will it ever be my turn, Auntie?"

I looked her in the eyes. "It will, Deihlia. You might not be up there right now, but you'll have victories of your own. I promise."

The dancers left the stage and the teacher walked out, mic in hand. An older woman, she stood erect like a ballerina, her wavy brown hair pinned back on one side with a sparkly flower that glittered under the stage lights. She wore a pale pink Capezio dance dress and white tights with her white Mary Jane dance shoes. Her dark-red lips moved as she thanked the audience, the parents, and the dancers. "They worked so hard this year. You should be very proud of each and every one of them."

The lights went on. I got out and turned Deihlia's chair around, towards the doors. I was as happy for Chelsea as I was aware of Deihlia's hurt. Both feelings sat together in my heart, just like the girls.

Nana slipped out of the row and walked beside Deihlia. We both had long legs and our strides matched as we walked out of the school. "Your sister did an excellent job up there today. She really loves to dance, you can just tell."

Deihlia was quiet. We walked out of the school. Going from the dark into the bright light hurt our eyes.

"Don't you think so, Deihlia? Wasn't your sister good?" Nana asked.

I bent down over Deihlia's chair, putting my arms around the front of her, hugging her from behind. Deihlia nodded at her grandmother, blinking up at her in the bright sun.

A Day at the Races

Parents, kids, and teachers stood on the side of the track, watching the race. It was a late fall Saturday. Bare trees stood in dark clusters against a bright blue sky on the edge of the school grounds. The children had been training all season, practicing a couple of days a week after school. I walked into the crowd, looking for my sister. Traffic had held me up and I arrived just as the race was about to start.

A voice bellowed out of a megaphone. "We're ready to start! Racers, take your positions!"

I moved to a spot in the crowd where I could see, closer to the fence. At the start of the track, children aged eight to eleven were spread out, getting ready to go. Each racer sat in their own racing chair, their hands on the wheels, waiting for the signal. Deihlia was two over from the left, wearing a helmet and a colorful racing jersey, seated in a red racing chair, her legs tucked underneath it. The school purchased or received donations of racing chairs and other equipment, so each chair was different. Deihlia was smiling, her hands on the wheels, looking sideways at the boy to her left.

The signal went off with a pop, and the racers shot out on their track, their arms pushing the wheels furiously as they sped along the course, the wheels' silvery discs rotating in the sunlight. I smiled and tears sprang to my eyes. Deihlia whizzed past me, smiling fiercely, her eyes on the track ahead, her sky blue cape flapping in the wind behind her along with the multi-colored capes of the other children in the race. I was glad to see her enjoying herself. It had taken some convincing to get her to come to the after-school sports program at the Mass Hospital School. Though she'd gone to their pre-school and had a great experience there, she was hesitant about joining a sports program for children with disabilities. She wanted to play with the kids in the neighborhood and get into local mischief. She didn't want to miss out on anything by being in an after-school program many miles away.

"You're going," Donna had said.

I whistled as she turned the corner, and shouted her name. There were six other kids in the race with her. I didn't know them, but Deihlia talked about them at dinner when I came by a few weeks earlier. "Sterling's been in a wheelchair since he was shot one day when he was out playing ball on the street in his neighborhood," she said "and Rachel was in a car accident and lost a leg. Jimmy was born without legs. Everyone is pretty nice there, but some of them don't have parents. It's sad," she said, reaching over to get her Game Boy off of the table.

"What do you mean, they don't have parents?" I asked.

Deihlia put the Game Boy on her lap, keeping her eyes on me. "Auntie, some of those kids were brought there as babies by their parents and left there. Their parents just gave them up and never came back."

I was quiet for a minute, taking it in. "That's so sad, Deihlia. Did they just tell you this stuff?"

She nodded. "I've known most of them since pre-school. Plus, we all talk about stuff after the races. We have snacks and hang out. Everyone there has some big medical issue. They wouldn't be there if they didn't."

I didn't know what to say. She carried around more than we did, all the time. "It's hard to imagine parents doing that, no matter what the problem is."

Deihlia shrugged. "Yeah, I can't really imagine it. I don't think too many of them are in public school like I am. Most of them go to school there."

"Do you like the program?"

"Yeah, I like it okay. Basketball is kind of funny. It's pretty hard to dribble the ball and push your chair at the same time. We've had some major crashes," she laughed, her shoulders shaking.

Her ability to be both in the story and outside of it looking in impressed me. She made fun of herself first, before she cracked on someone else. Even painful moments were saved by her sense of humor.

Here she was on race day, competing against her friends with disabilities. I cheered louder, whistling and clapping as they reached the finish line. Deihlia came in third, putting her fist high in the air as she crossed the finish line. Her face was flushed, and she was beaming. I was beaming too.

I walked through the loose-knit crowd, making my way towards Deihlia. As I walked, I suddenly became very aware of the ground beneath my feet. Of my feet, stepping on the ground, the way my ankles turned, how my long legs moved of their own accord to follow the direction my eyes wanted to go. I breathed in the fall air, feeling an appreciation for my body that I'd never felt before. It traveled like a tiny star from my heart down to my feet then back up again, catching in my throat.

I stopped where I was in the middle of the crowd and looked around at all the people: some standing, some sitting, some in hand-powered wheelchairs, others in motorized chairs, some kids in braces and crutches, some of them smaller than normal, with prosthetic limbs, with no limbs, and I looked at the coaches, parents, and siblings. Something in me opened and expanded, going outwards. I felt connected to all of them. Each person was someone very important, and I was just another one of them. They were people who cared, people who were pushing hard to do more with what they had, who were getting over themselves, and had disproportionately more to get over. I was nobody special there, but I was somebody too. I was pushing to get over myself too. The parts of me that weren't working well weren't really visible to the eye, but I knew they were there.

A bright pink and lime green jacket darted through the crowd coming towards me, a ponytail bopping above it. "Auntie, you made it!" Chelsea said, putting her arms around me. I wrapped my arms around her and hugged her tight. "Did you see Deihl?" she asked.

"I did, I sure did. She did great! I want to go congratulate her and see how she's doing."

She nodded and took my hand, leading me through the crowd towards Deihlia and her mother, saying hello to the people she knew as we walked between them.

The Net

Sean knocked on the kitchen door then opened it, his hockey stick in hand. "Deihl, come out and play." It was a cool March day, but it was windless and dry. The trees were still bare and the lawns were brown. Hockey was still on Sean's mind.

"I'm in here," Deihlia yelled back from the living room.

Sean walked into the living room and found Deihlia on the floor playing Nintendo. She didn't move her head when he came in, she just kept playing, her eyes on the TV and her hands moving quickly. Sean was always at her house, or she was at his.

"Come out and play hockey with me Deihl. I want to practice." Sean swung his hockey stick towards her so that it swiped the air next to her, missing her face by an inch or two. She turned her head and looked at him. His blonde hair was in a scraggly mullet, and he wore a black and gold Boston Bruins jersey.

"C'mon, I'll set up the net in the street."

Deihlia looked back at her game, then paused it. "Do you have another stick? I don't have one."

Sean nodded vigorously. "I'll go get it!" He turned around and ran out.

The kitchen door slammed behind him. Deihlia pulled herself up into her wheelchair, then reached over and grabbed her army hat. She put it on and wheeled herself into the kitchen, where she put on her jacket, then went out the door and down the ramp. They lived in a development off of the highway, and their end of it was a circular road with seven houses dotting the perimeter. The only people who drove down the street were the residents, because it didn't go anywhere else.

Deihlia saw that the goalie net was placed in the middle of the road, and Sean was picking his second stick up off of the ground. "Here you go Deihl," he said, coming over and handing it to her.

Deihlia took the stick then looked around. They had the street all to themselves. "I'll play the goalie," she said.

Sean nodded, dropping the puck and running after it down the road, then turning back to chase it towards the goal. Deihlia put her stick to the ground, trying to hold on to it with one hand while she steered her chair with the other.

Thwack! Stick met stick and Deihlia grabbed on to hers with both hands, trying to push the puck back. Sean maneuvered around

59

her, moving his body in a half circle while keeping the puck in tight between them. Then, *swoosh* - he sent the puck sailing under Deihlia's chair, into the net.

"Under my chair! That was a good one," Deihlia said, pushing the brim of her hat up so she could see. She turned her chair around and dragged the puck out with her stick, then hit it hard, sending it across the road into the grass.

Sean ran after it then pushed it back into the street.

An old green car approached, slowing down as it got close to them. Deihlia moved over to the side of the road.

Their neighbor rolled down his car window, scowling at them as he shouted. "You shouldn't be playing in the road you two! Get out of the road!" Sean moved the net to the side so that the car could pass. "And *you* really shouldn't be playing in the road," the driver pointed emphatically at Deihlia as he drove slowly past them.

Sean stood on the other side of the street, squinting at the car as it turned into the driveway of a house a few houses down. Deihlia looked at him, then over at their neighbor as he got out of his car. He didn't look back at them or see them watching as he entered his house.

Sean put the net back where it had been in the street. "Jerk," he spit, pushing the puck back into play. Deihlia ventured back out, raising her stick in the air as if she was going to bring it down on someone's head. Suddenly Sean smiled so big that his cheeks became round like small apples, and he went back over to the grass. He rummaged around in the dirt until he found what he was looking for. Deihlia watched him, both hands on her stick as it rested on the street, ready for action.

"This'll work good," Sean said, dropping a stone the size of a racquetball onto the ground. Deihlia smiled, raising her eyebrows as she pushed her hat up again. "This is what you get," he said, raising his stick high in the air then bringing it down against the stone.

Clunk! The stone made a hollow metal sound as it hit the side of their neighbor's green car.

Deihlia put her hand over her mouth and started laughing. "What if he catches you?"

Sean shrugged, stepping towards her. He was mad. "I don't care. He didn't have to be such a jerk to you."

"I want to do one too."

Sean went over to the grass again and nosed around until he found another rock. He placed it on the pavement in front of Deihlia. "You've gotta swing hard so it goes far," he said.

Deihlia adjusted her seat and lifted her stick high in the air, twisting her torso as she aimed it at the stone.

Sean could tell that her stick was going to drag along the street and not hit the rock the right way, so he hit his stick against Deihlia's as it skimmed the pavement and together they struck the rock so hard that it went high in the air, sailing over the car and hitting a tree.

Deihlia laughed as the rock smacked the tree then bounced off it and hit the side of the house. Sean grinned, snickering.

"Let's play hockey again tomorrow, right in front of his house," he said, moving towards the puck.

Moving the stick around her wheels, Deihlia leaned out over the side of her chair trying to stop Sean from pushing the puck away from her. "I can't play tomorrow, I have to go to the hospital."

Sean stopped, halting his next goal, and looked at her. "To the hospital? I didn't know you were going in the hospital." It seemed like Deihlia was always going there. He didn't like it when she was so far away.

Deihlia turned her chair around towards him. Her hat fell, sliding down over most of her eyes. "Are you gonna get the goal or what?"

Sean continued to look at her. He was feeling something that he didn't have words for. She was his best friend. He knew what that felt like. It felt true, it was something solid. Why did she have to go into the hospital tomorrow? He'd forget about what it was like when she was gone until she disappeared again, reminding him of the hole that he'd felt the last time she was away.

Deihlia looked at him, bending forward as she moved her stick slightly, seeing her chance.

Sean recovered and lifted his quickly, sending the puck flying into the net.

Through the Door, 1993

I went down the hall and had to stop myself from taking the first left, which led to a different part of the hospital now. Suffolk Universal had completed their renovations last year, and Starfish Five didn't exist anymore. Deihlia was staying on the Harmony Seventeen ward now. I got off of the elevator and said hello to the nurse behind the nurse's station. This ward was a big fast forward in time from Starfish Five. "You can go right in, Deihlia's just hanging out before dinner," she said.

I walked into the room she'd been sharing with another girl for the last two weeks. "Hi, Deihl," I said, going over to stand on the other side of her bed. The new ward was well equipped and had a new kind of chair next to every patient - one that could be pulled out into a narrow bed for family members. I put my bag down on it. I'd slept on it once, staying over with her. Donna had used it more than once.

Deihlia lay in bed, watching TV but not really paying attention to it. "How are you today, Bug?" I asked, leaning over to give her a hug, avoiding the tubes and wires. She put her arms lightly around me, half-heartedly. She didn't say anything, just continued to keep her eyes on the TV.

The Simpsons yellow and blue characters were running across the TV screen, the familiar "D'oh" shot out in the air above us. Trish, her long-time nurse popped her head into the room. "Dinner will be coming shortly, Deihlia. I'll be in to clean you up after dinner."

Deihlia didn't turn her head towards Trish. She kept watching *The Simpsons*.

"What's going on, Deihl? Are you feeling okay, or...?" I asked, standing next to her bed.

I noticed that her roommate's bed was made and her things were no longer scattered around her section of the room. "It looks like Courtney went home today," I said.

Ever so slightly, Deihlia shook her head no, and her eyes began to shine like glass.

My heart clenched and I grabbed her hand. "Oh honey, I'm so sorry," I said, tears springing up in my own eyes. Her hand firmed up, holding mine. Tears began to roll down her face slowly. She nodded her head yes this time, and I leaned over her bed again to give her another hug. She held on tight and began to sob.

"It happened this morning. They closed my curtain, but I could hear everything. She was supposed to go to Disney World next month," Deihlia said, her face blotchy, her lips quivering.

A woman in light-purple scrubs walked in, placing the dinner tray down on to the cart next to the bed. She looked at us but didn't say anything.

"She was really looking forward to that trip. That's all she talked about. She gave me her Mickey Mouse yesterday," Deihlia said, pulling a small stuffed toy out from under the sheet.

"I'm so sorry Deihl. I'm sorry Courtney is gone and that it happened right next to you. It's so sad that she won't get to Disney World." I felt helpless. There was so much we couldn't protect her from. So much was out of our hands. I handed her a tissue.

Deihlia looked at me. "She was my friend. We were gonna play chess today. I beat her yesterday." She sobbed.

I continued to hold her hand. "She was a sweet girl. She was always asking you what you thought about everything, wasn't she?"

Deihlia half-smiled, nodding her head, rivers on her cheeks. "Yeah. She was younger than me. I liked to make her laugh."

The room felt hollow, yet full of Deihlia's grief. I guess the Bus Driver had come in that morning and picked up Courtney, sliding out of the room with her cradled in his arms.

"Do you want me to ask if you can move into another room, with someone else?"

Deihlia thought for a moment, then looked over at the empty bed as she wiped her face with the tissue. "No, that's ok. I'd rather just stay here and miss Courtney right now."

It was going to be a long night for her. I was grateful that they had thought of adding the convertible chairs to the new ward. You never knew when you might need to spend the night.

The Quest, Boston, 1993

It was May. The trees had blossomed, birds were nesting, and everything was starting to come back to life. People were outside all the time, shaking off their winter coats. Deihlia was in the city spending the weekend with me. We were going to the movies, to Newbury Comics, strolling around Back Bay. We took the orange line into Back Bay, and later that day, we took it home. On the subway home, rainbow-hued flyers fluttered and flew as the doors opened and closed at each stop. A pink flyer slipped under the footrest of Deihlia's pink wheelchair. She bent down and picked it up. "Pride afterparty at Fritz. What's that, Auntie?" she asked, looking over the black and pink image of a crowd underneath a rainbow made of balloons.

"Oh, that's a party that happens after the Gay Pride Parade. There are a bunch of them."

"What happens at the parade?" She asked, looking up at me.

I looked at her, in her backwards baseball cap and her ninja-print hammer pants. She'd fit right in at Pride. "It's a big parade where people who are gay dress up and ride on floats and celebrate their community. They're proud of being gay so they're getting together to dance and have fun. It's a real mix of people. It's lots of fun."

"Are you going?"

"Yeah, probably." I said. Some people brought their kids to Pride. Deihlia was nine. She was asking about it. "Would you like to go?"

Deihlia nodded. "Yeah, I think I would."

"Let's ask your Mom when I bring you home tomorrow," I said.

The second Saturday in June came up fast. Deihlia was excited about going to a parade full of gay people. What would it be like?

"What should I wear for the parade?" Deihlia asked over dinner the night before.

"Let's see what you brought in and we'll pick something out," I said. I wanted her to feel good about herself, and I didn't want her to be disappointed. I picked up the bag her Mom had brought in with her when she'd dropped her off earlier. I went through it, pulling out different pieces. After spreading them all out on the couch, Deihlia pointed at her 'Save the Whales' t-shirt. "How about that?" she asked. It certainly was appropriate, I thought. Then she picked out a pair of grey sweatpants, and her baseball cap, which she always wore backwards.

"Don't forget your cool bike gloves," I said, placing them on the small pile of clothes being made ready for morning. Deihlia smiled, nodding.

The next day, we boarded the orange line, locking Deihlia's wheels into place so that her chair wouldn't roll around the train as it sped up and slowed down. She hung on to the pole, keeping herself steady as the train lurched into movement. When we arrived at Back Bay station, we discovered that the elevator was out of service. My friend Peg shook her head and looked around at the crowds heading towards the stairs and escalator. Deihlia looked up at us.

"I guess we'll have to take the escalator," I said, watching the crowd thin as it ascended.

"Is that okay?" Deihlia asked.

"If the elevator is out, then we have no choice. We're not going to get in trouble, and if we do, we'll just point at the elevator. What do they expect people to do?" Peg said.

Deihlia kept looking at us, wondering.

"It's ok Deihl. You wouldn't get in trouble anyway - it would be us. Don't worry."

We moved over to the escalator, and I got on first. Then Peg pushed Deihlia's chair onto a stair and stood behind her, holding the chair steady as it went up. Deihlia put her hands on the escalator rails, looking down over the side as we went higher.

Cops lingered around the turnstiles, keeping an eye on the crowd. One of them watched us get off of the escalator. As we opened the gate, he approached us. "That's not too safe," he said, gesturing to the escalator, "you really shouldn't put a wheelchair on the escalator."

"Elevators out of service," I said matter-of-factly as we kept walking. Deihlia looked up at me, as if to say *I told you so*. I gave her the same look back, smiling.

As we stepped out of the station, we were in a throng of rainbow-hued men and women. Leather, feathers, Bermuda shorts, ripped jeans, spandex. From glam to grunge, every style was covered within a twenty-foot radius. Deihlia looked around and slipped on her sunglasses, checking everyone out. We moved along with the crowd, heading towards Boylston Street, where most of the action took place.

We maneuvered through the crowd, trying to get as close to the street as we could so that Deihlia could see the parade better. "All I can see are people's butts," she said, so we tried to squeeze her into the front of the line, between the grunge chicks and the queens. The parade began, and the dykes on bikes thundered past in full leather gear. After them, floats began to roll by. There were bunches of people from different gay organizations or groups, from different towns and states, carrying banners to show "We live here too. We're part of your community." Theater groups, random clusters of gay men wearing rainbow suspenders and spandex, the queer fairies in their diaphanous skirts, the lesbian auto workers union, and so on. Deihlia sat and watched, and we stood right behind her, checking to make sure she was okay.

After a while, the Quest float came along. Quest was a nightclub with three stories and three different dance floors, so the float had buff gay men dancing on its makeshift stage to loud house music. They waved at the crowd, tossing out pink crowns as they went by. A crown flew through the air towards us, landing on the edge of Deihlia's foot. She bent over and picked it up, turning in her seat to show it to us. She had a big smile on her face. "Put it on," I said, "it was meant for you. It even matches your wheelchair!" She placed it over her baseball cap, where it fit perfectly, the word QUEST encircling her head.

She smiled up at me, and I snapped a photo of her wearing it. "What do you think so far? Do you want to stay, go, or do something else?" I asked.

Deihlia shook her head. "Nah, this is pretty interesting Auntie. I've never seen so many different people like this before."

"The world is full of all kinds of people, Deihl. It's not like elementary school." I said.

She listened, then turned around to continue watching the parade.

I knew that Deihlia was going to be in many environments in which she'd be the one deemed to be "different." I wanted her to experience a full-on celebration of people who were labeled "different." I wanted her to see a spectrum of people being boldly themselves, wearing their queerness like a badge of honor, wearing it like a crown, happily blowing kisses and waving to the people on the sidelines. I wanted her to know there were different kinds of people and communities out in the world - places where she could belong. Elementary school is not the whole world, but she wasn't out of it yet. I was trying to show her that it wasn't always going to be like that. She might have to go searching for her tribe, like a lot of us do, but they were out there to be found.

Later, we sat on Boston Common for the stage show and speeches. We ate lunch. My friends came by, seeking us out, stopping to say hello to Deihlia, to see how her day was going. She sat in the sun with her sunglasses, hat, and her black fingerless bike gloves, soaking up the attention, trying to be cool, even if it made her a little bit more shy than usual.

"How are you feeling about this, Deihl? Do you want to stay, or go? We can do whatever you want," I said.

Deihlia was quiet for a moment. I couldn't see her eyes through her dark sunglasses. She looked around. "Let's stay for a while longer," she said. "Let's see what happens next."

The Mountains, New Hampshire, 1994

The sun was just starting to brighten the hills around them. They'd left home early that morning, before sunrise, half asleep and cold in the car. It was early February, they still had another week to go before school vacation started. Chelsea slept against the car seat with her knit cap pulled down over her eyes. She was wrapped in a pink and white afghan crocheted by her great-grandmother. Deihlia was awake, looking at the world outside the windows as Green Day's song *When I Come Around* thrashed on the car stereo. Her long, blonde hair framed her face and spilled out underneath her ski cap. The girls didn't mind getting up before the crack of dawn on a Saturday, because they liked going to Loon Mountain, a ski resort in Southern New Hampshire, about an hour or so away from home. Donna found out about an adaptive skiing program at Loon, and had been bringing the girls up to learn how to ski that winter.

"Finally! Here we are," Donna said, "wake your sister up." She pulled into a parking spot.

Deihlia reached her arm over and started to shake Chelsea. "Chels. Chels! We're here. Wake up!"

Chelsea lifted her head and opened her eyes, yawning.

They made their way up to the central ticketing area. The program was staffed by volunteers, and Deihlia had the same coach each week. Donna and Chelsea dropped Deihlia off with her coach, then went off for their ski lessons. Jeremy was all in black, his cheeks were red, his goggles sat on top of his head over the knit hat. His blue eyes glittered in the early morning sun. He went to college a few towns over and spent his weekends volunteering for the adaptive program.

"Deihlia! I wasn't sure you were coming today. I'm glad you made it," Jeremy said.

Deihlia smiled up at him. "I made Mom bring us up this week. She almost wasn't going to come because she has so much work right now. Anything new with you?"

Jeremy shrugged his shoulders. "Nothing. Just a lot of good skiing this week between classes. Life's pretty good in my world."

Deihlia nodded. She liked his attitude. He made everything sound so simple. "Every day in school this week I kept thinking about skiing."

68

"That's good. That helps you learn faster. When you imagine doing it, you ski better. And now you're here, so let's get to it! I was hoping you were coming up, so I set aside the bi-ski we used last week for you. That one seemed to work the best for you, don't you think?" Jeremy asked.

"Yeah, I think so too." Deihlia said. The bi-ski was a kind of sport seat with two skis on the bottom. She'd get strapped into it, then Jeremy would tether her to him and he'd ride behind her to help her learn how to use it as they went down the slope.

A few minutes later, he picked her up and helped her get into the bi-ski, tightening the straps so that she couldn't slip out of it. It was a simple configuration that allowed Deihlia to develop her own senses on the slope, and her skills in navigating the snowy terrain. They'd been on this trail for the past two weeks. It wasn't the bunny trail, it was the next one up. She was ahead of her mother and sister.

"Here are your outriggers. If you hold on to those, I'll grab my gear and we'll head up the mountain." He handed her the light poles that had small, hard, ski-like flippers on the ends for helping to push off or maneuver over the snow.

The other volunteers helped them get Deihlia in her bi-ski into the lift, and took Deihlia's wheelchair and put it inside the building.

Deihlia and Jeremy sat in the lift. Deihlia liked the first ride up the mountain the best. She felt like she was leaving her life behind: rising up the mountain, gliding skyward against gravity into a different part of the world. The higher they went, the more her heart lifted. It made her feel like everything was possible.

"What a perfect day for skiing," Jeremy said, breathing in the cold air.

"It's a perfect day," Deihlia replied. Her lungs felt like they were expanding, like she could breathe in the blue sky. It happened to her last week too as they approached the top of the lift.

Jeremy hopped out quickly and then pulled Deihlia off the lift. He pushed her over to the top of the slope and put the tethers on her, then attached them to himself. Deihlia sat snug in her bi-ski, grinning in the bright sunlight. She pulled her goggles down over her eyes.

"Ready?" Jeremy asked.

"Yep!" Deihlia replied, pushing off with her outriggers. Jeremy skied behind her, helping to keep her from propelling like a bullet down the side of the mountain. Deihlia watched the terrain in front of her, moving her outriggers to push her skis over the small hills that surfaced. It felt good hopping over them, and then landing and speeding down the hill. She knew Jeremy was behind her, but he seemed to let her choose the pace and the path down the slope. Deihlia pushed her outriggers into the snow, harder this time. She liked to go fast, she liked the white wind against her face, how the other skiers were dark blots that blurred as they sped past them.

"Whoa, Deihlia! You're going pretty fast for this slope!" Jeremy shouted behind her.

She didn't answer, she just pushed again to go even faster. All of her thoughts and frustrations disappeared in the air behind her, neutralized by the sun and wind.

A minute later, Jeremy leaned back and went sideways to slow her down, pulling the bi-ski in a sideways direction as it met the base of the trail. Deihlia turned and looked up at him as he approached. "Can we go down the next trail? I want to go faster. We've been on this trail for two weeks now."

Jeremy paused and looked at her. He couldn't see her eyes behind the goggles, but he could tell by her face that she was in the zone. First ski of the day and she was already there. Deihlia was becoming a speed junkie just like him. They were a good match. Though their pairing was random, created by chance, it seemed like chance knew what it was doing. "I think you're ready for the next trail, Deihlia. You've got this one down."

She grinned in reply and adjusted her helmet and goggles.
At the top of the next trail, Jeremy spoke to her before they took off. "This trail is a lot steeper than the last one. There are more moguls and those dips in the snow can be tough. We can ski on this one all day if you want, so you don't have to go 100 miles an hour on the first run." He had to say it. It probably wouldn't do any good with Deihlia, but he had to at least try.

Deihlia looked up at him, then over her shoulder at the side of the mountain below them. It was a completely different trail. She wanted to fly over it and master it at once. Going slow would only take the fun out of it. "Yeah, sure thing," she said.

Jeremy knew she was going to gun it anyway, and he was right.

Deihlia hit her outriggers against the snow, giving it all she had, and they sped off down the trail. The first mogul appeared below them, to her right. She aimed for it, and they went over, her bi-ski airborne for a few brief seconds before it landed back on the snow.

"Deihlia! Slow it down a little!" Jeremy yelled into the wind.

Deihlia saw a bowl in the slope below them, and aimed for it, wanting to swoosh through it.

Jeremy saw where she was heading and hoped they didn't wipe out in there. He'd seen other new skiers flip over as they went in. All he could do was trust that the lessons he'd been giving Deihlia would hold her in good stead. And he was with her if they wiped out.

Deihlia put her right outrigger down against the snow and tilted her body in that direction so that the skis turned and arced. She didn't tilt too far, or she'd end up on her side. It was a delicate balance, but her body told her exactly how far to tilt, and when to let go. She lifted her outriggers horizontally and let the trail take them down, walls of snow on either side of her. She stared in front of her. Jeremy was still behind her. He was a skilled and experienced skier. But he knew they might wipe out as they came out of this. Suddenly, the walls of snow cocooning her on the side were gone, and she was in the air, sailing out over a small edge. She landed with a bump, and kept going, letting gravity determine their speed. "Deihlia! Slow it down!" Jeremy added some resistance to slow her down, because she wasn't listening to him.

It felt good, flying down the side of the mountain without constraints. Deihlia was wide open inside, like the sky was streaming straight through her heart. For a few seconds she forgot about Jeremy behind her, about the bottom of the trail coming up below her, about the kids at school. She was sky and speed, elemental.

The bottom of the trail came into view, she could see people walking off it in their skis. She turned her skis slightly by moving her torso one way then the other to start slowing down, weaving to the left and then the right to bring it to a slow gentle stop, but Jeremy was doing a lot of the work too.

He skied up next to her after her skis stopped at the bottom of the trail. "Deihlia! You're a demon on the trail. That was too fast for a first run on that hill. I thought we were gonna wipe out a couple of times." He said, bending over halfway with his hands on his thighs.

71

Deihlia looked up at him, pushing her helmet up off of her forehead. "But we didn't wipe out!" she said giggling. "This trail was so much better. That was awesome."

What could he say? She was right. If it were just him skiing it for the first time he would've done the same thing. "True enough, but we could wipe out at any time on trails like this."

Deihlia was quiet for a moment, then she pushed her outrigger down into the snow. "I don't want to go slow just to avoid wipeouts. If they're gonna happen anyway, I'd rather have a blast and go fast. If we wipe out, we wipe out."

Jeremy heard her clearly. He'd never worked with such a fearless kid before. He hadn't thought about it this way either, especially with the students in the adaptive program. He was extra careful with them because they each had such particular handicaps, he didn't want their wipeouts to cause extra problems for them. But Deihlia, at eleven years old, had something figured out for herself. She was right on that one too, but it was his job to be the voice of reason and teach her how to have a sustaining relationship with the sport. He squatted, then sat down in the snow next to her.

"I hear you. But I don't want you to hurt yourself and then not be able to ski at all. You have a real affinity for this sport and I want you to be able to keep doing it."

She nodded, pushing her outrigger back and forth, making a cut in the snow. "I like going fast. This is the only place I can really fly," she said, saying out loud something she hadn't realized until now.

Jeremy felt for her. He didn't know what Deihlia's life was like. He only knew her in the program. She had a fierce spirit. *It must be hard for that spirit to be so restricted*, he thought to himself. "Tell you what. We'll spend the day on this trail. I promise we'll go fast, but you've gotta listen to me when I tell you to slow it down. I know this trail well. Just slow it down with me when I tell you to and we'll have a great day without any wipeouts. I don't want to get fired," he added, chuckling. He knew that would work.

Deihlia giggled and looked him in the face. "Alright. I don't want you to get fired either." He was her skiing buddy. She didn't want to lose him.

People walked by them, heading back towards the lift, or towards the lodge. The sun was high in the sky. Jeremy put his hand out towards her, and Deihlia reached over and smacked her gloved hand against his.

The Junior Counselor, Maine

Deihlia was in the car with her father. It was mid-July. Linc was driving her up to summer camp in Maine, where she would spend the next two weeks at Camp Explorer. She'd gone to the Easter Seals sponsored camp for children with disabilities for the past three years, spending two weeks there. The camp was located in the woods of Maine, set on a small lake nestled in the mountains. Though she hadn't wanted to go that first year, this year and last she looked forward to it. She was going to be in their junior counselors-in-training program. Next year she could be a junior counselor.

Woods surrounded them on either side of the car. Dark green evergreens and pines cast a cool shade along the road. They were about forty-five minutes away from camp. Deihlia never had her father alone all to herself; this was a rare occasion. It was usually her and Chelsea, or they'd be with a few of his five step-children from his second marriage. They talked about family history on the way up, about how his ancestors, the Cooks, had come from England with the first pilgrims, settling on Cape Cod. "You come from hearty stock, Deihlia. The Nye's were whalers back in the day. The sea is in your blood, just like it's in mine."

Deihlia couldn't swim, she never went in the water. She looked over at her Dad, trying to picture him as a sailor or a whaler. As far as she knew, he didn't ever go out in boats. She couldn't visualize it. All she could see was her Dad: his slim body in jeans and a Harley-Davidson t-shirt, with his short blonde hair, the moustache he'd had for the past few years, and his mirrored aviator sunglasses that reflected the road in front of them. She looked like him. They shared the same oval face, button nose, and smile. But neither of them went in the ocean. "I couldn't ever kill a whale, Dad. They're kind of special creatures."

Linc smiled and laughed, looking over at her. "Yeah, come to think of it, I don't think I could either. Good thing we don't have to, huh?"

Giggling, Deihlia nodded.

Later, after they registered her in the lobby and brought her things to the cabin she shared with three other girls, her Dad turned to her. "I guess I should head back now. You're gonna have a great two weeks."

They left the cabin, walking along the sidewalk to the drive that circled in front of the main building. "Thanks for bringing me up, Dad," Deihlia reached out to give him a hug.

"Have a good time and don't get into too much trouble," he said, his arms around her shoulders. They stood like that for a moment and then he pulled his arms back. "Love you. I'll see you soon."

"Bye Dad, love you too," Deihlia said. She stayed on the sidewalk and watched him as he walked back to his car, disappearing from view.

Ten days later, Donna and I were on the same road, on our way to Deihlia's camp. Donna had called me late two nights before. I was getting ready for bed. She was sobbing on the phone. Linc was on his motorcycle. He was hit at an intersection by a man who went through the red light. He'd been rushed to Boston to the medical center with the best trauma unit in the area. I told her I'd meet her there. When I arrived, she stood in the emergency room waiting area, shaking her head, tears streaming down her face. Linc didn't make it.

Donna called the camp to let them know we were coming to get Deihlia, but they didn't tell her. There was no need to ruin her time there any earlier than was necessary. She'd been having a great time at camp, seeing her old friends and assisting the counselors. She liked being able to help. "She's really made the new campers feel comfortable and get into things quickly," her counselor said on the phone, "she's really becoming a leader at camp. Deihlia is a very caring and thoughtful kid."

We arrived, parking the car in the shady area of the parking lot. It was quiet and peaceful, the air smelled like pine, birds chirped in the trees. Even though it was beautiful, we walked into the building with heavy hearts. As we approached the front desk, Donna told the woman behind the desk who we were, and she nodded, disappearing to get Deihlia.

A few minutes later Deihlia came in, an unfinished red and blue lanyard in her lap. She was surprised to see us, and a look of confusion, then worry, crossed her face. "What's going on? Why are you here?"

"We need to bring you home, sweetie," I said. I could tell Donna was going to burst out crying, and I knew she didn't want to do it right there in the lobby.

75

"Let's go outside for a little bit," I said, putting my hand on her back as we moved towards the door.

"Mom, what's going on? What's the matter?"

Donna shook her head, unable to speak yet, her eyes filling.

As we got further away from the building and closer to the car, we stopped under a tree and knelt down beside her. I kept my arm around her. Donna squatted, facing her daughter, her hands on her arms. "Your Dad was in an accident," she said, choking as she continued. "He was on his motorcycle and was hit by someone going through a red light. He didn't make it Deihlia. I'm so sorry."

Deihlia burst into tears, and we all wrapped our arms around each other, sobbing. A few minutes later, she looked up. "Where's Chels? Does she know?" she asked, wiping her face.

"She's in Vermont with Chrissy. She doesn't know yet. She'll be home tomorrow, so we'll tell her then."

We went back to Deihlia's cabin, packing her things. Her room was neat. There were two books stacked next to the bed, and a couple of envelopes. Back in the main building, the counselors were gathered in a group as the campers ate lunch. They rotated in and out of the dining room. Deihlia found her counselor and went over and touched her on the arm. She turned and looked at Deihlia.

"I have to leave now. My mom is here. We have a family emergency."

Her counselor looked at her with concern, then over at us, and bent down to give Deihlia a hug. "I'm sorry you have to leave. It was such a pleasure to have you here, Deihlia. You'll make a great junior counselor. I hope we'll see you next year."

Nodding, Deihlia said goodbye, then turned towards us, putting on a strong face. She wheeled into the main office and told the woman at the front desk that she had to leave. She didn't know that we'd already called them to let them know.

The day was bright, the sky cloudless blue as we walked through the parking lot towards the car. It felt unreal, like a fake backdrop that had been brought in and put around us.

"I wish Dad had made it," Deihlia said, fresh tears rolling down her cheeks. "Chels is gonna be devastated. Why did he have to die?"

"I don't know Deihlia. I wish I knew," Donna said, opening the car door to let her in.

"How are we gonna tell Chels?" Deihlia asked.

I looked over at her. "Deihlia, we'll figure it out. Probably the same way we told you."

"I'm worried about her," she said as her mother lifted her up out of her chair and put her into the backseat of the car.

Behind the Scenes

I don't know exactly when it happened. Was it when she was nine, or eleven, or thirteen? At what point does something we're very aware of blend in, then settle under the surface of our thinking? The awe we had for Deihlia and the protectiveness we felt for her became part of our everyday lives. Deihlia was just being Deihlia. Surviving, growing, figuring herself and her world out like every other child. She was wise, funny and prone to joking, good at school, and good with people. She made things look easy. She cracked jokes to lighten up tense moments. Her concern for the people she loved, her family and friends, was deep and clear. The way she loved us was to make our lives a little easier, and to shield us from some of her difficulties.

She was energetic, focused, and naturally independent. A leader. Though she shared some of her struggles and asked for help, it wasn't as often as it should have been. That's just how she was. She gave us her love and attention generously - she focused on us. I'd never experienced that kind of pure attention before. She had so many gifts, and the way she loved and saw each of us was one of the most powerful ones.

But the older she got, the more we expected her to sail through every surgery, come through her challenges just fine, and get her homework done while she recovered in the hospital bed. Without meaning to, she'd set our expectations high. She was bigger than life to us, and whether it was conscious or not, she tried to live up to it. She'd been living up to it since she was born, but eventually that image stopped being in the forefront of our vision - how much she handled every day without complaint. The superhero image we had of her slid under the surface of conscious awareness, settling deep.

New Games, 1996

Julia opened the kitchen door, letting herself in. She came over to Deihlia and Chelsea's house almost every day after school. They'd met through her cousin Mary who lived down the street. Though she was good friends with both Deihlia and Chelsea, she and Deihlia had a special bond, cheering each other up when things were hard. Both misfits and rebels, Deihlia was like the wise older sister that Julia never had. She was an only child. After school, they roamed the neighborhood together like a pack, with Deihlia dispensing wisdom as they went.

"Hey, what's going on?" Julia asked.

"In here," Deihlia said. She was in her bedroom finishing her homework. Chelsea was over at her cousin's house.

Julia stood in the bedroom doorway. Her wavy black hair had been cut, and curls framed her heart-shaped face. Four years younger than Deihlia, she was tall for her age. Deihlia looked up at her.

"What do you feel like doing today? Wanna play a game of Magic or something?" Julia asked. Magic was a fantasy card game that Deihlia and her friends played often.

Deihlia looked over at the stack of Magic cards on her shelf. She'd had the same set of cards for almost two years now, only adding new ones occasionally. She needed some new ones to progress in her game. Magic the Gathering, a battle card game in which creatures fought against each other, sometimes picked up magic spells that gave them more power, or were outranked by their opponent creature's characteristics, was one of Deihlia's favorite games. It had a complex set of rules and was always coming out with new cards. "Nah. I need some new cards."

Julia shrugged. "We can always go up to Reeves game store and buy some. I'll walk up there with you if you wanna go."

"I don't have any money."

Julia scrunched her face. How could Deihlia have no money at all? "Come on, a packet only costs like $2.50. You must have enough to buy a pack or two."

Deihlia shook her head. Ever since her dad died a couple of years back, there wasn't ever any money for anything. She couldn't babysit like other kids did; no one would hire her. Her mom was painting and babysitting, and she couldn't drive Deihlia to get to a job even if she could find one. "I don't have any money, and there's none around the house. Believe me, I was looking in the sofa the other day."

Julia hated to see her friend so broke. She was having a rough day herself but Deihlia's problems made hers feel a little smaller. How could she have no money at thirteen years old? "I have like $8 on me. Let's walk up and get you a couple of packs of cards."

"It's okay, Julia."

"No, I mean it. I want to go up there. My mom will give me another ten dollars if I ask her. It's not a big deal."

Deihlia relented. "Let's just go see what they have. I haven't been in there in a while."

They walked outside. Deihlia flew down the ramp and they headed up the hill, walking and wheeling towards the end of the development that took them out to Route 140. Reeves, a chain store that sold video games, movies, comic books, and games was about a mile away, tucked in a small shopping plaza not far from the liquor store and high school. Route 140 was a busy road that went from two lanes to four lanes in different sections as it crossed the highway. It didn't have sidewalks, and people drove fast along the stretch they were traversing.

"I can push you along here," Julia said as they turned out on to the busy street. Cars whizzed past them. Deihlia was in front of Julia, facing the traffic that blew by.

"No, I'll do it," Deihlia said. They walked on the narrow shoulder of the road. Cars honked as they drove by, annoyed that a teenager in a wheelchair and her friend were walking so close to the cars. It was late afternoon when traffic started to get heavy, so it was a noisy walk across the highway overpass as one car after another honked at them. They had to stop for five minutes at the entrance to the highway, until someone took pity on them and let them cross.

Deihlia wheeled quickly across the entrance, pushing fast. Julia ran behind her. "Just let me push you," she said as they approached another hill. The side of the road was bumpy, full of pebbles and trash. She grabbed on to the handles of Deihlia's chair and started to push. A few minutes later they were at the top. Reeves was in sight, across the road and down a bit. They waited at the stop light for a walk signal, and crossed.

Deihlia was starting to get excited to see what new games and cards they had at Reeves. Then she got a pit in her chest because she wouldn't be able to buy any of them. She was mad at her dad for dying, and she felt bad about it. Why did he leave them like that?

Julia held the door open. The bell tinkled, and Deihlia went in. The guy behind the counter recognized Deihlia. She'd been in many times, but he hadn't seen her lately. He didn't know her friend. "How ya doin' today?"

Deihlia waved at him and said "Hi," as she went over to the new game section. Julia went with her, perusing the shelves. She wasn't into video games like Deihlia was, but she could play a little in a pinch. The bell on the front door tinkled and a cluster of teenage boys came in, joining Deihlia at the new game shelf. The new Super Mario Brothers role playing game was out. Three of the boys next to her grabbed a copy off the shelf. She looked sideways at them. They were teenage boys, probably about fourteen. One of them was smaller and younger looking, and the other two were lanky. One of them spoke and his voice cracked. Deihlia wanted that game too. She felt frustrated, and moved over to another shelf on the other side of the store, checking out the Magic cards and comic books. There were a couple of comics she wanted to read, but she didn't even pick them up. What was the point? The boys wandered around the store, picking up different items as they went, joking and bantering.

Julia stood next to her. "Let's get a couple packs of Magic cards."

Deihlia reached up and slipped two packs off of the hanger, handing them to Julia. She could hear the boys at the register, paying for their piles of stuff. "Why don't you go pay for those and I'll meet you at the door?"

"Ok," Julia said, walking to the end of the store and getting in line behind the six boys. Deihlia peeked around her. No one was there, or watching. She reached up and took three more packs off the hanger, and slipped them into the pocket of her hoodie. She wheeled casually towards the door and waited there. The boys passed by her on their way out. Each one looked at her as they passed through the door, bags hanging lightly in their hands, as if they contained nothing. She ignored them and waited for Julia.

Cash went across the counter, and the two packs of cards were handed back to her, with some change and the receipt. "I don't need a bag," Julia said. She turned and came towards Deihlia.

"Bye now!" he said, waving to them as they left the store.

They walked back to the busy road, and stood at the lights waiting for the cross signal. "Here you go," Julia said, holding out the packets. A breeze ruffled their hair as cars sped by.

"You can keep those for your deck. I got my own," she said, slipping the silver edge of the packets out of the side of her hoodie pocket.

Julia's eyes widened. Then she laughed. "No, you didn't!"

Deihlia nodded. She wasn't proud of what she'd done, but she wasn't going to hide it, either. She didn't want Julia to feel like she had to buy her stuff like she was some kind of charity case. And she didn't want to feel like one either, so she took matters into her own hands.

"Shoot, Deihlia," Julia said. She was only half surprised.

Deihlia looked down at the road. The light turned green and Julia took a step into the crosswalk. Deihlia saw her legs go past. The pavement glittered in the sunlight. Pushing her wheels, she went forward to catch up with her friend. Everything was different now, and there was no going back. She wanted to figure out how to make some money, because this didn't feel good to her at all. It weighed like a heavy ball around her neck.

Visiting, Boston, 1996

I picked up the ringing phone. "Hello?"

"Auntie, it's me, Deihlia. I miss you."

"Deihl how are you, Bug? What's going on?"

"Nothing much. I just need some Auntie time. Can I come in and stay with you this weekend?"

"Yeah, of course. Anything special you want to do?"

"Nothing special, just some time with you at your place."

That Friday night, I parked my car on the street in front of the old Victorian house where I lived. The house was on the inside elbow of a street lined with old Victorian houses painted with sedate historic colors punctuated by bright trim. Though it was just off the main street, it was quiet and peaceful. I'd bring Deihlia into Back Bay tomorrow, go to Newbury Comics, lunch, maybe a movie, but tonight we were just going to hang out. My apartment was on the third floor, a small garret apartment with sloped ceilings and a tiny kitchen.

I held Deihlia's chair steady as she jumped out from the car, pushing off with her arms as if to jettison herself into the open cockpit of her wheelchair. I helped to push her chair over the concrete walk that led to the house. Deihlia then pushed herself out of the chair and clambered up my front stoop, four wooden stairs, her butt on the stair treads, her arms behind her pushing up as she lifted her body to the next step. I opened the front door to the house and she pulled herself over the threshold, and then across the dirty oak foyer floor, going backwards the whole way. She got to the first step on the first floor stairs and went up, her hands on the stair treads as she lifted her body up to the next step. There were landings and halls between the three floors. Rather than getting in and out of her chair each floor, she simply pulled herself along each floor, moving backwards all the way to the top. I felt terrible that I wasn't strong enough to lift her.

After ten minutes, she reached the top of my third floor stairs. I stepped beside her and unlocked my door, carrying her chair into my apartment. The landing was narrow, so she had to slide into my apartment several feet before she could get back into her wheelchair. "I'm sorry, Deihl. I really am," I said.

"It's ok, Auntie," she said as she climbed up into her chair. My dog was all over her, licking her face, wagging her tail madly, pushing her nose into Deihlia's neck. "Rudy! I see you, girl," Deihlia said, patting her on the head. Rudy was a three year old Dalmatian. She was born deaf, and was spared being euthanized because they didn't realize she was deaf until they'd put her in a shop to sell her. They'd asked only for payment of her boarding fee, and I fell for her sweet and sensitive face with the black spots around both eyes.

I turned on some music and lit a couple of votive candles in the red glass holders I kept on my table.

"What do you want to do? Wanna play a game of chess?" I asked. We started to learn chess together a few years prior, but she quickly eclipsed me in the game.

Deihlia went over to my table, looking around at my apartment. She hadn't visited in a couple of months, but nothing much had changed. "I like your place, Auntie," she said, "Can I bring Julia with me for an overnight sometime?"

I looked at her sitting there all nonchalant, like she hadn't just climbed Mount Everest to get into my apartment and spend the night. She was already thinking of coming back again. "You and Julia are always welcome. You know that."

"Maybe I'll live in the city one day," she said as she leaned over to give Rudy a kiss.

I put the chessboard and pieces on the table. "Maybe you will. You could get around better here with public transportation than in the suburbs."

We set up our chess pieces on the board. She was always white. She moved a pawn out two squares and waited for me to make my move. "What do you like about the city?" she asked.

I moved my knight, jumping over the pawns.

She moved another pawn on the other end of the board.

"What do I like? Well, I like the mix of people. I like being able to walk around my neighborhood. Not having to drive. There's always something going on. Even if I don't get into the museums as often as I'd like, I like knowing they're there. I always hated the suburbs." I said, pushing out a pawn timidly - only one square.

"Yeah, I don't hate it, but it's not that easy to get around."

"You really need a car out there, that's just how it is."

A third pawn slid out on to the board, forming a small spearhead that was coming in my direction. Keeping her eyes on the board, she asked, "Do you think I'm ever gonna have a car?"

I hadn't thought about it until that moment. She was still in middle school. I looked up from the board at her face. The candlelight flickered across her cheeks, lighting up a section of her dirty-blonde hair. "I don't know Deihlia. I wish I could say yes, but I really don't know."

She nodded, never lifting her eyes from the game board.

I moved my second knight out front. "What's making you ask that question?"

She shrugged. "I don't know. Chels is starting to babysit. Mom drives her over there or they come and pick her up. I'd like to make some money too."

She was thinking further ahead than I was. It was all I could do to get through this month, never mind two or three years from now. Suddenly Rudy jumped up, putting her paws on the table, knocking our chess pieces over.

"Aww. Rudy!" Deihlia said, laughing. "Game over!"

I laughed too. Rudy was always trying to steal things from the table; she was the court jester. I told her to lie down. Deihlia giggled, watching me hand signal once, twice, three times to my deaf dog to get her to lie down.

"Seems like she has selective hearing," Deihlia said, watching as Rudy ignored me and tried to get me to play, pawing at my legs. Finally I put my hands on my hips and gave Rudy the angry face. She got down on the floor, with a look of hurt surprise that I was being so adamant.

Deihlia laughed again.

"Can I get you something to drink or a snack or anything?"

She shook her head. "Nah, I'm good." She wheeled back, moving into my living room area. It was small and cozy. She hopped out of her chair, sitting on my futon sofa. I went over and sat beside her. It was dark out, the large window was black, reflecting only my candles and the table lamp.

"What do you do here all by yourself?" she asked.

"Well, I'm not really all by myself," I said as Rudy came and sat next to us, right on cue. "I write, I read, I listen to music, cook, I have my writing group here, have people over."

She kept her eyes on my face. "Oh yeah, I forgot you write, Auntie. Will you read me something you wrote?"

Her question made me feel quiet, naked for some reason. I didn't talk about my creative life with my family much, but it was Deihlia. She and Chelsea were closer to me than anyone.

I smiled. "Ok, sure, if you really feel like hearing something. And it's ok if you don't like it."

"I would, Auntie, I haven't heard your writing," she said, putting her hand on Rudy's head.

I went over to my desk and pulled out my notebook from under the small stack of books. "It's funny that you should ask Deihl, because I just wrote a piece about you."

She looked up at me, blinking. Her face was open, without expectation.

I always felt more myself when I was around her and Chelsea. I was solidly in the world for a reason, and stronger parts of me fell into place.

I sat back down on the sofa next to her, opening my notebook. "You know, I think I needed this weekend too," I said, and started to read.

The Beckoning Sky

It was afternoon when they arrived at the campground in southeast Massachusetts. LP helped his father unload the tent and gear from the car. They'd been coming to this campground for the past few years, discovering new areas each time they stayed. LP grabbed the stakes and began to hammer them into the ground. His Dad was tall and stocky with a ponytail trailing down his back. His dirty-blonde hair was starting to recede at the forehead. He lifted his bushy eyebrows as he extended the tent pole up. He was a gentle, quiet man who loved to be out in nature. Deihlia sat in her wheelchair on the edge of the campsite, watching her cousin and Uncle. She held the other tent poles, waiting to hand them over. LP was still petite, but at eleven and a half he was skinny and strong. Long gone were the days when he wore dresses, but he did pay careful attention to his style. He wasn't into sports but he liked to go camping with his Dad. Deihlia turned from watching them and looked around. There were clusters of trees between campsites; the ground was covered in pine needles. The air smelled like Christmas. In the distance, she saw a triangle of blue through the trees: the pond. LP's father promised to take her kayaking, and she wanted to try it.

"Almost done," LP said, helping to pull a tarp tight across the top of the tent.

His father knotted the last cord. "There we go. You two can do your own thing now if you want." He stood back, looking at their work.

"I wanna show you around the campground," LP said as he got behind Deihlia and started to push her pink chair. He was glad that she was finally able to come camping with them. He had so much he wanted to do with her. This trip brought three things together that were important to him: his Dad, camping, and Deihlia. They walked by a pop-top camper that had an awning stretched out over a card table and two chairs.

Deihlia looked to her right. It felt peaceful, like the trees held the stillness in place with their spiky green fingers. "This place seems pretty cool," she said.

LP pushed her down a narrow path over protruding tree roots, behind a couple of empty campsites. Suddenly the trees got thicker and she couldn't see through them. "What's over that way?" she asked, pointing.

LP turned his head to the right. "Oh I think that's a hill or something. I was going to take you to the hidden dock. It's around the other side of the pond. It's not really hidden, I just call it that cause it's harder to get to, and everyone uses the main dock."

"Let's go see the hill first."

He stopped pushing, looking ahead at the area before them. Tree branches bent low over the path and weeds were overtaking it in sections. He could hardly see it. He looked to his right again at the clear trail leading to the hill. Maybe Deihlia wants an easy trail ride, he thought, even though he was the one doing the work. "Ok, we can do that if you want," he said, bearing down on the handles and lifting the front of the chair up to pivot and turn it.

He pushed her along the trail for five minutes, past the outermost campsites. They came to a clearing at the base of a large, grass covered hill. Deihlia looked up, then turned to face LP. "Can we go up there?"

He looked at her, then he looked up. He knew she wasn't asking if they were allowed to go up there, but rather if he could get her up there. The top was high, empty. Blue sky beckoned. No one else was nearby. "If you wanna go up there we'll go up," he replied.

Deihlia turned around in her seat and LP began to navigate her up the hill. As it began to incline, he stretched his arms further, pushing off with his feet. He had to exert himself to get her up there. He pushed and stretched, keeping her facing skyward. After a few minutes he stopped to catch his breath. They were halfway up. Could he get her to the top without losing the chair? His legs felt wobbly, and he was breathing hard.

Deihlia's chair was at an angle facing up. She couldn't see behind her. "You ok?" she asked.

LP took a deep breath and continued his trek, pushing hard. The chair rattled over the grass and bumps. Deihlia held on lightly to the frame but kept her eyes focused on the top of the hill. That was her goal and destination. She wasn't going to let her mind wander to the possibility of LP slipping along the way. She could hear him breathing behind her. As they got closer to the top, something inside her shifted. The sky kept getting bigger around them the closer they got to the top. It expanded, surrounding them as far as she could see. She felt like she could lift her arms and take off like a bird. She closed her eyes and imagined flying over the grass, over the tree tops, catching a current of wind and soaring away. Her chair stopped rattling.

"Well, here we are," LP said, pushing her chair onto the flat terrain at the top. He stood next to her, looking down at the woods on the other side of the hill, then up at the open sky. "The sky is so cool," he said, his head tilted back, his heart pounding.

Deihlia smiled, nodding.

He turned around, looking back at the way they'd come, then turned her chair around. "Check it out," he said. From up there, the hill looked steeper, more dangerous; a shiver of fear slid up his spine.

Deihlia looked down and giggled. "This is a lot higher than it looks from down there, huh?" She liked seeing the tops of trees against the sky and being so high up.

LP nodded, trying to regain his equilibrium. He could see the pond in the distance, dark blue between sections of trees. Then he tried to see if he could locate their campsite, and thought of his Dad. "How are we gonna get down?" he asked. "I didn't even think of that!"

Deihlia grinned mischievously, lifting her eyebrows. "That's the best part!"

His eyes got wider. "You can't just go down, Deihlia. You'll crash and have to go to the hospital. Our camping trip will be over."

She continued to look him in the eyes. "You'll have to hold onto my chair, it's the only way."

LP wasn't sure he could do that. "Well, you could get out of your chair and go down that way. I could carry your chair down."

She shook her head adamantly. "No. I don't wanna do that. Let's go down together."

LP looked at her. She always came up with fun ideas, and she usually found a way to make them happen. Being part of her adventures made him feel daring and free. He was torn between worrying about her safety and wanting to have this thrill with her.

"You can do it, right?"

He looked down the hill one more time. What if he lost control of her chair and she got hurt? What if they both toppled down? He felt the weight of the responsibility on his chest, and he didn't want to do it. Pushing her up was one thing, riding her chair down was another. He didn't want anything bad to happen to her.

Deihlia saw him hesitating. "I know you can do it. If my wheelchair goes down, I'll try to jump out. Come on, it'll be fun!"

The hill seemed long - far longer than when they came up. LP looked away from it, turning to look Deihlia in the eyes. She looked back at him expectantly. He couldn't say no to her. He ignored the tightness in his chest, his stomach fluttering. He wanted to match her bravery, her comfort with risk.

Nodding slowly, he took a step and got behind her. "You'd better hold on tight," he said, pushing her chair to the edge of the decline, where the grass started to slope down. Leaning the top of his body over her chair, he let it start to roll down. Then, once it got going, he put his feet into the grass to create resistance. The front of Deihlia's chair tilted up, and they were flying down now only on her big wheels, the silver spokes turning brightly in the sun.

She held onto the frame as the wheels turned and the grass flew up under them. LP kept his feet against the ground so they wouldn't go down like a runaway shopping cart. They both looked down as the chair's metallic rumble brought them downhill faster and faster, the sky and grass a blur. They picked up speed the closer they got to the bottom. LP noticed blue fabric beating the wind out the back and side of Deihlia's chair. It flapped in small triangles, then disappeared when he looked up. If he could have looked behind him, he would've seen his own cape - an orange stretch of shiny material streaming behind him down the hill.

Deihlia let go, putting her arms out in the air, exhilarated. Her chair was a boxy chariot, not a racing chair, and she wanted to see how far she could push it, what it could do. The feeling of danger combined with speed made her giddy. She knew LP had her back. It felt as if they were diving into the warm summer air and the chair could eject them out into it at any second. Her outstretched fingers caught the wind. She began to laugh as the bottom of the hill came up towards them, meeting them like a friend they'd outgrown.

When they reached the bottom, LP leaned way back, pulling her chair to a stop. Then he put it down gently, the small front wheels landing back on the ground. His heart was beating fast. Deihlia's cackle was infectious, and he began to laugh hard too, bending over to hold his stomach. "That was incredible!" he said.

Deihlia nodded, her face beaming a big smile. "I knew we could do it."

LP felt something explode inside him, making him feel strong and light. There were things he could do that he didn't know about. He looked back up at the top of the hill. He felt like he could run up there, stretch his arms out, and take off, flying up and away.

Just then, a hawk glided out over the top of the hill, its tawny red outstretched wings circling high in the sky above them.

Deihlia watched it sail effortlessly through the air in a large circle.

She turned to LP, who was still looking up. "Let's do it again!"

Turning of the Wheel

What becomes of a summer day? The years when Deihlia didn't have any big surgeries were like long, luxurious, sun-filled days. The absence of trauma was its own reward; we were all coming out of a kind of intimate battlefield, leaving Deihlia's surgeries behind. Our baseline had been a rollercoaster for over a decade. Who were we once we got off that ride? Could we look back and see how far and how fast we'd come?

We could, but we didn't want to. We were catching our breath and stretching our wings. Seeing a future beyond the next hospital stay felt unreal at first - a trick -and we didn't trust it. But as each month passed, time flowed more smoothly, uninterrupted by emergencies. The future approached us differently, waving at us through the kitchen window like a long lost friend. It was satisfying, watching Deihlia turn towards new unknowns. She didn't discard her cape. Instead she wore it casually, fluttering behind her as she wheeled down the ramp towards other pursuits. Her cape pointed to, but didn't contain her power, which was made up of so much more than the mortal combat she'd fought and won. It contained love, patience, humor, vision, cunning, sacrifice, leadership, and vulnerability.

The Demotion, Provincetown

Provincetown is a world unto itself, where artists, writers, actors, and musicians find inspiration on the outermost tip of Cape Cod. A mini New York/San Francisco for three months a year, it's a gay resort town, a fishing village, and a New England icon. In the summer, its beauty and light rivals parts of Greece and is a muse for visual artists and dreamers. I'd been visiting there every summer since I was a teenager.

"It would be cool to meet someone down here," my friend Thea said. She was visiting from San Francisco. Her short, punky hair was dyed electric fuchsia, and she was in a phase of wearing daring, sexy, femme outfits that made her stand out in any crowd. We'd met when I spent a few months in San Francisco, taking a short break from my life on the East Coast a couple of winters before. We met in a writing group, and became fast friends. After I returned to Boston, we visited each other when we could.

I laughed. "Provincetown isn't exactly a hotbed of single lesbians. Everyone who comes here seems to be coupled up already."

"We can still try," she said.

I nodded and looked at her sideways. "Yeah, we can still try. Let's go out tonight before Deihlia arrives. You can go out looking for trouble when she's here, but I'm not going to leave her alone."

Thea smiled. "Of course you wouldn't leave her alone. Let's see what we can find tonight." She proceeded to put on a lace-edged silk slip and merlot lipstick. She scrunched up her shocking pink hair and slipped on some chunky-heeled shoes.

She didn't find any trouble. I didn't find any trouble. I didn't even know what I was looking for, if anything, but we had fun bopping around Commercial Street, running into friends. The next day, Donna arrived and dropped Deihlia off to spend the weekend with us. We carried her chair up the dark wooden steps into the cottage. Luckily, her chair fit into the doorways of the old house.

"Deihlia, this is my friend Thea." I said.

Deihlia looked up at Thea, her eyes going up to the shock of pink hair. "Nice to meet you," she smiled shyly.

"Same here," Thea replied. "Diane has told me so much about you. I'm glad we've finally met."

"Have you had a good week?" Deihlia asked.

I nodded. "Yeah, it's July in Provincetown. There's so much going on. How was your week?"

Deihlia shrugged. "Just regular. Nothing much going on. I've been kinda bored."

"Well we can kick around P-town if you'd like."

"Yeah, I'd like that."

Thea stood up. "I think I'll go upstairs and rest for a bit and give you guys a little time alone. Come wake me up when you want to go into town."

I poured us both a glass of water and then Deihlia and I went out on the deck and sat in the late morning sun.

"Thea seems pretty cool," Deihlia ventured, sipping on her water.

I nodded. "Yeah, she is. We became friends pretty quickly when we met."

Deihlia looked up at me, puzzled, trying to figure something out. She put her glass down on the side table. "Auntie, I'm just gonna ask you 'cause everyone is trying to figure out if she's your girlfriend. Is she? Are you moving to San Francisco?"

The water in my mouth caught in my throat and I coughed, putting the glass down on the table. I shook my head back and forth. "No, Deihl, Thea is just a good friend."

She smiled at me, her braces making her mouth look bigger than it was. "Well I had to ask. You haven't had a girlfriend in a while."

I figured it was as good a time as any to tell her the truth, something I'd come around to slowly over the past few months. I'd just started telling my friends. I could tell her. I'd been in relationships with women since I was about 19. Prior to that, I'd had boyfriends. I realized that my relationships with women were even more difficult than the ones I had with guys. I couldn't say I'd dated men because I'd been a teenager and had dated teenage boys. Being with women was a form of rebellion for me. It wasn't that for most other lesbians, and I knew that. But my rebellion was shortsighted. I didn't escape any of the relationship dynamics I'd inherited from my parents by being with women. One day I just woke up and knew that I was finished with that trajectory, but I didn't want to lose the great friends I'd made.

94

"Deihl, I'm not really dating women anymore. I just kind of hit a wall with it and I'm done."

The air between us felt thick, loaded. I knew that she liked having a gay auntie. It was part of my rebellion, my outlaw status, my defiance. I hated letting her down, but I wasn't going to lie to her. We'd always been honest with each other.

She raised her eyebrows and looked me in the eyes. "Well Auntie, you've been demoted in my book. I had a feeling something was up. That's why I asked."

I was crushed. It was hard enough to handle my friend's disappointments and my own changing feelings, the end of a part of me. But being demoted in Deihlia's eyes was the hardest blow of all.

"I'm sorry to disappoint you Deihl. But hey, I'm not moving to San Francisco. I'll still be around, gay or not." We'd been through harder things than this. And the truth was, I loved San Francisco and wanted to move there. But I couldn't bring myself to leave her and Chelsea. They were still young.

"You're still my Auntie no matter what," she said.

"Well I better be!" I said.

Later, the three of us walked down Commercial Street. It was crowded like it usually is on a Friday night with tourists arriving for the weekend, furry, chunky gay men in tight shorts, families, lesbians holding hands, teenagers on skateboards, and party boys. They filled Commercial Street, spilling out of bars, restaurants and shops. I pushed Deihlia's chair through the throng.

"I have a couple of shops down the other end of town I think you might like," I said, leaning over. "Or we can check out the Pirate Museum if you want."

She nodded, watching three men who looked exactly alike walk arm in arm down the center of the road, stepping together in time to a song they were singing. A guy on a skateboard wheeled through the crowd, navigating his longboard with his husky dog standing on it out in front of him. It was a bit like being at the gay pride parade, except the mix was different. Another skateboarder glided between people, reaching out his hand towards Deihlia as he went by. She put her hand out and they lightly slapped each other as he sped past. People stared at us, too; at Thea with her hair, at Deihlia with her long blonde hair in her black Smashing Pumpkins t-shirt and

95

pink wheelchair, and at me in ripped jeans and a tank top, my spiked belt slung low at my hips.

As we walked past the drag queens handing out flyers to their shows, one of them spotted us and hurried across the street, trying not to trip in her large platform pumps. "Oh goodness I adore your hair!" she said, putting her hand on Thea's shoulder. "Did you have that done here?"

Thea smiled her dark red smile, shaking her head. "No, honey. I'm from San Francisco."

The queen batted her big false eyelashes. "Oh, I should've known!" Then she looked down at Deihlia, who was peering up at her Technicolor makeup and sequined gown. "And look at you! Your wheelchair matches her hair. You must be what, twelve or thirteen? What's your name?" she asked.

Deihlia giggled. "I'm fourteen. My name's Deihlia."

"Well, Deihlia - that's a pretty name, isn't it? I'm afraid you're too young to come to my show. But I want to tell you something," she said, putting her hand on her hip and bending down close to Deihlia, the hair from her long red wig dangling near Deihlia's face. She lowered her voice. "Don't let anyone bully you because you're special. There are a lot of fools in this world, and you can't help running into them on every other corner. Just enjoy being who you are."

Deihlia blushed and didn't know what to say. The red-headed queen stood up and started to walk away.

"Have a fantastic night girls! Don't do anything I wouldn't do!" She said, winking over her shoulder as she turned and crossed the street.

I looked down at Deihlia. I wanted to make sure she was ok. Thea took a few steps, walking ahead of us.

Deihlia caught me checking on her, and turned her face up to me. "I like this place, Auntie," she said.

I put my hands on the handles of her chair and continued pushing her through the crowd, smiling at the people who stared at us as we went by them.

Up in Smoke, Franklin

Another weekend, another Friday night. Julia sat across from Deihlia at the small kitchen table against the wall. Deihlia was fifteen, Julia was twelve and a half. Donna liked vintage furniture, and the table was old pine, with a single drawer underneath. It was sturdy but battered around the edges from decades of use. Deihlia and Julia had already eaten the pizza that was delivered, and the empty pizza box lay open on the table. Julia was quiet and distracted. Her black wavy hair was pulled back in a loose ponytail. Deihlia's attempts at drawing her out weren't working.

"What's the matter, Julia? Is something wrong?" She finally asked.

Julia traced across the pizza cardboard with a blue marker, doodling a spiral. She shrugged, and began writing on a section of the box. Deihlia watched her friend, trying to see what she wrote. When she was done, Julia ripped off the piece of cardboard and handed it to her. Then she moved on to another section of the box, writing some more. Early evening sun spilled into the kitchen. Grey tracks from Deihlia's wheels criss-crossed across the white tiled floor.

Deihlia took the piece of cardboard and began reading it aloud, a poem Julia had written in haste. It spoke of parents fighting, ignoring their daughter who stood nearby, their home filling with the pus of an infected relationship. Deihlia looked over at Julia and placed the cardboard poem on the table next to her. Julia handed her the second one. This one was darker, more internal: the story of a daughter poisoned by her parents misery. Deihlia shook her head as she read it out loud, glancing over at her friend.

A third poem was ripped out of the pizza box and dropped on the table in front of her. The text spiraled to a desperate place, a lonely place, a precipice. Deihlia read it out loud, her heart starting to beat hard. Her friend was in trouble. She put it down neatly in the pile of other poems. Julia sat across from her, scribbling away. The marker was running out of ink, the darkness of the letters faded in and out, making it hard to read.

"Julia, things aren't as bad as you think. Your parents aren't going to keep this up. Something has to give. You have to hang in there until it gets to the next place. I promise things will change."

Julia shook her head and pulled out her lighter. She'd started smoking when her family life had begun to go up in flames. Deihlia didn't like that she smoked, but she was more concerned with her friend's mood. She knew what it felt like to feel hopeless, and that things weren't going to get better. But she'd shaken those feelings off when they came along, because if she sat in them they'd engulf her. And Julia always helped her get out of it when she was in a funk too. "This is just one moment in time. I know it's a hard one. Things will change, they always do. You can come over and stay with us as much as you want."

Julia flicked her lighter. The flame flared up and went out. She did it again, then again.

Deihlia picked up the small pile of poems. "How about we go out in the backyard and burn these?" she asked.

Julia looked up at her, and took her thumb off the lighter switch.

"We can build a little bonfire! We can throw some of my mom's bills into it too," she said, glad that her friend was interested. She pulled out the drawer beneath them on the underside of the table. "See, there's a whole bunch of them in here," she giggled as she started to pull out the papers and envelopes stuffed into the drawer. "There's a bunch more over there we can burn too!" Deihlia said, gesturing with her head towards the counter next to the refrigerator.

Julia smiled. Her friend always knew how to pull her out of rough spots. "Ok, let's have a fire."

Deihlia was giddy with relief, and went over to the counter to grab the pile of bills with both hands. She put them onto her lap. Julia picked up the stack of poems and papers, and the remains of the pizza box, and opened the kitchen door.

They went down the ramp together, Julia marching down behind Deihlia. She could have taken the stairs, but she wanted to go the same way Deihlia was going. It felt important to stay together as they made their way into the backyard.

Deihlia pushed her chair over the hard, lumpy grass. It was April. Everything was still solid from winter. She pulled up next to the iron hibachi, a small rectangular iron grill that sat on the patch of pavement near the cellar door in the back yard. "We can use this," she said, dropping a few envelopes and bills into the open rectangle, rusty and black from sitting out all winter.

Julia pulled a bench over from the picnic table and sat next to Deihlia. Pulling out the last poem she'd written on cardboard, she held it with one hand while she switched her lighter on with the other. "Ready?" she asked, looking over.

"Yeah," Deihlia said. She was so ready to put this sorrow behind them, to burn it away.

Julia put the flaming piece of cardboard down on top of the bills and papers in the hibachi. Deihlia nodded. The papers were catching, curling black at the edges. She looked over at her friend. "Things are gonna get better. They're gonna change. Just come over here whenever things feel crappy," she said.

A small breeze blew quickly through the bare trees surrounding the yard, flitting across their fire and flaring it up a little. Julia lit a cigarette, cupping her hand around the lighter. She inhaled, then held the cigarette down low. She didn't want the smoke to blow into Deihlia's face. She thought about what Deihlia had said. If anyone could tell her that things were gonna get better, it was Deihlia. She trusted her more than anyone else in the world. Being with her always made her feel better. Their pranks and talks made life bearable. "Can I stay over all weekend?" she asked.

Deihlia smiled. She knew her Mom would say yes. She liked having their friends around. "Yeah, of course. You don't even need to ask," she replied, leaning over and tossing another bill into the small fire at their feet. Then they heard a car pull in, and two car doors slam. Julia snuffed out her cigarette. Donna came around the side of the house, following the line of smoke.

"What are you doing back here?" She asked as she approached, looking at the small fire in the hibachi.

"Just burning our pizza box."

Donna looked at Deihlia pointedly. "Looks like you're burning more than a pizza box. Where did you get those papers?"

Deihlia and Julia exchanged sideways glances and started laughing. "In the drawer?"

Donna went over and grabbed the papers off of Deihlia's lap. "My bills! I hope you didn't burn anything important! What were you thinking?"

Deihlia shrugged. "Most of the ones I burned were in the drawer. They've been in there forever!"

Donna shook her head. "Don't burn anything else. Make sure you pour water on that fire when you're done." She turned around and headed for the kitchen door.

Deihlia watched her Mom walk away and when Donna was out of sight, she turned to Julia, smiling. "What else can we throw into this fire?"

Magic, Franklin

It was one of the first times that LP stayed for an overnight with Deihlia. She had made a concession for him, finding the easiest videogame in the store that wasn't a young kid's game - a simpler one that she could still stomach - so that he could play something with her. The two of them were starting to spend a lot of time together, even though they were four years apart. They went into Reeves and purchased *Critical Depth* when he came over late Saturday morning. She was trying to teach him how to use the controller for the video game, to have better hand-eye coordination, to become a better gamer. But technology wasn't really his forte. He could sit and watch her and Sean play all day, but him? He lost his stamina after five or six hours, which was nothing for her.

They'd been playing all day. The sun started to disappear outside, making a watercolor of the sky behind the bare trees in her backyard. Her charcoal-gray room was suddenly dark, lit only by the flashing light of the game on the TV screen. "Oh well," LP said, putting down his controller "I'll never beat you at this thing."

Deihlia shrugged. "Nah, don't say that. You're getting better." She put down her own controls and looked up, noticing that it was dark. "Let's play a different game," she said as she turned off the game, "What number am I thinking of, from one to ten?"

"What? Oh, six." LP said, without thinking much about it.

She looked at him, surprised. "Yeah, that's it. Now you think of one."

He paused, leaning back in the chair. "Ok."

"Eight," she said, the first number that popped into her head.

"What the heck? How about a color now," he said, looking her in the eyes.

"Bright green," she said, really fast.

"Oh my god! Now your turn. Let me see... orange."

They went on like that for a while, guessing numbers and colors until it was ridiculously funny, because they kept getting it right. LP was having a great time with her. Though there was always some fantasy element to her games, they weren't childish - they felt like they were on another level.

Deihlia got into her chair, put on the light, and wheeled over to her closet, opening the door to rummage around in some boxes. She pulled out a candle, some incense, and a thick book. Putting them on her lap, she wheeled over to LP. "It's a good night for doing a little magic," she said, placing the candle down on her bedside table, and handing him the book.

"What kind of magic?" he asked.

"Take a look inside, and we'll do one of those spells tonight."

With her hands on her wheels, she wheeled back and forth in place, watching his reaction to the title of the book: *The Big Book of Spells.* "Remember when we were talking last time about wanting our lives to be different?" she asked, pushing her hair back behind her ear.

LP nodded, opening the book gingerly, holding it lightly at the edge of the cover, as if something might come flying out of it. He was 12, but he wanted to be grown up more than anything. He was always trying to be more mature than his classmates, more than anyone else his own age. They both wanted to be older, further along inside and out. This was something they shared: a desire that pulled them both forward together, on parallel paths, but that neither one let their other friends in on.

"I was thinking we could do a spell or something to help us change things," she said, raising her eyebrows to emphasize that it was a question, not a statement. She wanted him to be into it too, just like the video games, because they were so close. Deihlia didn't have any formal training or experience with magic, but she'd started reading some books - the kind that are easy for teenagers to find at the mall if they're looking.

LP looked at the table of contents, reading the list of spells, then turned to a few of them, looking them over. "Which one do you think we should do?" he asked.

She leaned in next to him and turned to a page she'd already thought about, and pointed to it. "I think we should try this one. But first, we have to think about what it is we want to change. What we want to happen."

He looked at her, wide eyed, serious. "Well, I need to think about that for a few minutes," he said, "there are so many things I want to be different."

She nodded. "I'm gonna think for a little bit too." Then she laughed. "Nothing too crazy, you know. I'm not gonna wish that I can stand up and go for a walk or anything."

LP kept his face serious. "I understand what you mean, Deihlia."

She lit the candle and then the incense, placing it in the holder next to her bed. She switched the light off, and for a moment all the words written in chalk on her bedroom walls stood out against the darkness, as if they were floating in mid-air. There was Julia's poem, and Chelsea's swear word, and Sean's pun. There was her half-serious quote, and some punk lyrics. Her mom had painted her entire room with chalkboard paint last year, and each of her friends wrote on it whenever they were hanging out in her room.

The entire house was dark, because no one was home. It was just the two of them, and the dog and cats. She was fifteen and a half, and wanted some things to change. She wanted to see more of the world, she wanted to have adventures, meet new people, and not be stuck in the house for the rest of her life. She wanted to be able to get around on her own somehow, to make her way in the world, not have to rely on other people so much. She wanted to have her own money. Deihlia sat there and thought about it, letting her eyes drift past LP, out the window, out into the night.

She let herself imagine what it would be like to go around in other places like she sometimes did in Boston. That feeling of freedom, of seeing new things, turning corners she'd never turned before, deciding she wanted something and then cruising around the streets to find it. Taking the subway, and seeing a lot of different kinds of people. Maybe it was like skiing too. She tried to hold on to that skiing feeling and make it bigger. As if she were going out into places that existed but she couldn't see yet. Like she'd wheel off into nothing then find herself somewhere, some curb cut that led into a new place, kind of like in her video games.

"I think I'm ready," LP said.

Deihlia looked at him from that other place, that other city, from far away. "Ok," she said, opening the book, holding it near the candle. "Let's say this together," she said, and he turned and got closer to her, trying to read by candle light, looking at her, then at the page. The incense was almost burned down to nothing, making the room smoky. "To the angel of the East," she began, and LP joined in. The window rattled, and something banged out in the hallway. They looked at each other, silently agreeing not to let it spook them, not to let it stop them, to keep going. They finished calling on the angels, and recited the spell, following Deihlia's finger as she traced underneath the words. Her room felt still. They heard the dog walk by, stopping to sniff under her door. A tree branch scratched against the side of the house, and they both sat up quickly, then giggled nervously.

"Do you think it will work?" LP asked, touching the page lightly.

"I don't know, I've never really done this before. But I sure hope so. We're just setting our intention for the future, right?"

LP nodded, his eyes wide as he looked back into the candle flame.

The Rookies, Boston

It was another Friday night, so that meant that Julia was hanging out at Deihlia's house, spending the night. As they ordered pizza, Deihlia remembered that she had to get up early and go into Boston the next day.

"Julia, come into Boston with me tomorrow. My mom and Aunt signed me up for this young entrepreneurs program for kids with disabilities and tomorrow's the last day. It's kind of beat, but I've gotta go."

Julia picked up the black cat off the floor as it sauntered by, and held it against her chest. "What kind of program? That doesn't sound too fun," she said, petting the cat.

"Yeah, just come with me. We can go somewhere afterwards and do something fun in Boston."

"I don't know..." Julia replied, shrugging her shoulders, "I don't have any money on me. I don't know if I want to go."

The next morning, Donna woke Deihlia up early. "Come on Deihlia, get up - last class today."

Deihlia rolled over and shook Julia, who was asleep next to her. "Hey, we've gotta get up."

Julia grumbled, turning over to face the wall.

"We're going in. My mom will pay for the train. Come on, get up."

Deihlia sat up and shooed the cat off of her wheelchair and scooted into it. She kept it next to the bed with the brakes locked. At night she had to attach a catheter bag to herself to catch her urine. She removed it, and got into the chair.

Donna popped her head into the room again. "Are you up? There are bagels on the counter for breakfast. We need to leave for the train in forty five."

"Mom, I'm up. Julia, GET UP!" Deihlia said, shaking her friend more vigorously. Julia rolled back over, looking at Deihlia through half closed eyes. "Alright," she moaned, swinging her legs over the side of the bed.

Deihlia went into the bathroom and shut the door. She emptied the bag of urine into the toilet, then proceeded to do the same with her colostomy bag. She washed herself all around the area with a soapy washcloth then soaped her hands under the running water to rinse them off. She reached over to the shelf above the toilet where her toiletries were, and got out her face cleanser, swishing it around on her face then wetting it with her hands. After washing up, she went back into her room to get dressed.

"Where the heck are we going?" Julia asked as they got off the Commuter rail train at South Station and Deihlia started wheeling through it, past the pretzel stand, the bakery, and the chocolatier.

"The red line is downstairs. We're gonna take it to Downtown Crossing and get off there. It's only a couple of stops." Deihlia said, turning around to speak to her. Julia had stopped in the middle of the station, looking around. She hadn't taken the train in alone before. People crushed past them, heading for the subway. "The elevator to the Red Line is right over here," Deihlia said, gesturing with her head towards the left. The elevator was over on the far side of the station, where people had to search to find it. Julia regained her composure and caught up with her friend, joining her at her side.

After they got off the Red Line at Park Street station, Julia helped to push Deihlia up the incline of Beacon Street, past the Boston Common, and up and around the State house. The class was held in a big gray room on the first floor of a government building behind the State house on Beacon Hill. Julia didn't know what to expect. What kind of class was this? She walked in next to Deihlia, entering a room full of other teenagers. Some were in wheelchairs, some had arm or leg braces, some had obvious disabilities, some didn't. Black, white, Spanish, Asian - a real mix.

They went in and sat down at a metal folding table with a couple of other kids. The teacher, a middle-aged woman wearing glasses who taught business classes at a local college, welcomed the students. "This is our last class. I hope you all had a good week and did your homework. Your homework was to create something you could go out and sell today," she said. "We'll create a list of all the materials we used to make our items, with their prices, and tally them up so we can track our expenses," she said, handing out copies of a blank spreadsheet to each student. Deihlia looked around the room for her friends Jimmy and Fernanda, but they weren't there. She was disappointed she wouldn't get to say goodbye to them.

"What did you make?" Julia asked Deihlia, whispering as she watched the other kids rustle through their bags and pull out their goods to show the others.

Deihlia shrugged. "Nothing. I kind of forgot about the homework," she said.

Julia giggled, her eyebrows raised. "What are you gonna do?"

Deihlia shook her head, looking at the spreadsheet, then put it down on the table.

Each student spoke about the things they brought in to sell. One girl crocheted potholders, another kid made keychains out of Playmobil figures, someone else made lanyard bracelets with suede cords and beads. When it was Deihlia's turn, she looked around at the class. "I didn't bring in anything but my friend, Julia," she said. A couple of the students gave her a sour look. One shook his head. The teacher just looked at her. "Well, it will be hard to make any money today without a product," she said.

"I guess so," Deihlia replied.

"Let's have lunch. Then we'll go out and sell our things," the teacher said, waving at the table on the side of the room. There were lunches in cardboard boxes lined up on the table, and sodas. Each student got up slowly and went over to the table to grab a box, returning to their seat to eat.

Deihlia and Julia went over to the table and peeked in a couple of the boxes. Ham and cheese. Turkey and cheese. An apple. A bag of chips. A cookie. Deihlia looked up at Julia. "I'm not into these lunches, are you?" Julia shook her head. Some of the other students watched them, thinking that Deihlia thought she was better than them, bringing her friend with her and turning her nose up at the lunch. Plus, she didn't even bother to do the assignment.

Deihlia and Julia sat by themselves, talking about what they'd like to have for lunch. Something warm, like stir fry or lasagna. As the other students finished eating, the teacher sent them on to their next task: to go out and sell their products. There were tables set up outside the building so they could put out their wares for people passing by. Parents and friends were also invited to attend. Of course, they could purchase each other's goods as well.

"What should we do?" Julia asked.

Deihlia wasn't sure, but she had an idea. She looked over at the table full of boxed lunches. There were two stacks of them left on the table. "Let's grab those lunches," she said.

Julia looked at her. "You're kidding, right?" she asked.

"If you carry them for me, I'll sell them. Grab as many as you can!"

Julia went over and picked up several boxes, stuffing them into her backpack. Then she grabbed five more, carrying them out of the room as Deihlia wheeled out. Deihlia had some piled on her lap. Outside, the other students were placing their goods on the table, putting out signs they'd made with markers and poster board. The teacher saw them go by, lunch boxes in hand.

"We'll be back in a bit," Deihlia said to the teacher.

They went past the State house and back down Beacon Street, crossing it to get into the area near Park Street station. Julia had to pile more of the boxes on Deihlia's lap so she could hold on to Deihlia's chair and help keep her from speeding down the hill. As they approached the open area near Park Street station they saw a group of Hare Krishna's playing music on the other side of the station, smiling in their orange clothes, and a religious zealot shouting to people who passed by, telling them they were damned. Deihlia looked around for a good spot not too far from the subway entrance, but not too close to the crazy guy. When she found it, she took one of the boxes from Julia and opened it on her lap, facing it out so people walking by could see it. "Let's make some money," she said to Julia.

"Ham and cheese lunch for sale - four bucks! A real deal! Freshly made today! Come on people, you know you're hungry!" Deihlia said as a small crowd of tourists walked by. Julia laughed. One or two people slowed down to see what was going on. Who was this kid in a wheelchair selling sandwiches? Was it a joke? An elderly woman with blue hair in a matching raincoat paused then came over to them. "What kind of sandwich did you say it was?" she asked, holding on to her flowered purse. "We've got ham and cheese, or turkey and cheese," Deihlia replied, "Four bucks." The woman opened her bag, careful to pull out her dollars inside the purse so no one could see or grab her wallet. "I'll take the turkey and cheese," she said, handing Deihlia the dollar bills with her pale, petite hand. Deihlia closed the box and handed it to her. "Thank you Ma'am," she said, taking the dollar bills and giving them to Julia to hold. "Why thank you," the woman said, walking away, disappearing into the crowd of people walking towards the park.

"Four bucks for a box lunch! You can picnic in the park! Four bucks - turkey or ham! Comes with chips, a cookie, and an apple,"

Deihlia shouted. A father and son approached them tentatively. The father placed his hand on his son's back and pushed him gently towards Deihlia. The boy stood in front of her, looking at her and her chair. Deihlia could tell that he was really curious about her, but she wasn't sure why the father had pushed him forward like that. Were they going to buy lunch or just gawk at her?

"I like your Simpson's button," the boy said, staring at the button pinned to Deihlia's jacket. It had a picture of Bart, Lisa, and Maggie on it.

"Aw thanks," Deihlia said. "Who's your favorite character?"

The boy stood smiling at her. "I like Bart!"

"Yeah, Bart's pretty cool," Deihlia said nodding. "Are you and your Dad hungry? We're selling lunch boxes."

"Why are you selling lunch?" he asked.

Deihlia looked at him for a moment before answering. She could see his father standing a few feet away, watching. "We're trying to make some money so we can go and do something fun," she said.

The boy looked over at his father, a silent question on his face. The father walked over and joined him, his dark green windbreaker matched his son's jacket. "How much did you say for the lunches?" he asked, pulling out his wallet.

"Four bucks each," Deihlia said. "Ham and cheese or turkey."

The man handed her a ten dollar bill. "This'll cover it, right? We'll have two turkey lunches please."

The boy smiled, taking the boxes from Julia, then he looked at Deihlia again. "I'm sorry you can't walk," he said.

Deihlia folded the ten dollar bill in her hand. "Yeah, I am too," she replied. "Thanks again, enjoy your sandwiches!"

A small crowd had gathered, watching the transaction. The father put his arm around his son's shoulder and they walked off, boxes in hand.

"We've got sandwiches for sale. Apples! Cookies! Chips! A buck apiece! Good for a little morning snack!" Deihlia continued, and several people came forward, holding their dollars out, pointing to a bag of chips, or a cookie. Julia helped, managing the goods. She looked around at all the people going by, looking, stopping, and at the ones who made purchases, and those who didn't. It was so interesting, seeing all the different people and their reaction to Deihlia.

After forty five minutes they had sold all of the food.

"Hold on to the money. We'll count it when we get back to the class," Deihlia said as Julia got behind her and helped to push her wheelchair back up the hill.

"I'm getting hungry," Julia said. "I can't believe we sold all of those lunch boxes!"

Back in the classroom, the other students were putting away their things, writing on their spreadsheets, counting up what they'd brought in and spent and what they'd sold. Each one had to share their success with their classmates. "I made $6.50 on my bracelets," one girl said. "I paid like nine dollars for the materials, and I sold eight bracelets." They went around the room. Most of them had made between five and fifteen dollars after they covered the cost of the materials. The teacher turned to Deihlia last. "What did you do out there, Deihlia?" she asked.

Deihlia paused before answering. "We made thirty-six dollars selling the lunches and the contents of the lunchboxes." She didn't want to gloat or appear to be bragging, so she didn't smile, just said it matter-of-factly. The others turned their heads and looked at her, some glaring, some curious. But Julia couldn't stop herself from smiling. She thought that her best friend was the coolest person ever, making something out of nothing. Talking to strangers and selling them leftovers.

The teacher smiled and wrapped up the class, congratulating them on doing everything themselves - from making their products, to selling them, to doing the accounting. Deihlia was hungry now.

"Let's go get a nice lunch," she said to Julia.

"Totally ready for this class to end," she replied.

"I know a good place. I've gone there with my Auntie, but we'll have to get back on the subway. I think I know the way," she said as they wheeled out of the building.

They took the Red Line to the Orange Line and got off at Back Bay station, crossing Dartmouth Street and walking into Copley Place, the chic uptown mall. They rolled through it, then across the catwalk to the Prudential Center. Julia followed Deihlia's lead. She didn't know where they were.

They sat and ate their lunch at Marche, a fancy, Swedish, cafeteria-style restaurant. Stir fry for Julia, steak and fries for Deihlia, with pie for dessert. Julia looked at Deihlia across the table, smiling. "I had no idea what we were gonna do today. I had such a blast! I'm so glad I came in with you."

Deihlia grinned. "We still have like fourteen bucks left. You wanna go to Harvard Square and check it out? They have a couple of comic stores and a great ice cream place."

The Applications, Franklin

Chelsea put her backpack down on the sofa. She just got back from babysitting overnight. Deihlia was playing a videogame and didn't look up when she entered the living room.

"I made seventy-five dollars last night. I think I'll be able to buy a car when I get my license," she said, taking off her jacket.

Deihlia stared at her game. She wanted a car. She wanted a job. Chelsea had been babysitting for years now, and giving her money to Nana to put into her savings account. She nodded to Chelsea and put down her controller, pausing her game. "That's really good Chels," she said, feeling frustrated. She'd dyed her hair black and cut it shorter, putting on heavy gothic makeup every day. Chelsea had dyed her hair pink, and was wearing the wide army green pants she'd bought at the mall last week. They looked like lots of other teenagers in the late nineties, but hadn't progressed to tattoos and piercings.

Donna walked downstairs into the living room. Though no mean words were being said, she could tell that Deihlia was bothered by something. A mother just knows these things. "What's the matter now?" she asked.

Deihlia looked up at her. "Mom, I want to get a job too. I just want to be able to make my own money. It's not fair! I'm always broke. I want to work."

"I'd like it if you'd get a job Deihlia. You're sixteen. You can legally work. Let's go up to the plaza and apply at all the stores you go into all the time." She saw other teenagers working in them, so it was worth a shot.

Deihlia thought about it for a minute. She could easily work at Entertainment, Inc. They rented and sold movies and videogames. She went in there all the time and she knew all of their stock. Reeves was another option, she was a regular there too. Maybe even the giant Shop'n Go would hire her. She could wheel around and help people. She was too low to work the register, but who knows?

"Let me put on some nicer clothes," she said. "Will you take me this afternoon?"

Donna nodded. "Yes, dress up nice."

That afternoon, Donna parked the jeep in the giant parking lot, and tossed the handicapped tag on to the dashboard so she could park in one of the open handicapped spots. She pulled the wheelchair out of the back and brought it around to the side. She picked Deihlia

113

up out of the car seat and put her into it. Donna's biceps were like rocks from lifting Deihlia all her life. It was getting harder each year as she got heavier, but she stayed fit partly so that she could carry her daughter. "Do you want me to come in with you?" She asked.

Deihlia shook her head. "No, I don't think that's a good idea."

Chelsea got out the other door. "I'm gonna run into Shop'n Go and get some snacks for later," she said. "Good luck, Deihl."

Deihlia wheeled into the plaza and down a few stores into Entertainment, Inc. She rolled up to the counter. The man behind the counter looked to be in his mid-twenties. The blue tag on his shirt read "Isaac, Manager." "Can I help you?" he asked, looking down.

"Hi, Isaac. My name's Deihlia. I come in here all the time."

He remembered her, and nodded. "How are you today, Deihlia?"

"I'm good. I was wondering if you're hiring. I'd really like to work here. I know all of your stock and I'm really good with kids. I could work on the floor stocking shelves and helping customers."

Isaac didn't know what to say, he was caught off guard. "I see," he said, stalling as he tried to figure out what to say. "We aren't hiring right now, but you could fill out an application and we'll keep it on file."

Deihlia's disappointment showed on her face. "Oh. Ok. Well, I guess I can fill out the application now and maybe you'll have an opening sometime soon?"

Isaac rummaged around in the shelves under the register, trying to find an application. He'd never hired a handicapped person before. It seemed like it might be a lot more work to have someone in a wheelchair working in the store. Plus, what if something happened while she was here? They'd be held liable. He stood up, producing a piece of paper and a pen. "Here you go," he said.

Deihlia got closer to the blue counter and moved further down, out of the way of customers. People were drifting in. Moms with small children went directly for the brightly colored kids section. She filled in all of the information on the form, but it felt like a futile exercise. She didn't want to let it show, just in case there was a slim chance he might hire her later. When it was completed, she returned to the register, handing it to him. "I hope to hear from you soon, Isaac," she said.

He took the application from her and smiled. She was a nice kid. But he couldn't hire her. "Thanks for your interest, Deihlia," he said, looking it over then placing it on the counter next to him.

"Have a good day," Deihlia said, smiling at him as she went through the door. She thought she did a pretty good job outlining her skills and what she could do there. As she went out, a teenage girl in the Entertainment, Inc. uniform walked past her, opening the door. Deihlia turned and watched her go in, chatting with Isaac. Knowing that they wouldn't hire her, she turned around, heading for the Shop'n Go.

Her mother was standing on the sidewalk. "How'd it go?"

Deihlia shook her head. "Probably not gonna happen Mom," she said. "I'll try Shop'n Go next."

Donna watched her wheel through the automatic door into the supermarket. She wished there was something she could do to help her get a job. She'd brought her babysitting a few times, staying with her to make sure everything was ok. But that didn't really work. Deihlia wanted independence. That's what she was really after. She waited on the sidewalk.

Chelsea came out, carrying a grocery bag. "I think everyone's gonna hang out at our house tonight," she said.

Donna reached into the bag and pulled out a bag of chips and ripped it open, grabbing a few.

"Mom! I bought those for tonight! Now they'll be all stale." Chelsea reached in and scrunched the bag, trying to close it tight. "Can I have your keys so I can wait in the jeep?"

Donna pulled them out of her sweatshirt pocket and handed them to her.

A few minutes later, Deihlia came out through the other automatic door. "Well, I put in my application, but they said that they need people who can lift at least fifteen pounds."

Donna looked back at the store. Unfortunately, it made sense, and Deihlia couldn't lift that much without straining something. It was too far to the ground to lift with just her arm strength. Deihlia's body was twisting oddly as it was. Her doctor was concerned about her being able to survive without strong abdominal muscles. Her upper body could crush her organs over time. All of this ran through Donna's mind as they made their way back to the car. "We'll figure

115

something out Deihlia, I don't know what to say. There has to be something you can do."

Deihlia looked down at the ground. She knew she could sell things. But where? Who would hire her? What was she going to do when she was older? She wanted to live on her own and have a real job. She didn't want to stay stuck living in her Mom's house for the rest of her life. She looked past their car into the parking lot, at the cars driving in and out, people coming and going. She wanted that mobility. She didn't know how she was going to do it, but she was going to do it. She felt it in her heart. She knew it. But like so many things, it wasn't going to start today.

Her mom opened the truck door and she wheeled in close. Then Donna lifted her up, placing her in the passenger seat. She tossed the wheelchair into the back. As they drove out of the parking lot, Deihlia looked out the window. She was tired of coming to this plaza all the time anyway.

117

The Laser Pointer, France

Deihlia's class was planning a trip to France. She was in her junior year of high school and third year of French, Naturally she wanted to go, because she had never traveled more than six hours from home before. Her mother had to go with her. That was the only way she was able to go on the trip, since she would need assistance to get around. Deihlia was looking forward to the trip. She'd been studying the French language and culture for the past three years. In class, they talked about French food, culture, art, history, and made mousse au chocolat. *Parlez vous Francais? Oui, je parle le Francais. Tres bien!* French was in Deihlia's blood from her Nana's side of the family, and she wanted to experience it herself. Her Auntie was into Paris and shared photos of her trip there - the farmer's markets, flea markets, restaurants, the Seine, the Marais, the museums, the churches, the way the Parisian monuments and bridges were lit up at night. It would be cool to see them for herself.

But there were things that the French teacher didn't teach them about France - things that the teacher may not have known, that her Auntie didn't know - information that lived invisibly side by side with the Bastille, Versailles, the Louvre, and Monet's gardens at Giverny.

Once they arrived in France, Deihlia and Donna discovered them slowly, one by one. Serge, their French tour guide, took a liking to both of them and tried to take extra good care of them, even though they continually ditched the tours to do their own thing. He was a petite, slim Parisian, with dark hair cut close to his head. He'd been a tour guide since his early twenties, ten years prior, and was great with students and their parents.

One day, the tour was going to a museum, but like a lot of Americans, Deihlia and Donna wanted to go to Pere Lachaise, the famous Paris cemetery, and visit Jim Morrison's grave, which wasn't on the tour. The hotel called a cab for them.

When the cab arrived and Deihlia wheeled out to the curb to get in, the driver was rude and cursed "*merde*," complaining and snorting, not wanting to let her into the car. Deihlia's French was pretty good so she understood most of what he was saying. She didn't know what to do so she just sat there at the curb, looking at him.

The hotel concierge stepped in and said something to him, trying to do his job, speaking low and fast.

118

Deihlia and Donna stood on the curb, waiting, watching, listening. Donna didn't speak French, but she knew the driver was mad about something.

Finally, the concierge opened the back door of the car, waving his hand to usher them in. Deihlia hurled herself into the backseat while the driver got out of the car, scowling. Donna got in. The driver, a man in his forties wearing a newsboy cap and sporting a beer belly, picked up Deihlia's wheelchair and shoved it into the trunk of the car, slamming the door on it over and over. They could hear the trunk door coming down on her chair, metal on metal, the driver's curse punctuating each slam.

Deihlia stuck her head out the window and said in French: "Please don't break my wheelchair! Please! Please! It's all I have!" She couldn't believe he was being so brutal with it. "That's my only chair! Please don't break it!"

The driver banged the chair this way and that, finally pushing it deeper into the trunk and slamming the hood shut.

He drove through the streets of Paris, pushing his way through and around traffic. He stared at them in the rearview mirror, swearing as he drove. Donna and Deihlia held on to each other, staring back at him in the mirror. Paris was an indifferent mistress outside of the cab windows. It came at them in the driver's acceleration around corners and in between cars, blurring at the rotary. Fifteen hostile minutes later he pulled over by the entrance of Pere Lachaise, popping the hood of his trunk and saying "fourteen euros" at the same time. Donna handed him the cash and hopped out of the car, pulling the chair out of the trunk and putting it next to the open back door. As soon as Deihlia was on the curb in her chair, Donna shut the back door and the cab sped off, gunning it so that the wheels squealed and burnt rubber clouded the air around them.

"What was his problem?" Donna asked.

Deihlia looked up at her mom, hurt mixed with anger visible on her face. "He didn't want me in his cab. He didn't want to take someone in a wheelchair," she said.

A look of shock crossed Donna's face then, too. "What an asshole," she said, wondering briefly it if it was just the characteristic French rudeness. Then, after her shock settled in, she turned towards the entrance and said "Let's go," trying to put the cab ride behind them.

Inside the gate, they picked up the cemetery map and set off, winding their way through the clusters of beautifully sculpted graves and headstones, snapping photos. The graves were clustered together, some with figurative sculptures, some without. Each section was like a densely woven story, grave upon grave squished against each other in beautiful, unique shapes. Large oak trees dotted the grass and lined the road, dappling the graves with sun and shade.

"Auntie was right, this place is magical," Deihlia said, stopping to look at one unique headstone and crypt after another, each one an exquisite sculpture that expressed something about the person or family inside it. She took out her camera and snapped, not knowing that it is hard to take photos that do the crypts any justice. The headstones are black and grey, the white marble or stone weathered by decades of weather, exhaust, tree droppings, and the eyes of tourists. There was the balloonists' grave, and Oscar Wilde's - full of lipstick kisses. After a lot of wheeling, walking, and pushing they found Jim Morrison's grave and hung out there for a bit, soaking in the vibe of the place, watching as others came by, and looked at all of the offerings scattered around the spot. "We're clichéd Americans, Mom," Deihlia laughed, immersed in the moment.

"I don't care," her mother said, "we have as much right to be here as anyone else."

Pere Lachaise is a well-guarded, walled in cemetery, and when the guards come around and announce that it's closing time and time to leave, you really need to start heading back to the exit. If you don't, they will sit in their car near you, creeping along and following behind until you reach the exit and leave. They will not offer direction on how to get back. They will only follow along, reminding you that the cemetery is closing. It was under these circumstances that Donna and Deihlia made their way back to the gate where they came in, and left. "That was definitely better than a museum," Deihlia said, her smiling, gothic made-up face pink and warm with wheeling.

They went to the curb, and Donna stuck out her hand to hail a cab. Taxis whizzed by, ignoring her raised hand. One after another, the drivers acted as if they didn't see them. Or if they did, they spat with disdain in that way that the French are known for, with their mouths turned down in a haughty, cursing frown. Thirty minutes went by, and they saw people get in and out of taxis that pulled up to the curb near them. The empty cabs sped off as they approached.

"Let's find a payphone," Donna said, so they crossed the street and headed down the sidewalk towards a block full of Tabacs, the small tobacco shops that was ubiquitous around France, and brasseries. Donna called Serge, who'd generously given them his number. "We went to Pere Lachaise but we can't get back. The cabs won't pick us up. Can you come and get us, Serge?" she asked. The buses were not handicap accessible, nor was the metro. They were too far to walk, and didn't know the way.

"Oui, yes, I will be there in twenty minutes," he said, arriving in his little French car, stuffing Deihlia's dismantled chair into the backseat. "You had quite an adventure today, no?" he said, smiling at them as he drove through traffic.

"The cab driver was so rude," Donna said. "He didn't want to give us a ride because Deihlia is in a wheelchair."

Serge nodded, keeping his eyes on the road ahead of him. "Welcome to France," he said. "but you saw the rock star's grave, eh?"

"That place was so cool," Deihlia ventured, smiling at him from the passenger seat. "It was worth all the trouble. And thanks for coming to pick us up."

Donna was squeezed into the backseat of the tiny car, because Deihlia couldn't get back there. She listened to their conversation, and agreed that it was worth it - but that Serge was key to their adventure.

A few minutes later, he dropped them off in front of their hotel. "I will see you tomorrow morning for Chateau de Chenonceau," he said as he got back into his car.

The next day they gathered with the rest of the class to get on a bus to the Loire Valley. Later that morning, they walked along the tree lined paths that led up to the Chateau, marveling at the perfectly manicured grounds. Everything was orderly and clean; there wasn't a piece of trash anywhere. Once in the main courtyard, they waited in line with other school groups, restlessly standing around with their backpacks, unsure that their trek to the Chateau was worth it. While it had been updated to allow for hundreds of thousands of tourists to walk through the gilded halls and rooms, it had not been updated to accommodate wheelchairs in 2001. And, the bathrooms were not placed in easily accessible places.

"How are we going to do this?" Donna wondered aloud. She could only carry Deihlia so far, and it meant someone else had to carry her chair up the stairs.

Deihlia sat by the stairs, watching her classmates go in. Crossing her arms over her chest, she looked at her mother. She was getting mad. "Mom, I'm not missing out on another site because of the French stairs. We're at the Chateau de Chenonceau," she said, holding out her arms, "I'm never gonna be here again in my life!"

Serge stood next to them, looking up at the stairs. He knew the Chateau very, very well. He didn't want to Deihlia to miss it either.

"I will carry you," Serge said to Deihlia, turning to look at her.

Deihlia looked at him. He was only a little bit taller than her Mom, and he was a typical Frenchman, small and thin, wearing jeans and a button down shirt. He always had a five o'clock shadow. She thought of her cousin LP, smaller and thinner than Serge, and her nickname for him was "The Human Ant." Serge had spent extra time with them during the trip, running away from the group with them to go on spontaneous adventures. He'd gone out of his way to show them things off the beaten track and to help Deihlia get into places that were really inaccessible. She felt okay about being on his back. She nodded. "Ok. I want to see this place."

Serge squatted so that Deihlia could climb onto his back, encircling her arms around his neck. He put his arms behind him, underneath her bottom. Donna carried the chair up, walking behind them to make sure Deihlia didn't slide off of his back. There was simply no other way to get up and down the stairs. Deihlia would have preferred to be in her chair, but it wasn't possible.

"France is so inaccessible," Donna said, walking along beside Serge and Deihlia, her eyes on the simple, opulent bedroom of the king.

"Yes, it is inaccessible. It is an old country. Buildings are old." Serge said, sighing as he shifted Deihlia in his arms behind him, trying to keep her on his back piggyback style. "And we do not have our handicap people out in the world like this. In France, they stay in institutions. They do not mix with the rest of the people. The French do not want to see them."

Donna looked at him aghast and stopped. Her eyes went to her daughter hanging on to his neck. Deihlia looked hurt. She was listening, her eyes wide.

122

Serge stopped too, realizing the deep waters he was standing in. He knew that it was going to come to this, that he would have to tell them point blank how France was. Now that he'd been helping Deihlia and Donna around France, searching high and low for the accessible bathrooms, carrying her up and down stairs, he knew how difficult it was. He liked Deihlia. She was funny, smart, and sweet. She was another student in his care. He wanted to help her. *The tyranny of the perfect*, he'd been thinking to himself as they searched for ways into places. He'd never once noticed or thought about it before he'd met Deihlia.

People moved around them, casting curious glances at the couple with the goth girl on the man's back stopped in the middle of the King's bedchamber. Then he continued, looking directly at Donna. "I'm sorry to tell you both, but it is true. If I had a disabled sister and she was coming towards me down the street I would turn the other way. I would not acknowledge her. It is just how the French are." He admitted. He hated saying it, but up until he'd met Deihlia, this is how he thought.

"That's inhuman," Donna said. "My daughter is a real person just like you are."

Serge nodded. "Yes, I know that," he said. "She is a very real person. She is the most real handicapped person I have ever met. You are lucky you were born in America then, no? If you were French, you would not be visiting Chenonceau." He raised his eyebrows to emphasize his point, turning his face to the side to speak to Deihlia. "Come Mon Amie, let's catch up with the rest of the tour, we don't want to miss the Madame's pissing room," he said, and they continued on, letting the reality of French culture sink in.

When they finished the tour of the Chateau and returned to the first floor, Serge put Deihlia back down in her wheelchair, squatting as her mother pushed the wheelchair into place behind him and Deihlia leaned back into it. She looked at Serge differently, seeing him more clearly. It hurt to know how he felt about people with disabilities, but she knew it wasn't about her. He liked her; she knew it. She felt it. He gave her all of his attention, so it wasn't that. It was his culture, and his lack of experience.

A few nights later in another part of France, the tour had gone off to another mostly inaccessible iconic restaurant for dinner, but Deihlia and Donna didn't want to go and face yet another hurdle.

They wanted to relax and chill out at the hotel. Her classmate Aidan wanted to as well. He knew there was more fun to be had hanging out with Deihlia than going to another stuffy restaurant serving dinner banquet style to a bunch of high school students. Donna and Deihlia went to the local supermarket, where Donna picked up a bottle of wine and some bread and cheese: a quintessential dinner for anyone visiting France.

"I just want to relax," Donna said, opening the balcony doors. Then she poured the red wine into the small hotel water glasses.

"Chin chin," Deihlia said, holding her glass up. "Here's to France, the country that hides its cripples."

Aidan raised his glass. "Here's to you, Deihlia and Donna. Merci." Aidan had dark hair and ruddy cheeks. His French was impeccable for a senior in high school, and he didn't fit in well with the other kids. He hadn't come out yet, but he knew he was gay, and so did everyone else. The knowing but not really expressing it created a kind of tension in him that made him aloof and self-protective. But he and Deihlia were always friendly.

"Back at ya," Deihlia said, taking a sip of wine.

Donna split the baguette by hand, and sliced cheese to top it with. The crunchy bread fell in small crumbs with each bite, but it tasted better than any bread they'd ever had at home. "Why is French bread so good?" Donna asked, eating another piece. They sat at a table by the balcony, looking out at another apartment building across the street, and at the people walking along the sidewalk several floors below.

Deihlia pulled out the laser pointer she had purchased from the pushy street vendor at the foot of La Tour Eiffel on their last day in Paris. Aidan's was in his pants pocket, so he pulled his out too, pointing it around the hotel room as they drank the last of the wine and Donna relaxed after days of walking and hauling and not speaking or understanding French, which is quite exhausting.

The sun went down and their spirits went up. Deihlia and Aidan started beaming their red lasers into the windows of the apartment building across the street. They played a game to see if they could both get their lasers into the same windows but in different spots. Or they'd venture away and try to hit every window on every floor, the shutters wide open to let in the warm night air. Then they'd return to a window for a second or third time, especially if there was some kind of light on, making it clear that someone was home.

A fat man in a t-shirt came out on to his balcony wearing a scowl, so Deihlia and Aidan ducked down, hiding behind the balcony wall, laughing and snickering. They did this for hours, taunting the residents to come out and figure out where the laser lights were coming from, conversing with their neighbors over their balconies, pulling the shutters tight as they tried to figure out who was shining the small red lights into their homes, and why. Then they shined their lasers down at the people walking on the sidewalk, drawing squiggles on the pavement like little red fairies frolicking in front of them.

"Aren't you glad we got these laser pointers?" Aidan said, his face shiny with laughter and wine.

People looked up as the red goblins twirled on the pavement in front of them. Deihlia and Aidan clicked off their lasers quickly, laughing hard. Sometimes the best moments in a trip are the unplanned ones, silly moments when you get to act crazy and be yourself with a friend.

The crowning trek for many trips to France is Mont Saint Michel, the small medieval island dedicated to the Archangel Michael. The monastery was built on top of and around an island, over a span of centuries. A small village grew like barnacles around its base. The paths up to and into the monastery are all old stone paths with uneven stairs. They are a challenge to climb for most everyone who goes there, except maybe small children with excess energy and a lot of sugar in them, of which there are many. They eat candy and sweets and ice cream and bump into weary tourists pausing to catch their breath in a tiny spot of shade. Then there are the thieves, who are well acquainted with Mont St. Michel. They stand leisurely on the edges, trying to look inconspicuous in touristy clothes, bland and blending in with their sunglasses on so that you can't see them scanning your body for wallets and openings in your bags. They don't get winded walking up the hill, either. But that's about it. Everyone else is trying to take in all the interesting details, hear the snatches of information being dispatched by the tour guides, and breathe without stopping as they climb higher and higher.

Donna, with her defiance and physical strength was determined to get Deihlia in too. She pushed her up and over and around, going higher and higher, over the cobblestones, looking into the old rooms used by monks to create illuminated manuscripts. She was determined. She was a force to be reckoned with. Then someone kindly pointed out that going down would be an entirely different matter. Deihlia's wheelchair would not maneuver so easily downhill. Mother and daughter looked at each other, eyes wide. "Shit," Donna said, and Deihlia nodded. They both looked down the mountain at the height they'd already traversed, and started laughing. "Let's see what we can see at this level before we start heading down again," Donna said.

They went into the section of the monastery that had once served as a prison. The halls were narrow, the cells small. The grey stone walls seemed to retain a feeling of desperation and death. Deihlia shuddered, imagining what it may have felt like to be locked up there, knowing the ocean was lapping at the base of the island. Even if escape was possible, there was nowhere to go. She looked up at her Mom. "I think I'm ready to go back down."

Donna looked ahead at the crowd moving forward on the tour. "Ok, if that's what you want."

Deihlia nodded, and they turned back the way they came. Back to the main path that led through the monastery and down the hill. When they reached the narrow cobblestone road still jammed with people coming up, Donna looked out past the buildings. The sea glittered in the distance. They'd come up pretty high. "We'll have to go diagonally down this road so your chair doesn't go flying down." She knew people were going to be annoyed as they cut through, but there was nothing she could do about it. She began to push Deihlia over the bumpy path, steering her chair sideways. People had to look up from the ground when they crossed. "Excusez moi," Deihlia said, over and over. She was met by one scowl after another as each person adjusted their route to accommodate them. It took them 35 minutes to get to the bottom of the hill.

The next morning, most of the other students were already on the bus. Their luggage had been put into the storage area, and the driver was busy checking things on a piece of paper before he took them to the airport. Serge stood on the sidewalk. Donna stood next to him. Deihlia was rummaging around in her bag.

Serge looked down at her, then looked around at the people walking past them on the street, at the cars passing on the other side of the bus, then over at Donna. "You were quite a soldier, Donna. I

126

have never seen a mother so strong before, all you do for Deihlia. This trip was not easy for you," he said.

"We'll never return to France, no," Donna replied, laughing, shaking her head. "You took really good care of us though, Serge. We couldn't have done it without you. Thank you."

Serge nodded, then squatted and looked at Deihlia. "I'm going to miss you Mon Amie," he said, "you are quite the girl. What will I do now without you joking on my back?"

Deihlia lifted her sunglasses up off of her face, sliding them on to the top of her head. She wanted to say so many things to him, but the words caught in her throat like feathers. She nodded instead, blinking back the tears that were forming, and held out her hand. "This is for you," she said.

Serge reached over and gently plucked the small trinket from her palm: a keychain with one wing dangling from a silver chain. He held it up. Sunlight caught the edge, throwing a sparkle across his face that skittered back and forth over to Deihlia's cheek as it twirled in his fingers.

"I am so glad I got to spend this time with you, Deihlia," he said, folding the souvenir in his palm. "I learned so much about France from you," he chuckled, putting his hand on her knee.

Deihlia reached her arms up. She wanted to hug him. She didn't want to say goodbye. They'd forged a strong bond during their time together. Serge put his arms around her as she buried her face against his shoulder. "I'll miss you," she said into his shirt.

Serge's eyes were glassy as he looked her in the face one last time. "I will never forget you, Deihlia."

France is a beautiful country. The French value beauty, and privacy. The city of Paris has a budget line item just for lighting the monuments, bridges, and sculptures. To show them in the most magical and flattering light. Paris at night is a remarkable thing. Paris in the daylight is stunning too: the architecture, the ancient Roman walls appearing and disappearing throughout sections of the city, the Seine and the grand boulevards, the cafes, the wide expanse of blue sky above the old white buildings. It is a deeply evocative place.

Deihlia never wanted to come back to France. It was too hard to get around in a wheelchair, and the French people viewed her as a shameful alien. It felt awful, worse than the stigma she experienced in her own country. She couldn't wait to get home, where she could wheel herself into buildings. And though she cried all the way home on the plane, knowing she would never see her friend Serge again, she had made a decision. She liked speaking another language and being able to connect with people whose primary language wasn't English. Using her French in France was empowering and interesting. Deihlia decided she wasn't going to give up on languages, but her next one would be Spanish. She was done with French.

New Wheels

Chelsea pulled into the driveway and put the car into park. At 17, she'd sold her first car and purchased a used Camaro, pearl white with a blue stripe down the center. She and Deihlia shared a love for speed and physical risks, something they'd inherited from both parents. Her 1989 Camaro was the culmination of working several jobs after school - babysitting, hosting at a restaurant, painting with her mom, and taking portraits at the photo studio. She liked having her own money and thus her freedom. It was work, but it was worth it. She reached over and ran her hand over the red vinyl car seat. The guy she bought it from had detailed it nicely for her. She got out of the car and went into the house.

Deihlia was in her room reading. She was 18. Chelsea stood on the threshold of her door. "My new car is in the driveway. Wanna go for a ride?"

Deihlia looked up from her book. She had mixed feelings about Chelsea's car. She was jealous. She wanted freedom and mobility so much that it hurt sometimes. She often painted that hurt onto Chelsea with a giant brush. But she also knew how hard Chelsea worked. They shared the same circumstances, so hurt or not, she was secretly proud of Chelsea, and happy for her. The car was part of their family now, she may as well go see it. What would be the point of waiting, of stretching it out?

"Yeah, take me for a ride," she said.

They left Deihlia's wheelchair in the driveway. As Deihlia put on her seatbelt, Chelsea turned the key in the ignition. The car growled and roared as it started. Deihlia smiled. She couldn't help it. It was such a cool car. It reminded her of their Dad's blue '69 Chevelle. It had the same macho feeling, only with Chelsea at the wheel it was more mischievous. Deihlia ran her hand over the dark red leather. "This car is badass Chels. It's so cool. I'm so happy for you," she said, and she meant it.

Chelsea turned out of their development onto Route 140, then took the exit to the highway. "Hold on," she said, merging into the traffic on route 495. Deihlia couldn't see over the dashboard, she wasn't tall enough, but she could see out the side window. Cars appeared and disappeared beside them as Chelsea stepped on the gas, moving into the fast lane. She looked behind them, then accelerated again, hitting 70, then 75. Deihlia beamed. That's how she'd drive if she could - fast. She felt a kinship with Chelsea that she normally didn't let surface because of their rivalry. It felt good. Underneath it all, she thought her sister was really cool. She just didn't like living in her shadow, and wanting the things Chelsea had. Jobs. Money. Cars. Freedom.

Freedom most of all.

"I'm glad you like it, Deihl. I knew you would. It reminded me of Dad's Chevelle. That's one of the reasons I got it." She smiled, looking over at her sister. Chelsea was enjoying this rare moment of sisterhood. Deihlia's constant jealousy, sometimes expressed as criticism, was like sandpaper on her skin. They'd been comrades and rivals as far back as she could remember. She'd always protected Deihlia, but she also expected her to hold her own. She wasn't going to treat her like an invalid or a child. Her sister had the same blood she did. She was strong, too. That's why they fought and that's why they shared some of the same friends. She really did want Deihlia to have things of her own. Maybe with this car she could help her sister out, too.

Chelsea sped down the highway, watching the road in front and back for cops.

Deihlia reached over and turned up the volume on the car stereo. Led Zeppelin filled the car. The pitter-pat start of *Ramble On* mirrored their feelings. The night felt open and clear, like an adventure into new territory.

A few weeks later, Donna drove Deihlia into Cambridge. They were finally able to purchase a Hall's Wheels wheelchair for her. Hall's Wheels was Bob Hall's wheelchair design/build company. He was the first Boston Marathon racer to cross the finish line in a wheelchair. He'd fought to be in the race, and finished in under three hours in a chair he'd designed and built for himself. His fight to participate allowed other people with disabilities to race from then on. Later, he started his own wheelchair design business, revolutionizing their design so that they were lightweight, fast, and allowed the user more flexibility and control, like his racing chair. Deihlia was secretly in awe of him, and had wanted one of his chairs for a few years, but they were more expensive than her mom could afford, and the state health insurance she was on wouldn't pay for one. Eventually her grandmother on her father's side agreed to pay for it, but first they had to meet with Bob so he could measure Deihlia and get a feel for her strengths and abilities. His design workshop was in Cambridge, and the drive was a little over an hour from their home in Franklin.

As they drove through traffic along the side of the Charles River, Deihlia started to get excited. Not just about starting the process for getting her new chair, but about meeting Bob. She'd watched the wheelchair racers come in at the end of the Boston Marathon line one year, and she knew that Bob had blazed the trail for them. Meeting him was a special moment for her.

Donna and Deihlia parked the truck and went into Bob's shop, which was in an industrial section of Cambridge, in an old brick building that was once a factory but now was home to the studios of artists and designers. Bob's shop was right off of the parking lot. Donna and Deihlia went in. Chairs and chair parts were organized around the edge of the room, and a low workbench was situated in the middle. Bob was in his chair, working on a chair on the workbench. A man in his early fifties, he looked up and turned towards them as they approached. His hair was thinning, and he had a moustache and thick, beefy arms. "Hi there. Donna and Deihlia I assume?" he asked, extending his hand.

"Yes, hi Bob. Thanks for meeting with us today. This is my daughter, Deihlia." Donna was feeling a little shy herself. This guy was a superstar.

Deihlia smiled and reached out her hand to his. "Hi, Bob. It's really nice to meet you." She could tell she was blushing.

Bob angled his head and looked at her chair. "The Spinny, huh? I've seen a lot of those in my time."

Deihlia nodded. "Yeah, it's a Spinny. You know how limited these chairs are. I feel like I'm on a kitchen chair with wheels. I used one of your chairs at the Mass Hospital School when I did racing there. It was so fast and light. It felt so different than any other chair I've ever been in."

Bob smiled at her. She had dyed black hair and was wearing heavy goth makeup, as well as clothes that were all black. She looked like a lot of other teenagers. "Then you're in the right place, Deihlia. We're gonna build you a chair that will make the one you're in seem like an old Roman chariot. I think the Hallmark chair is probably the right one for you. Why don't you hop into the one I have over there and try it out? Tell me a little about what you like to do."

131

"Well, I like to ski. I like to go around Boston and check out new places. I go for walks with my friends all around Franklin. I don't really play sports anymore but I do like to be active. I think I'm going to college next year." Deihlia said as she went over to the chair he had gestured to. Donna followed her and held onto the handles of her Spinny so that Deihlia could get out and into the Hallmark. Bob watched the scene. The Hallmark's aluminum frame was one piece. Multiple parts made it, but they were together in one square, S-shaped frame with a small footrest. When a person sat in it, you saw the person first, not the chair.

Donna looked around at the parts and chairs he had in the shop. They were sleek, sturdy, and low to the ground. She knew that one of his racing chairs was in the collection at the Museum of Modern Art. His chair designs were art and science. Something else was different from Deihlia's other chair, though.

Deihlia rolled back and forth in the Hallmark, turning it this way and then the other way. It turned easy and tight.

"No handles," she heard Bob say to Deihlia.

"None?" Donna asked, turning to him. How would she push her up hills, or carry her up and down stairs? Her latest chair was still boxy but she and someone else could grab it from in front and behind.

He shook his head. "This chair will allow you more freedom and independence," he said, talking to Deihlia. "But also more responsibility."

Deihlia nodded her head back at him. She wanted all of those things. The chairs she'd had up until now were just that, seats that she sat in, seats that had wheels. But the new chair would be more like a part of her, built to hold her as she moved freely. Plus, it was cool.

She smiled at him. "I'm so ready. I can't wait to have my own Hallmark! This chair is awesome!"

He smiled back. She was going to do just fine, this girl. The new chair would set her free.

"Thank you for making these," she said seriously.

He nodded. "I think you'll do great. Like I said on the phone, it'll take me about two months to build it."

Deihlia nodded. It was worth the wait.

Two months later they drove into Cambridge to pick it up. They entered his shop and the chair was sitting off to the side. Deihlia knew which chair it was. She could just tell, even though there were other chairs just like it nearby. As if it called to her, she went over and touched the wheel, then the smooth silver aluminum frame.

"This is it, isn't it?" She asked, pulling her eyes away from the sleek little vehicle to look at Bob.

"Yep. That's all yours. Go ahead and get in it."

Deihlia pulled it out next to her. It was so light she could probably lift it with one hand if she had to. She reached over and put her hand on the inside frame, on the other side of the chair. She put her left hand on the frame of the chair she was in, lifting her body over into the new seat. Donna stood nearby, letting her do it alone. The new chair wiggled a little, but stayed put as she nestled into it. She was a bit lower to the ground, but she felt sturdy, grounded. She put both hands on the wheels and began to move around his shop. Her body was the center of gravity in this chair, it felt so different. She turned the wheels this way and that, backwards and to the side. It could turn angles easily. It was so light. "Wow, I love this chair," she said, looking over at him.

Bob sat near the workbench and smiled back at her. "You'll do great in that. You have so much more control."

Control is something Deihlia wanted more of. "Feels good already," she replied.

Donna went over to him. "Thank you so much, Bob," she said, reaching out her hand.

He shook it vigorously. "No handles, Mom. This is a big adjustment for both of you, but I trust you'll do just fine. If you have any problems with it, give me a call. But I don't think you will. That frame is aluminum. You'll have to replace the gel cushions once in a while, and the tires, but other than that it should last forever."

Deihlia went over to him and extended her hand. "This chair means a lot to me. Thanks for making them. Thank you so much."

"You are very welcome. Enjoy it. Get to know it before you do anything too risky!" He said as they left the shop.

Donna pushed Deihlia's old chair out the door, and Deihlia followed. The industrial section of Cambridge wasn't pretty. The highway ran next to it. But Deihlia looked around and wheeled past her mom, past the truck, maneuvering around the parking lot. Back and forth she went, as fast as she could. In addition to not having handles, there were no brakes. Every part of her ride was now in her

133

hands. Her connection to the wheels and the ground beneath her felt different. She looked at the traffic and wanted to roll out into the road and zoom up the highway. Everything looked traversable to her in that moment, even the overpass that carried cars into Boston. This chair was going to be her partner in crime. The light turned green at the intersection and cars began to move.

"Deihlia, let's go." Donna shouted to her, smiling to herself as she watched Deihlia zoom around the parking lot.

Deihlia moved her wheels back and forth a little, rocking in place, then pivoted her seat up into a kind of wheelie. She dropped back to the ground and moved back towards her Mom.

She was smiling. "I'm ready to go now," she said.

Chrysalis, Boston, 2002

Deihlia had been accepted into a college down south, Saint Michaels, a college known for its handicapped accessible campus and program for students with disabilities, a mix of students with disabilities and without. It was in North Carolina, 700 miles away from home, from the hospital, from her friends and cousins. Deihlia wanted to go. But before she could do anything else, she had to have another surgery. Without enough muscular support, her spine was twisting and bending. If left untreated, it would bend her over so badly that her upper torso would crush her organs, killing her from the inside out.

Deihlia and Donna sat across from the back surgeon, Dr. Moore. He had grey hair, and wore khakis and a sweater vest over a light-blue button down shirt. Dry but genial, he drew them a diagram on white board to illustrate what he would do for her. He'd insert a titanium rod next to her spine, attaching it to her bones so that it would hold her upright.

"When are you supposed to go off to college? This year or next?" he asked, peering at them over the documents he held in his hand.

"September," Deihlia said.

He looked down at the paper in his hand, trying to determine the best way to say it. "Deihlia, this surgery is critical. Dr. Zee and I agree it is absolutely necessary for your survival."

Donna felt like her heart stopped for a second. Deihlia looked at him intently. She knew what he was going to say before he said it. She'd had a sinking feeling all day before the appointment. "I know," is all she said in reply.

"I'm glad you understand. This is major surgery and it will take you months to recover. I'm afraid you'll have to put off starting college until the Spring semester."

Her eyes became wet, but she caught the tears before they fell, blinking quickly several times to make them disappear. After a moment, she replied to him. "I knew you were going to say that."

"If we don't do it now, you won't be going to college at all. I'm sorry to be so blunt."

Donna turned to her and put her hand on her arm. "Deihlia, you'll just start college a semester later. It's not the end of the world. It's just a few months. You'll still be able to go."

135

So many parts of her life had been put on hold or put off forever because of her body. Deihlia was used to it, but she was really looking forward to college, to being on her own with new people and new experiences. Even though she was used to it, even though she knew it, the reality of it still came as a blow. She looked down at the floor. She was not going to cry. "I'll do whatever I need to do, Doc. I want to go to college, I want to do other things too." Her options were clear to her: death, or surgery. Surgery meant college and doing other things, it meant more life.

Deihlia resigned herself to it, and spent her summer having as much fun as she could, because recovery was going to take a while.

It had been a number of years, but the surgical response mode was still inside our family. The day came and it was the same core team there that day - Donna, me, and Nana. Dr. Moore was calm and confident.

"Ready?" he asked Deihlia. She shook her head, and reached up to give each of us a hug. It wasn't our usual hospital, our usual nurses, our usual neighborhood. We had to trust that he would do well and that Deihlia would survive and come out whole.

"We'll see you in a while," Donna said. Deihlia shook her head. It was going to be another very long day, at least a twelve hour surgery, if not more. I hated to think of Dr. Moore working that long on his feet, focused intently for such a long time. I hated to think about it at all - about what they were doing, where she was.

We sat in the light blue waiting room. It filled with sunlight as the sun moved from east to west, glancing over this section of the hospital. There were no other families in the room with us. We were tense, trying not to think about it, this weird in-between space of waiting, hyper-awareness, and denial. We got lunch, we read magazines; we waited. Twelve hours creeped by and there was no word from the surgeon. I scanned the waiting room. Our old friend the Bus Driver was nowhere to be seen. I thought he'd at least make an appearance and check in on her, but not this time. We wanted to know what was happening, why it was taking longer than expected. Three, four more hours went by. We started to get really wound up. Donna started pacing the hall. I caught myself holding my breath. It was late, and the windows were dark, the waiting room filled with our anxiousness.

136

Finally, Dr. Moore came out, smiling and relaxed. He didn't look as if he'd just spent seventeen hours doing surgery. "It went well, but I ended up having to put two rods into her back instead of just one. That's why it took longer. But it went well and I think she will be good with this." He said it so matter of factly.

"Two rods?" Donna asked, taken aback.

"Yes, once I got in there I realized that one would not be enough." We glanced at each other, then directed our gaze back at him.

"It went well," he said, gently emphatic. "She did well. She will do better with two rods, I assure you it was necessary. You can go into the ICU and see her shortly."

Thirty minutes later, we went in to see her. Deihlia was lying on the bed on her side, a pillow beneath her arm and chest, so that she was not on her back.

As she started to come out of the anesthesia, Donna leaned over the bed, looking at her. She still looked out of it.

"Mom, I'm fine," Deihlia said, opening her eyes.

Coming out of surgery was just the first hurdle, there were still many more to go. But this was a good sign, and we breathed a bit easier. We huddled around her. Grateful, relieved, and on another level amazed. She was sometimes hard to comprehend, hard to take in and this was one of those times. She was resilient on a level I couldn't fathom.

Donna looked at me, and I looked back at her, then at Deihlia. Nana stood there too. We were silent. We had no words.

A few minutes later Donna said "The surgeon said it went really well." She touched Deihlia's arm, rubbing it lightly. Deihlia nodded, closing her eyes.

"We should let you rest," Nana said.

"Ok," said Deihlia, shaking her head slightly in agreement.

"I love you Deihl," I said as we got ourselves together to leave. "Love you too, Auntie," she replied, her eyes still closed, ready to go back to sleep. "I love you all."

Deihlia spent a couple of weeks in the hospital after the surgery, then went home. The incision took a long time to heal, having to heal from the inside out. Six weeks after the surgery, Nana was over at the house. Her nursing skills had come in handy with Deihlia many times over the course of her life. She'd been checking on Deihlia every week since she came home from the hospital, but she'd been away the week before, so it had been two weeks since she'd seen her. When she walked into the house and saw Deihlia, her stomach clenched. "How are you feeling? You look awfully pale."

Deihlia looked up at her. Her Nana's tall frame looked bigger than usual, her short brown hair was fuzzy around the edges and her pink top had some sort of bird on it, but she could only make out a wing, a beak. She felt really weak, and tired. Everything looked hazy, like she was seeing the world through a light fog. "Kinda tired I guess."

"Let me look at your back." Nana said, sitting down on the bed next to her. She lifted Deihlia's t-shirt. Deihlia's skin felt hot. The wound had shrunk, only a small hole the size of a thumbnail was left open, but Nana had a bad feeling. "Where does your mother keep a flashlight?" she asked.

Deihlia's eyes were closed. She rested her head on her arm. "I think maybe on top of the fridge, or one of the drawers next to it."

Nana got up and went into the kitchen. There was no flashlight on top of the fridge. She pulled open one drawer after another, cursing as she rummaged through the junk and papers in each drawer. Mixed in with tools and markers in the bottom drawer she found a small blue Mag-Lite. She turned it to make sure it worked, then returned to Deihlia's side. Deihlia lay still, almost sleeping. Nana pointed the light beam into the wound, and gasped. The inside was red and raw, infected. It wasn't healing.

"Sweetie, I need to take you to the hospital right now. Your back isn't healing."

Deihlia opened her eyes. "What?"

Nana pulled Deihlia's t-shirt back down over her. "I'm taking you into the hospital right now. I'm going to try and reach your Mom but we need to go now."

"I don't want to go back in the hospital," Deihlia said, starting to cry softly. Tears rolled down her face sideways, landing on the pillow.

That's when Nana knew for sure that Deihlia was really sick. She never cried. Nana hurried into the kitchen and picked up the phone, trying to reach Donna at work. There was no answer. She scribbled a note and left it on the table, then went back to Deihlia's room. Moving Deihlia's chair closer to the bed, she asked "Do you think you can get into your chair?"

Deihlia sat up slowly, woozy. Nana could see that she couldn't do it, so she squatted next to her and gathered her up in her arms as best she could, sliding her over to the edge of the bed and placing her in the seat.

An hour later they were at the hospital. In the emergency room, Nana spoke efficiently to the admitting nurse. She spoke their medical language, using words like "temperature," "blood pressure," "infection," names of medications. As she stressed Deihlia's fragility and the state of the wound, the nurse made a call and Deihlia was admitted immediately. The waiting room was full of people, some grimacing, some crying. Deihlia barely noticed them as they wheeled her back past registration into one of the rooms. A doctor met them there, hurrying in, nodding at Nana. "We're getting a room ready for her upstairs."

Deihlia's head dipped down, she couldn't keep it up. She felt so tired. The doctor reached his hand out towards her as she passed out.

She woke up hours later in a room that was all too familiar. Her Mom and Nana sat on chairs next to her bed. "What's going on?" she asked.

"Your wound is infected and wasn't healing at all. You're gonna be here for a while until it heals." Nana said.

Donna got up and stood next to the bed, putting her hand on Deihlia's arm. She shook her head. "You could've died if Nana hadn't brought you in." Her eyes were wet. How many times did Deihlia have to go through this? Why hadn't she seen it this morning before she left? Deihlia had been upright and seemed fine.

Deihlia didn't say anything. She'd been in this exact same hospital room at least three times that she could remember. The window looked out over the top of the parking garage. She looked out at the darkening sky, then closed her eyes again.

Crash Landing, North Carolina, 2003

Donna, LP, and Deihlia drove down to North Carolina to bring Deihlia for her first semester at college. Deihlia was eager to start a new life, a new chapter. It was a two day drive. The three of them arrived on the campus exhausted and worn out from driving, a truck crammed full of stuff Deihlia couldn't live without.

Donna pulled up in front of the dorm, and they got out. No one in the family had actually gone down to visit the campus prior to Deihlia's arrival that first semester. Donna worked for herself, painting the interior and exteriors of houses, and ploughing in the winter. She had all she could do to keep the house and put food on the table. She didn't have the finances to fly or drive down to visit while Deihlia was a senior in high school, and then there was her surgery. So as Deihlia went inside the dorm and into her room, she discovered that while the bathroom was technically accessible, the accessible shower stall had no door. There was also no bench, or seat, or anything in the shower. The facilities were kind of old and in poor shape, and Deihlia was disappointed and upset. She needed privacy for the shower, and a way to get in and out of it.

"Mom, this stinks. I can't live in a place like this. The building's so rundown and I just can't believe this bathroom."

Donna looked around, and LP stood by looking at the space. "We'll figure out how to make it work, just calm down," she said, but she was also feeling disappointed, and overwhelmed with the task.

"I'm not staying here," Deihlia said.

"We'll get a curtain and set it up so you have privacy, and we can get some kind of stool for you to use in the shower. We'll get it all set up for you, don't worry." She said. She was really good at making any space feel like home, and she was going to figure out how to do it there too. The three of them unloaded the truck, setting up Deihlia's things in her dorm room. Then they headed to the store to hunt down the things Deihlia needed to set up the bathroom on the first floor.

It took several hours to pull together the things that would work, but Donna did it, with LP helping to set it up. Meanwhile, Deihlia wheeled around the campus, venturing out past her dorm. While it wasn't a huge campus, she didn't know her way around yet, or know any of the other students. Everyone she saw was a stranger. It felt daunting. She started to feel scared to be there on her own, with no one to call to come over or help.

140

Back inside, Donna showed Deihlia their handiwork, the curtain hung across the open shower door, the bench, the little things she'd set up for the shower. It had taken some creativity and some labor, and it had been a long day. The wind had long since been knocked out of everyone's sails.

"I don't think I can stay here, Mom. This place isn't what I expected. It's not fully accessible. I mean, what the heck?" Deihlia's face was long, scowling.

Donna was wiped out, and cheerful optimism after a long day of driving, unpacking, and setting up was pretty hard to come by. She let out a long, frustrated sigh, walking out of the bathroom.

LP went over to Deihlia and squatted, looking her in the eyes, face to face. Her arms were folded across her chest, an unusual stance for her. He put his hands on her arms. "Just try it, Deihlia. If you really don't like it you can always come home. Just give it a try. What do you have to lose?" he said.

Deihlia looked at him, still scowling, and didn't answer. They spent the night sleeping in her dorm room on a single twin bed, then got up the next day to check out other parts of the campus.

"Deihlia, this will be better than staying home in Franklin. What would you do there? Last Fall while you were recovering from surgery all you talked about was starting college late. Now you're here and you want to go home. It's not just about the buildings. It's your classes and other students and everything you'll learn."

Deihlia wheeled along beside them. Other students passed them on the sidewalk. Her mom was right. What would she do in Franklin?

"Just try it for a semester. If you don't like it, you don't have to come back." LP said.

Part of her wanted to go home, but the other part wanted to see it through. "Ok," she replied, "One semester."

The Mixer

Michael knocked on the door. He could hear the party from outside. No Doubt's song *Hey Baby* was shaking the window, and people's voices were loud rumbles, battling against the music. It was a typical Saturday night on campus, and he didn't have to go far to find a good time. He stood there a moment, knocking louder, but when it was clear no one could hear him, he opened the door and walked in. Southern born and raised, he had excellent manners, and could charm his way into any party. He was in a good mood and wanted to keep it that way.

He walked in, saying hello to a cluster of sophomore girls in their college t-shirts. They were already half drunk, and throwing attitude, which was really unattractive. He wasn't sure who would be there, but he saw a couple of dudes he recognized from the Lacrosse team and from one of his classes. It was his freshman year at Saint Michaels too. *Ok,* he thought to himself *I can handle this party for a little while.* A beer would help make the crowd look better, too. He pulled out a couple of one dollar bills from his jeans pocket, and went up to the keg, pouring himself a cup. He handed the bills to the keg master, who stood next to the table, and by the looks of it, had been fully taking advantage of his role for a while. "Thanks man," Michael said, pouring a third of the cup down his throat. He looked around some more, trying to find someone interesting to chat up. The girls in attendance were the bitchy princesses of the school, and he didn't want to get anywhere near them. He sighed, moving over to a different part of the room after refilling his beer. He was tired of the same old people with the same old stories.

As he moved over near the window, he saw someone sitting off in the corner by herself. A girl with dirty blonde hair, sitting in a wheelchair. She sipped a cup of beer, and sat alone, watching everyone. *She looks interesting,* he thought. "Hey there, I'm Michael," he said, offering his hand. Deihlia looked up at him and shook it. "I'm Deihlia," she said.

"You new to school?" He asked. He hadn't seen her around.

"Yeah, I just started this semester. Late start. How about you?"

Michael looked down at her, and she looked up. He was tall, and she was low. "This won't do," he said, speaking loudly over the music. "Come on, let's go in another room," he said, gesturing with

142

his head for Deihlia to follow. She picked up her beer cup and placed it between her legs, nestling it down between her thighs so it wouldn't spill as she followed him through the crowd. He led her down a hall, into a back bedroom. He sat down on the bed. Deihlia looked around and kept her chair in proximity to the door. She didn't know this guy.

Michael could tell Deihlia was not a southerner. Her accent for one, but also the way she held herself. Something said 'Northerner' in his mind, but he asked her to be sure. "Where you from Deihlia?"

"Massachusetts," she said, taking a sip of her beer. "But I can tell you're from around here."

Michael nodded. "Kind of a lame party," he said, trying to put her at ease and let her know he wasn't into this crowd either. "How'd you hear about it?"

Deihlia looked at him, trying to determine what his agenda was. "A guy in my English class invited me, but I don't even see him here," she said. "Thought I'd give it a chance and see if it got better. I'm new to campus and I want to meet people."

Michael sat across from her, his elbows on his knees. She was trying. She came to the party, but she was sitting alone in the corner when he'd arrived. "Seems like a hard bunch to break into at this party," he said. He could walk in, shoot the shit with a couple of guys, have a couple of beers, and leave. But this handicapped Yankee girl was gonna have a harder time connecting with these chumps. Even though it was a very mixed student body, with a lot of students with disabilities, there was still a thick line between the able-bodied students and the kids with disabilities, and people didn't cross it much. Michael didn't care what anyone thought of him. "So what kind of things do you like to do, Deihlia? Got to be some things on campus that are more up your alley than the jocks and princesses."

Deihlia relaxed a little. Michael was trying to get to know her; he wasn't giving her a hard time for coming to the party, which she'd gotten last weekend when she accepted another invitation. "I'm into a lot of different things. Video games, Magic the Gathering, Psychology, comics, stuff like that. I like to ski, but I can't do that down here," she said.

"Ski? You ski? Wow. That's impressive. I've never skied in my life. Going downhill fast on a pile of snow spells wipeout for me. Not too much skiing in these parts, either."

Deihlia nodded and smiled. "Yeah. I know. But you look like you could handle skis if you were on them more often."

Her smile was bright, pretty, hinting at a humor that hadn't appeared yet. Michael was captivated. Here was someone interesting, with some courage and depth.

Deihlia looked back at him, and was starting to sense someone gentler under the edgy guy who'd approached her, acting a little cocky and full of himself. She was warming up to him. "You didn't look too thrilled with this party, either," she said, taking another sip of her beer. "The beer is warm and the people are cold and acting stupid. College parties aren't really all that great so far."

"Deihlia, we're gonna find some better parties than this one," Michael said, raising his beer cup to her.

"We're gonna *have* better parties than this one," she said, hitting her cup against his, smiling.

"Whatd'ya say we blow this joint and go find something better to do? I'm not really into video games but we could wander around and see what else is happening."

"Sounds good to me."

Michael got up and waited for Deihlia to turn and exit the room before he did. He reached over, holding his empty cup out towards her. "I'll throw these out. Meet you at the front door." Deihlia put her cup inside his, and wheeled back down the hall towards the front the door. She opened it and went out, waiting outside on the front walk.

A few minutes went by, and no Michael. A couple of other people came out, almost bumping into her, then frowning as they maneuvered around her. She wheeled her chair back a little bit to help let them by.

"So many people in wheelchairs at this school, it's annoying," one of the girls said as they walked away. "I know," the other one replied, looking back over her shoulder at Deihlia.

Deihlia started to wonder about Michael. Was he for real, or did he just want to get her out of the party? Her instincts were pretty good about people, and she'd had a really good feeling about him as they talked. She'd felt herself relax and open, that was a good indication. Where was he? Was he just another jerk? She was starting to feel let down.

144

Another two minutes went by. The door opened and Michael appeared, slamming the door behind him. "Sorry Deihlia, I ran into someone who wouldn't let me get away. Sorry for leaving you out here," he said, waiting for her to start wheeling down the walk.

Deihlia sat looking up at him, relieved and glad that he'd come out. "No problem," she said.

Michael stood there waiting, and Deihlia didn't move. "After you," he said, waving his hand towards the walk.

"I'm not used to being around gentlemen," she said, turning them down the walk.

Something in Michael split open as he walked half beside her, half behind her. She clearly had guts and personality, but she needed some help navigating the world of campus life. She seemed cool but shy. This place was going to eat her up if she didn't develop a badder attitude. She didn't seem like she wanted to only hang out with the students with disabilities, she wanted to mix in. She skied. He thought about it for a minute, picturing her around campus.

"Deihlia, this place can be rough. I'd like to apply for the position of friend and navigator, if you're in the market. I don't mean to be pushy or anything, but I think I'd be pretty good at it."

Deihlia continued wheeling along the sidewalk. She didn't look up at him, or register his comment. The first two months of college had been so hard. People were just as mean as they were in elementary school, and she'd had a hard time finding people to give her a chance. She had wanted to give up and go home a few times, calling her mom crying, homesick and lonely. Deihlia kept looking forward, letting Michael's comment land, and settle. They wheeled a few more paces in silence. Michael wasn't going to push it. He knew she had pride. She had to have it. She was down here in college all by herself, by the looks of it.

Finally, Deihlia nodded. "I think you'd fill that position pretty well too," she said. "But there's a probation period, so if you can make it through that, you've got the job." She turned to him, smiling.

Yes, he liked this girl. She was already making her way into his heart. "Cool," he said. "First stop, Charleston Hall. I know there are always some guys playing video games in there. I want to introduce you, then we'll move on."

Deihlia felt it - finally. A gate was opening. She knew enough to wait and see if Michael was good on his word, but so far, so good.

She had a positive feeling about him. She hadn't known she needed a campus navigator, but now that she did, she wanted one. "That sounds great, Michael," she replied, wheeling towards Charleston Hall, the three story brick dorm building that was two buildings over from her dorm. She knew how to get there.

Michael liked doing things for other people. It gave him something to focus on other than himself and his own problems. He walked beside her, marveling at how easily the universe had thrown them together at a party where neither one of them really belonged. "I think you're gonna like Stu and Billie. They're good guys," Michael said, holding the door open so she could wheel in.

Deihlia pushed her wheels past him. As she crossed the threshold of the door, a wave of good feeling washed over her. Everything was going to be okay.

Suddenly Last Summer

The house looked better than it ever had. With a fresh coat of paint, new bushes and plants in the yard, and a thick healthy lawn, it looked ten years younger. Deihlia had just arrived home from college for the summer after her second year. The house was the first thing she noticed.

So many changes were taking place. Her mom had gotten remarried the previous summer and had a baby a few months later. She'd met her husband white water rafting in Vermont, and they'd started to date not long afterwards. He lived in Vermont, and came down on the weekends to be with them and help get the house ready. Their son Kai, Deihlia's little brother, was six months old now. What was he like? The last time she saw him he was just an infant. She had mixed feelings about all the changes.

Donna came out of the house and stood on the deck holding Kai in one arm. "Wave to your sister," she said to him. He looked at the car that had just pulled into the driveway. She walked down the stairs and opened the car door.

Deihlia's Uncle Paul, the one who brought her kayaking and camping when she was young, had picked her up from college. He reached into the back seat and pulled out her wheelchair, popping on one wheel and then another. "Here you go," he said, pushing the chair over so she could get out of the car.

Deihlia hopped into her chair then looked up at her little brother. "Can I hold him Mom?"

Donna started to extricate her son from her arm but he pulled on her hair and held tight. "Sit with your sister Kai, come on," she said, looking at him. He looked scared.

"Kai, I haven't seen you in months." Deihlia reached her arms up towards him.

He squirmed in his mother's arm. "You can hold him later, let's just get your stuff inside."

Deihlia wheeled around the car to the ramp and went up. She could see into the backyard. It was all cleaned up. There was nothing left except green grass and a picnic table. She peered over the deck railing, looking out past the yard towards the trees. She had so many memories here. This was the only home she'd ever known. It wasn't a big fancy house but it was theirs.

147

"You ok?" her mom asked, standing against the screen door to hold it open while Deihlia's uncle carried her things in from the car.

"The house looks good," she said. She'd hated to leave school the weekend before. She'd been having such a fun time with her friends and in her classes. Now that she was home she hated the thought of leaving it behind too.

"Yeah, we're working hard on it. It goes on sale in August, just in time for the fall market."

Deihlia's heart sank. She rolled into the kitchen. The cabinets and floor had been fixed. She went through the kitchen down the hall to her bedroom and opened the door. At least they hadn't changed that yet. It was still pretty much the way she had left it. She went inside and shut the door behind her.

"Just put that in the living room for now," she heard her mother say on the other side of the door. She went over to her bedside table and picked up the dusty stack of Magic cards. She'd meant to take them with her to school but had forgotten to pack them. She got on to her bed and sat there, holding the cards in one hand. Holding them took her back in time to high school, and before that, middle and elementary school. She'd spent so much time in her room playing Magic over the years.

"What are you doing?" her mother asked, knocking on the door.

She didn't answer. She looked around her room, wanting everything to stay exactly as it was. She could feel Chelsea's absence too. She'd moved up to Vermont to teach snowboarding that winter. The house felt so different without Chelsea in it. She missed her. "I just need a little time to myself, Mom," she said. Without Chelsea, it felt like she was alone somehow. The feeling surprised her.

A few weeks later as her mother cleaned out the basement, Deihlia called Julia. "What's up? Are you gonna be around at all this summer?"

Julia hadn't seen Deihlia yet, and it was almost July. "Yeah, I'll be around the rest of the summer. What are you up to?"

"Just the usual," Deihlia said. Another summer without a job, another summer hanging around the house. Only this summer she wanted that. "You know my Mom's selling the house this fall."

Julia blew the smoke out of her lungs and sat down on a lawn chair in her own yard across town. "What? She's really gonna go through with it?"

"Yeah, she is."

"Shoot Deihlia. That sucks."

"I know. There's nothing I can do about it. I think we should have a weekend sleepover like old times. Whatd'ya think?"

"Yeah, we should. One last blow out." She was bummed. Deihlia's house had been her second home for years. "How the hell am I gonna see you after she moves?"

"I don't know," Deihlia replied. "I'm gonna call LP and see if he wants to come for the weekend too."

"Good idea. Have you talked to Chels? Is she coming back at all this summer?"

"Yeah, she has to. She has to get her stuff."

The enormity of the move started to settle on Julia, the way it had settled on Deihlia when she first arrived home. It felt like everything had been turned upside down, the contents of the house and the people in it spilled out all over the place, with nothing to put them back into.

A few weeks later, the white Camaro roared into the driveway, coming to a noisy stop. Chelsea got out, slamming the door behind her. She hadn't been home since last January. She paused and looked at the exterior of the house, at the new green paint, the bushes, the grass. The kitchen door opened and Deihlia sat in the doorway, looking out at her. Deihlia's dreads were getting longer, that was the first thing Chelsea saw. Something else was different about her too, but she couldn't put her finger on what it was.

"Chels, you're finally here," Deihlia said, wheeling out on to the deck.

Chelsea lit a cigarette, then walked up the stairs. "Yeah. What's going on? The house looks good." Deihlia nodded.

Chelsea leaned over the side of the deck, looking out at the backyard. "I can't believe Mom is really gonna sell," she said.

"Me neither. How've you been Chels?" she asked. They hadn't really spoken more than a hello on the phone all summer.

"I'm doing ok. Just working a lot." She was starting to feel sad and helpless being back at home and she didn't like it.

"I wish you were down here this summer," Deihlia said. She meant it.

Chelsea turned her head and looked at her sister. She'd never said anything like that to her before. "College seems to agree with you." She smiled.

Deihlia laughed. That was Chelsea, quick with the retorts. She was glad that she was home. "Julia was here last weekend. We did a final blowout weekend. Wish you could've made it down."

Chelsea turned around and looked out at the driveway, into the road, across the street to where Sean used to live. The past couple of years had been really hard. Deihlia off at college, her mom getting married and having a kid. Her job teaching snowboarding at the mountain had been her way through it. She'd made new friends and then found another job at the resort using her art skills. Her job was the only solid ground under her feet. "I wish I could've made it too. Maybe we can all get together again while I'm down here."

Deihlia nodded. She had the urge to go up and hug her sister, but they didn't roll like that. "Yeah, maybe."

"Where's Mom? I want to see Kai," Chelsea said, walking into the house.

Deihlia followed her inside.

"Wow," Chelsea said, stopping in her tracks.

"I know. This place never looked better."

As she stood in the hall looking into the living room, a scene flashed for a second then was gone. It was Christmas, and she and Deihlia were ripping open their gifts. The box in her hand started to reveal itself as she pulled the red wrapping paper off. The *American Girl* doll she'd wanted peered out from behind the plastic. "Look what Santa brought me!" she exclaimed to her sister.

Deihlia just looked on, watching. She didn't say anything, but she knew there was no Santa. Her mom told her not to say anything to her sister about it. Chelsea pulled the doll out, waving it around in the air. "Look! Look at her!" she said. But Deihlia looked kind of sad. "You didn't want an American Girl doll, I'm sure Santa would've brought you one if you wanted it," Chelsea said to her sister, holding her doll on her lap. They'd talked about it years later. It's funny how memories get layered with things you come to know over time, even if you didn't know them when the original moment happened.

Chelsea came back to the present. The house looked small to her now, but it had felt so big when she was a little girl. She had mixed feelings about selling the house, too. She didn't want to live here anymore, but she didn't want it to disappear, either. But when her Mom made up her mind, that was the end of the story. If it was time to let it go, Chelsea wanted to get it over with.

Deihlia sat behind her in the hall, watching as she paused in the living room doorway to take everything in. "Everything's different already," she said.

Chelsea nodded and walked away, heading upstairs.

Game Central, North Carolina

Deihlia grabbed her XBOX console and moved it over, plugging in the wires to hook it up into another console. Her friend Rickie helped her, plugging wires in here and there, connecting them to the TV that sat on the floor by the wall. He was blonde with a round face and beard. He wore big glasses, too, and got close to the TV so he could see clearly. Even with the glasses, he struggled a bit.

"How many people are coming over tonight, Dee?" he asked her.

Deihlia shrugged. "I don't know. A bunch. Let's just hook up as many as we can so everyone who wants to play can play. I could also use some help picking this place up a little bit."

Rickie looked around and nodded. "Sure. I'll take out the garbage and put some of this stuff away." As he turned back to the wires, light blue fell from Deihlia's shoulder, covering her arm in a swath of color. Rickie glanced sideways without moving his head to get a better look. A bright blue cape fell over the wheelchair and pooled on the floor around his friend. He grinned.

Deihlia noticed that he had stopped what he was doing and was staring at her kind of funny and smiling. "Everything ok?" She asked.

As she turned to him the spell was broken. No more blue, just Deihlia's purple hoodie and her tan pants. He shook his head like he was shaking off water. "Yeah, yeah. Everything's good."

A couple of hours later, the living room was ready for guests, and they started arriving, bringing beer and chips, and a couple of other XBOX consoles. "OK, we can hook those up too," Deihlia said, letting the guys rewire and reconfigure their setup. More people arrived, and the game got bigger, with enough consoles so that twenty-four players could play at once. The small apartment was crowded; people sat on every corner of furniture and on the floor. Deihlia looked around. She knew most of the people who were in her apartment, but there were a few who were strangers.

"Are we ready?" she asked, picking up her controller. Rickie sat next to her, and picked up his too.

Everyone looked up at them. Rickie turned towards her. "Let's go," he said.

The games began. Everyone stared at the TV and screens, moving their hands and shouting "Shoot," or "Damn it!" or

152

"Awwww" when they'd get taken out. They battled each other until one of them won, then that player went on to play another. Multiple games went on at the same time. A guy named Mitch, one of the students that Deihlia didn't know, who'd been invited by someone else, was playing against a player on the screen called 'Swiftie.' They played hard for over an hour, but Swiftie won. Mitch waited his turn for a while and played another game against Swiftie, who seemed to be staying in the games for the duration. Mitch prided himself on his game playing, and he'd played Halo a lot. Halo 2 was different but it wasn't that different. A few kids picked up and left, moving on to other activities. He and Swiftie fought again. Other players were duking it out. "Damn it!" he said out loud when his character was killed. What the hell?

Deihlia looked at the clock. It was 8:45. "Anyone else want to order pizza?" she asked.

Rickie shook his head yes, and a few others did too. People reached into their pockets, pulling out bills and handing them to Deihlia. She counted them, then added some of her own. "We've got enough for five pizzas," she said. Rickie called and placed the order. They started another round, and time passed. More people died. Swiftie was winning against someone else. The pizza arrived, and everyone paused their game and put down their controller. The pizza was devoured, a pipe was passed, and someone popped open another beer. The games resumed. Mitch jumped back in and played someone else and won. Deihlia was busy with her controller, at war with another player.

Hours went by and several players dropped out. "I'm heading out, thanks for the games Deihlia and Rickie," they said. Mitch watched them go. He figured Deihlia was the girl whose apartment they were at. He'd never spoken to her before. He knew Rickie. He picked up his controller and jumped into another game. Swiftie again! He played hard and they went neck to neck for a couple of hours, never lifting his eyes from the screen. Once in a while he'd look up, trying to figure out who Swiftie was. "Who's Swiftie?" he asked as he watched the screen, moving his controller up and over.

Guys shrugged. "I don't know," one said. Rickie and Deihlia looked over at him. Mitch looked puzzled. The game grew more tense as Swiftie continued to destroy him, and then it was over. No one else was left playing. Mitch put his controller down and stood up, his hands on hips. "Ok, who the hell is Swiftie?" He asked, looking around the room at the ten people who were still there. No one said anything. Who had been beating him all night?

From the couch, Deihlia started to wave. She grinned at him. "I'm Deihlia," she said.

Mitch was surprised. It showed on his face. He paused a moment before he responded. "You're one hell of a player," he said. Then he went over and extended his hand. "I'm Mitch. It's nice to meet you, Deihlia."

"You're a good player yourself, Mitch. It was a blast beating you." Deihlia giggled and looked up at him. He was tall and thin with black, wavy, shoulder length hair and a chin strap - a thin line of beard that was shaved sharp around his chin. He wore a blue plaid shirt and faded jeans with Nikes. The chin strap made him look like a rebel and a lumberjack, but his face was young and open.

Who is this girl?, Mitch wondered, standing in front of her. It was weird, he could swear she was wearing something bright blue, but she had on an orange Billabong hoodie. Rickie moved over and made room for Mitch to sit down with them on the couch.

Mitch felt a little awkward. Going from annoyed to amazed in a matter of seconds humbled him. Plus, how did he not know her? She was such a great player, they should've been beating each other long before this. Who was Deihlia? Where did she come from? Why was she such a good player? "How long have you been playing?" Is all he asked her, a hint of his North Carolina accent coming through.

"Ever since I was a kid. From Nintendo to Game Boy to XBOX, and here I am," Deihlia replied. "You look like you've been playing a long time too."

Mitch nodded. "Yeah, definitely since I was like fourteen or something. But I've never played anyone as good as you."

"That's such a compliment," Deihlia said, still smiling. "We should play together some more. It's good to play against the best players. That's how we really up our game."

Rickie sat near them, listening. He liked to watch Deihlia in action. She had a knack for disarming people, for winning them over with her charm. And, she was the best damn player at school. How did Mitch not know her already? She had gaming parties on a regular basis. He could tell Mitch was relaxing now, opening up, being seduced by Deihlia's attention. He'd seen it happen over and over -

154

how she made friends out of adversaries, how people stopped seeing her as girl with a disability and just saw her as a cool person. They usually didn't even know their idea of her had changed. "You know Deihlia - the girl with the dreads," they'd say. Not "the girl in the wheelchair."

"How about Tuesday night?" Deihlia asked.

Mitch nodded. "Yeah, Tuesday night works for me. I'll meet you after dinner."

"Cool," She replied. She was looking forward to playing with him again.

Mitch stood up to leave, then stopped after one step. "You need help taking these apart?"

"Sure," Deihlia said, pulling her wheelchair close to the couch so she could jump into it. Mitch watched her, then reached down and started pulling at the wires. *I can learn some things from her,* he thought to himself, sneaking another look over at her as he unhooked the wires. He felt like he'd just met the coolest girl ever, so he stayed and helped until everything was taken apart.

The Inspection, Ecuador, 2005

"It will be a long bus ride to my home in Cuenca City, Dee," Gabi said, grabbing Deihlia's bag and heading towards the bus. Deihlia noticed that her friend's long brown hair was even longer. Her big dark almond shaped eyes glittered warmly when she bent down to hug her. She hadn't seen Gabi since she graduated and had returned home to Ecuador.

"Yeah, I know. You told me. Five hours! I'm so glad we'll be riding together. Thanks for meeting me, Gabi." Deihlia replied, nodding, grateful to be off of the airplane and on solid ground.

"I cannot wait for you to meet my family and see my home. I'm so glad you came," she said. They were college friends and met in an English class. Deihlia had sat next to Gabi's desk, and started to ask her about what she had done for the homework assignment. They started to study together and share their papers for a first review before handing them in. They became good friends, hanging out and studying together. Gabi had returned home to Ecuador after graduation, and invited Deihlia to visit. Gabi knew Deihlia needed help getting around her country and village, and she would help, or ask others. It was Deihlia's first trip travelling alone on an international flight.

After getting their tickets, they waited in line at the bus.

"They will have to put your wheelchair in with the luggage on top of the bus," Gabi said, watching as people handed their luggage over to the bus driver. "I'll ask someone to help us get you on the bus."

Deihlia looked at the people around them, wondering who might be able to help. The line dwindled as people boarded the bus, a beat up old school bus that had been rigged to carry luggage on top. As they approached the front of the line, Gabi spoke in Spanish to the bus driver. Deihlia could understand her, mostly. She was asking the bus driver to help carry her friend on to the bus. The bus driver looked to be in his late thirties, and he wore a white short-sleeve button down shirt and blue khakis. He looked down at Deihlia in her wheelchair, in her grey jeans and t-shirt, her tawny dreads pulled up on the back of her head in a loose ponytail. "Si," he said, taking their luggage and putting it with the rest of the luggage on the sidewalk.

Deihlia handed her small backpack to Gabi, and the driver bent over and picked her up out of her chair. She wrapped her arms around him as he carried her on to the bus. He smelled a little sweaty and earthy as he walked to the back and placed her down on an empty seat. "Muchas gracias," she said. Nodding, he walked off, back to the other passengers waiting in line. A couple of people turned in their seats and looked back at her curiously. Her legs hung over the bus seat, dangling. After making sure that Deihlia's chair was secured with the luggage, Gabi came and sat down beside her. The bus filled. The driver looked back at all the passengers before he sat down and started the engine.

"I'm so happy to see you, Gabi," Deihlia said, reaching over to give her friend a hug. Gabi hugged her back. They hadn't seen each other in a year. Gabi was one of Deihlia's first friends at college.

"It will be a long ride to my village but we'll go through many different kinds of terrain, so I can show you lots of things as we go."

"Cool," Deihlia replied. Everything was new to her here. It felt good to be in a completely different environment, like all of her senses were clean and extra sharp. The bus took off, rumbling on to the open road as it left the city. Gabi pointed out different landmarks as the bus rolled along, and they caught up on what they'd been doing and news of their mutual college friends as the hours passed.

Three hours later, they were driving along a narrow road that snaked through the jungle. Suddenly the bus squealed and groaned to a sudden stop. Outside the window, trees with large leaves and wild underbrush lined the road. There were no buildings or bus stops, nothing but foliage.

"This may not be good," Gabi said, looking over at Deihlia with a concerned face.

"What is it?"

"Sometimes the police pull the bus over to inspect them for foreigners."

"I'm a foreigner!" Deihlia said.

"They are looking for drugs, I think."

Deihlia's eyes got wider. The only time she'd had any interaction with police was at the movies one night as a teenager, when the cop on duty had taken away her sharp-studded leather bracelets, calling them "weapons." "A cripple with goth bracelets is a danger to the general public?" Deihlia had wanted to retort back to him, but he was obviously a jerk, so instead she removed her bracelets and handed them to him, feeling humiliated and mad. What would the police do in Ecuador? Would her proficiency in Spanish be enough to understand what was being asked of them?

The bus driver stood up, looking out the door as someone shouted outside. The passengers could see him nodding, then he turned to the people on the bus and said something in Spanish about getting off the bus. He walked down the steps and got off. Gabi looked around frantically to see if there was a man who could help carry Deihlia out. The driver was already out the door. People were standing up and hurriedly shuffling off the bus. Only a few women and children were left around them, and they were moving towards the door. Gabi looked at Deihlia. "I cannot get you off the bus, Dee! I don't know what to do," she said, her eyes filling. "I'm sorry." She felt terrible. She couldn't lift her friend. She couldn't say anything to the police about Deihlia because they'd think she was trying to cover something up. She'd invited Deihlia to visit her and she'd come all the way and now this was happening. She felt helpless and scared.

"I guess I have to stay here," Deihlia said, a lump in her throat.

"Just do what they say, Dee." Gabi said. "I better get off now or I will get us in trouble. I'm so sorry!" She squeezed Deihlia's arm as she got up to go.

Gabi walked down the aisle and disappeared out of the side of the bus. Out the window, Deihlia could see a few people standing on the side of the road, silent and obedient. A moment later, three men in military uniforms carrying large black guns boarded the bus. They looked through the driver's area, then moved on to look in every seat, then under them, opening bags that were left as people scrambled out.

What should she do? What could she do? She wasn't going to get down on the floor and appear to be hiding. That seemed like a dumb move that would attract their attention and suspicion. Talking to them in so-so Spanish probably wasn't a good idea either. Deihlia watched them approach, trying to keep her head down a little so they didn't think she was being purposely defiant. She knew that her dreads made her look like someone who likes to smoke weed. Was that a problem? The men spoke in low voices to one another as they made their way slowly to the back of the bus, using the tips of their guns to overturn anything that was on the seats or floor.

Deihlia's heart was beating fast. Imagining an invisible shield enclosing her, she froze in place, not moving. Not lifting her head.

She wanted to disappear into the seat, but she couldn't. *They'll pass by me and leave me alone,* she thought to herself, trying to keep calm. *They won't even see me.* Though she was smaller than normal, her dreads clearly sprouted above the back of the seat in front of her.

The first man drew nearer, pausing. He stopped in place. She couldn't see what he was looking at because she didn't want to look directly at him. That would require moving. He was just out of her line of vision. He stood there a few moments, not moving, then took one slow step, placing his foot on the floor near her seat, crunching a wrapper. Deihlia remained still, her heart beat like a gong in her chest. Could he hear it? In her peripheral vision she saw the black gun, his finger on the trigger as he stood next to her seat. The other men had stopped too. The bus was quiet. It felt like an eternity before the man next to her said something, his voice low. One of his comrades grunted. They stood in place for another minute. The blood pumped furiously in her veins, beating in her ears. Then they continued on, looking into the last few seats of the bus. Deihlia held herself in the same position, trying not to blink. One of the men said something sharply and the three of them turned around and went back, back past all of the empty seats and opened bags, then got off the bus.

Deihlia lifted her head slightly and watched them go. As she saw the top of the head of the last one go down the stairs, she exhaled, relaxing her shoulders. She could hear them outside, talking to the passengers. She took a deep breath, gulping it in. Outside, she saw people standing on the edge of the road. The dense foliage behind them was a discouraging tangle. If she had to get off of the bus or the bus was taken from them, what would she do? She couldn't crawl around on her hands and elbows on a jungle road. She was too much for someone to carry, she knew that. There wasn't anything she could do except wait for the next moment to unfold.

She heard more shouting, then footsteps. People began to get back on the bus after the armed men searched inside the bags they held in their hands. Deihlia's heartbeat began to return to normal as the seats filled up. A few moments later, Gabi returned, rushing to sit down beside her.

"Dee, what happened? Are you ok? What did you do?" Gabi asked as she gripped Deihlia's arm, her face tight with worry. "I am so sorry. So sorry!"

Deihlia looked over at her as an older woman and two children slid into their seat across the aisle. Though she could feel that her face was still drained of color, she smiled mischievously. She didn't want her friend to feel bad. Her friend who'd already taken this five hour bus trip one way to come and meet her, and who would do it again round trip when she brought her back to the airport. The last thing she wanted was for Gabi to feel bad.

Deihlia shrugged. "I made myself invisible," she said.

Gabi looked at her for a few seconds, as if in shock, then let out a laugh. "You are so crazy Dee!" she said, a smile breaking out on her face.

Deihlia nodded her head in agreement. "I really did. They didn't even know I was here," she said.

The driver got on the bus and looked back at the passengers. He looked relieved, and eager to continue on. He sat down and turned the key in the ignition. The bus growled back into gear under them, bouncing slightly.

"Do you think my wheelchair is ok?" she asked.

Gabi nodded. "They didn't take it down off the bus, I kept an eye on it for you. We are lucky. This could have lasted for hours. And sometimes the men are cruel."

"I like being lucky," Deihlia said, gripping her seat as the bus lurched into the next gear.

Ten days later, they were back at the airport. The return bus ride was easier and undisturbed. Deihlia checked in, handing her passport to the airline attendant behind the desk, and Gabi placed her bag next to it.

"Here you go Ms. Nye," the airline attendant said with a Spanish accent as she handed Deihlia her boarding pass. "Have a nice flight."

Gabi walked beside Deihlia, heading towards security. The week had gone by so fast. "My family loves you Dee," Gabi said. "I hope you will come back again."

The airport was small but busy. A father walked by with a small girl on his shoulders. His wife held hands with two others. The father pulled two big pieces of luggage. American students with backpacks walked by in pairs. It was busy but not frenetic. A woman's voice came over the speaker system, talking quickly in Spanish about a change of gates.

Deihlia moved along, not looking up from the floor. Gabi's family was so warm and welcoming, they made her feel that she was one of them. It was really hard to leave. "I hope so too. Are you coming back to the states anytime soon? Visiting school or anything?"

Gabi shook her head. "No, I cannot afford to do that."

The security checkpoint appeared in front of them. People filed in, one after another. Deihlia's heart sank. She had an awful feeling that this was the last time she was going to see her friend. She stopped and looked up at Gabi. "You're such a good friend. Thanks so much for everything. This trip was amazing. I'll never forget the shrunken heads we saw at the museum!" Deihlia giggled. "Your family is awesome. I really loved getting to know them."

Gabi looked down at Deihlia. They had their whole lives to see each other again. Surely they would. Something would bring her back to the states, or maybe Dee would come back again one day. "I'm so glad you came. You have to come back again."

Deihlia looked hard at Gabi, as if she could memorize her face, then she reached out and threw her arms around her. Gabi hugged her back tightly. "We will see each other again Dee. We have to." She said into Deihlia's dreads. The announcer came on again, announcing the boarding for another flight. People walked by them, getting into the security line.

Deihlia pulled back. "I should go. Let's skype soon."

Gabi smiled back at her. "Yes, of course. I love you Dee. Thanks for coming all the way to Ecuador."

"Love you too," Deihlia smiled at her, then moved towards the line and got in behind a large tall man with a very small yellow suitcase. The sight of him and his tiny disproportionate luggage made her smile. She wanted to be smiling as she waved one last time to Gabi, and she was.

The Invisible Line

"I think that's a good plan. I'll come by later to see how it's going," Deihlia said. She was speaking to her friend Pitt. He'd recently transferred to her school and they became friends in one of her psych classes. Pitt had short blonde hair and blue eyes. His body was contorted from his condition. He was in a wheelchair too, but his was a motorized chair that he navigated with a small lever on the armrest. It had four fat wheels and a motor that sat underneath the seat in a grey box.

"Okaaay." He said, nodding his head in his own way, with a twist of his neck to the right.

"Is there anything else you need before I leave?" She asked.

"Nooo." Pitt replied. "I wanna play Halooo."

Deihlia grinned at him. "We'll play tomorrow night, I promise."

"Promissse!"

She left him, moving through the door, into the hall, then out on to the sidewalk. She liked Pitt, he was funny and smart. He'd been begging her to play Halo with him, knowing she had big gaming parties all the time and they seemed like fun. His hands were about the only part of his body that worked well, so video games had become his favorite pastime.

She looked at the University Center building as she approached. Clusters of students sat on tables outside on the patio. It was a warm spring day, so people were lounging on the grass and hanging around outside studying. In a small corner of the patio, students in wheelchairs sat together, their chairs askew. No two chairs were alike. Another student using a walker came out of the building slowly and joined them. Deihlia knew that the "regular" students didn't mix with the kids with disabilities, especially the ones with unmistakable ones like those needing wheelchairs or using walkers. It was a painful reality she had endured for the first few months of school, until Michael crossed that line, then others followed.

She paused on the concrete, poised between the students with disabilities, and the others. She saw her friend Jackson, an African American student with short spindly dreads in his big sturdy manual chair, drinking a soda. They'd met when she approached him to say that she liked his dreads. They'd been friends ever since. She looked at the group of other students. They were laughing, talking.

"Jackson! How's it going?" she asked, pulling up beside him.

"Not bad, shorty. I've got a paper to write but I'm loving this sunshine. What trouble are you getting into?"

"What are you implying? You know I'm a bonafied overachiever. All I do is study, study, study." She said.

"Right. I heard you were at that crazy party last weekend that got really out of control."

"How'd you know that?"

"Word on the street. I'm sure you didn't get in any trouble though, did you?" Jackson was dying to hear about the party. He was never invited. The kids who threw them wouldn't even talk to him or his friends.

Deihlia grinned and raised her eyebrows. "Me? I never get into any trouble! Y'know, it was alright. But some people get drunk way too fast and just show their ass to the world. That's what happened. Nothing too scandalous."

"Oh," Jackson replied, disappointed.

Deihlia could tell that he felt left out, like she had the first few months of school. It was a lousy feeling knowing that people didn't see you as a real person because you weren't built like them. The friends she had, with and without disabilities, were all awesome and appreciated her for being Deihlia, but she knew that wasn't the case for most of the students with disabilities. Yeah, all her friends were fantastic people. Why not have a party and let them all get to know each other?

"Jackson, I'm having a party this Friday night, 7:30. Put on your party hat and be there."

Jackson looked at her and smiled a big toothy grin. "7:30? I'll be there!"

"Cool," Deihlia said. "See you then."

She went back on the sidewalk, aiming for her friend Joel's dorm. She knew he was usually home in the afternoon. Tony and Joel came strolling out the front door of the dorm. Perfect timing. "What's going on?" she asked, rolling up to them.

Tony shrugged. Joel shook his head.

"Hey I'm having a party Friday night. Seven-thirty. Can you guys make it?"

Tony and Joel looked at Dee. She always had something up her sleeve, and it was usually a good time. "Yeah, I can make it."

164

"Me, too."

"Cool. Bring the usual suspects and some beer or whatever."

"Sure, ok." Tony replied.

Deihlia was excited. It wasn't that she had some brilliantly funny pranks or adventures planned for the party, it was that she was going to introduce her two sets of friends to each other. Up to now, she'd only introduced them in passing, between classes or on the quad. It wasn't that anyone was doing anything wrong, including herself, but she wanted to make the invisible line disappear and she could start with her own world. After all, the one thing they all had in common was her, and that was as good a starting point as any.

Friday night arrived and Deihlia put on some music. Her friend Bud had bought some beer for her, and she stowed it in the refrigerator. Her accessible apartment, built for people with disabilities, was often the epicenter of her friends' socializing. It was on the first floor, and was spacious enough for her to get around easily. Not all colleges have apartments designed specifically so that people with disabilities could live comfortably. St. Michaels had been a good fit, once she found her way in freshman year. She turned on her table lamps and lit a couple of candles. She thought of Pitt, and how hard it was for him to get around, the fat wheels of his chair subject to the herky-jerky movements of his hands. Looking down at her misshapen feet resting on the light silver edge of her chair frame, Deihlia felt grateful. She could get herself around okay, and her chair was light. Her friends could help her get in and out of cars and buildings. Neither Pitt nor Jackson could get around so easily. Their adventures were even more defined by their chairs, their sizes, the way their bodies functioned than hers were.

Boom boom, a loud knock announced someone at her door. Eric came in carrying beer, with a bong hidden under the flap of his backpack. His curly red-headed Mohawk bounced on top of his head as he came in, a counterpoint to the rainbow-colored hemp hoodie he wore.

"Dude, good to see you." Deihlia said.

A few moments later someone else knocked politely on the door. She opened it, and Jackson sat at the threshold. "Come on in!"

Looking around at Deihlia's apartment, Jackson said "Wow! Pretty clean for you, Deihlia."

Eric looked up, a little surprised. Jackson seemed to know Dee pretty well, but he'd never met him before.

"Jackson, this is my friend Eric." Deihlia said, waving at Eric who was popping open a beer. Eric looked over at Jackson. Any friend of Deihlia's was cool with him. "Jackson, nice to meet you man." He said, reaching for his hand.

Jackson smiled and shook his hand. "Looks like you've got something good in there," he nodded, noticing the top of the bong peeking out from Eric's backpack.

Eric patted the top of the satchel. "Some good stuff for later," he said.

The door opened and Joel walked in. His tall, dark haired, spectacled face was closer to the ceiling than any others. "Dee, everyone is on their way." He looked around. "Hey Eric." He was surprised to see Jackson. He'd never met him before. Deihlia was always bringing new people into the gang. "Hey man," he said, nodding to him.

"Jackson," he said.

"Joel."

The doorbell rang - *bzzz bzzz*. Joel turned around and opened the door.

"Let's get this party started!" Tony said as he came in, flanked by Lauren and Billie. Tony's light-blonde beard was scraggly. He wore a red t-shirt and jeans, which accidentally matched Billie's red jacket. Billie carried a case of beer and walked into Deihlia's kitchen, putting it down on the counter.

"Ok, who won the bet the last time?" Deihlia asked.

Tony looked around the room. Joel shrugged. Eric sipped on his beer.

They heard an odd scratching noise at the door. Tony opened it. Pitt turned the lever on his chair and it lurched into the apartment. "Hiiiii." He said. "You need a foot bell."

Deihlia laughed. "I'll add that to the list of improvements. Come on in. Everyone, this is my friend Pitt."

No sooner had the door closed than it opened again and Mitch walked in. He paused, glancing around the room to see who was there. He stood next to Pitt. "How's it going," he said.

Pitt shook and twisted his head in response.

166

"I saw a couple of Lacrosse players heading this way, Dee." Mitch said.

"What? Who invited them?"

"They must've heard one of us talking about coming over here."

Right on cue, someone knocked at the door. Mitch turned around and opened it. "Hey, we heard Deihlia's having a party," the brunette with flushed cheeks said.

"She is," Mitch replied. Standing in front of the door with his legs wide, he looked back over his shoulder at Deihlia.

She pushed her chair forward. "You guys are welcome to come in if you can be cool."

The tall auburn haired guy looked around the room, and then at his friend. He knew Deihlia was a cripple, but he didn't know there'd be other ones at this party. Maybe they didn't want to party here tonight after all. His friend with the pink cheeks paused, taking in the scene. He knew Tony and Mitch. They were alright dudes. He'd heard about Deihlia and her game parties. He turned and returned his friend's look. Why not stay and check it out? "Yeah, we'll be cool."

Jackson turned back to Eric. "You gonna spark that up?"

Tony approached Deihlia. "You're up to something," he said, smiling.

Joel began to talk to Pitt. "Can I get you anything?" he asked. While it was a little hard to understand Pitt, he could tell he wanted something.

Tony opened the case and began to offer beers to those standing without one. The two Lacrosse players reached out at the same time to accept a bottle.

Deihlia sat in the middle of the room, watching and listening. So far, so good. The night was young, but it was starting out really, really well.

Shangri-La, North Carolina, 2005

"I found the coolest bamboo grove out in the woods," Tony said one afternoon as he and Deihlia hung out in her campus apartment. "And I don't think anyone else knows about it."

"Really," she replied, turning her gaze to him. She didn't know much about trees, but she knew that her buddy Tony had a special affinity with nature. If he thought it was special, it probably was really beautiful. Tony grew up on a farm in New York state. He was earthy, practical, and warm, and they had an affectionate friendship that blossomed out of playing relentless video games. "Is that where you've been disappearing to?" she asked, smiling.

Tony nodded, looking absently into the distance, as if the bamboo trees were just on the other side of the apartment wall and he could see through it. "Yeah, it's really beautiful there. It's near this reservoir or something out deep in the woods. I like to go there and sketch," he said, reaching into his backpack and pulling out a sketchpad. He flipped open the cover and turned it towards her. "They're not great sketches or anything, but this is what I drew the last time I went."

Deihlia put her hand under the bottom of the sketchpad, careful not to touch the page, where fat and thin pencil lines brought the bamboo grove a little more into her view. Looking at the page carefully, she took a few moments before she asked "Can I see the other ones too?"

Tony nodded, turning the page. They spent some time looking at each of the pages in his pad. Deihlia looked each one over, taking it in, making small sounds to indicate that something on the page had reached her. She continued to hold the pad from underneath, balancing it on her open palm. "These are really awesome, Tony. That bamboo grove looks kind of magical."

"It is. I wish I could take you there to show you," he replied, slowly sliding the pad out of her hand and holding it closed in his lap.

"Why can't you?" Deihlia asked. "I want to see it."

Tony paused, trying to determine how he could bring her there. "Really? You wanna go?" He asked.

"Hell yeah!" she replied, "Let's go now."

Tony looked at the clock. "Yeah, I guess we can go if we leave now. Are you sure you're up for it?"

Deihlia nodded, beaming. "That's what we're doing today. You're taking me to the bamboo grove."

They put on their jackets. Tony opened the apartment door and held it for her as she wheeled out, closing it tight behind him. Together they made their away across campus, to the last building at the very edge of the woods that surrounded it. "I went in over here," he said, pushing her chair into the grass. He had to get behind her, and with his height, it meant bending way over to push her chair from behind. Deihlia pushed her wheels too, but it required two of them.

Tony traced his way through the woods, pushing her around trees, over roots and bumpy terrain. It wasn't often Deihlia got to walk through the woods, it was so much work for someone else to help her through it, and she couldn't do it alone. They talked and joked as she jostled along, and she lit a joint, passing it back and forth, stopping to inhale, one then the other. They laughed, squeezing her through the trees. "This is already a special place," Deihlia said looking up, her eyes puffy from the pot.

Tony stopped and inhaled the last bit of weed, looking around at the pines that surrounded them. They stopped for a moment, listening, and it felt like the trees embraced them.

"It is," he said, "but I want to show you Shangri-La." He began pushing her again, and she put her hands on the rims of her wheels and they continued on. After a bit, they were pushing harder, going up an incline. The pines were closer together, and they had to maneuver more tightly between them. Wings flapped overhead as they approached, then disappeared into the sky.

"I think we're almost there," Tony said, pausing to look around. They'd been out in the woods for a good 40 minutes, and the sun had moved lower in the sky. Deihlia looked around. She had no idea where they were or how they'd gotten there. It was Tony's path they had followed, the one in his head.

"Cool," she said, waiting for him to continue.

He bent over again and started pushing her up a steep incline, until they came out by the top of a ridge. Water glistened below. "It's not far once we get past this reservoir," he said.

Deihlia looked at the water, and at the narrow dirt and grass path that went across it. The body of water was large, and the path was a bit narrow. *Can we make it across?* She wondered briefly then looked past it, seeing more trees like the ones they just came through.

They weren't the bamboo trees. "Well, let's go. I can't wait to see it," she said, putting her hands on her wheels.

Tony started pushing her again towards the path that went across the water. The water shimmered a few feet below, reflecting sky and trees, the late afternoon sun a ripple of light across its surface. It felt peaceful, pristine. They were the only ones out there.

As he pushed her along the bumpy dirt and grass path, the land started to slope and get slippery on the edge. As they moved forward, a patch of wet grass gave way and they lost control of her wheelchair. There were no handles on it, just the small aluminum frame. It teetered, spilling Deihlia out towards the water as it rolled downhill then rolled over her into the water. She tumbled out and slid down, trying to grab hold of grass or anything she could. She was slipping towards the water.

"Tony! I can't swim!" She cried out as he tried to find a way down over the steep scrabbly earth so that he could reach her.

"I'm coming!" he shouted back.

Her legs were in the water and she had one hand holding on to a small tuft of grass, but she was sinking. The water was up to her waist. She had no way to keep her upper body afloat. Tony slid down, down to the water, and got in beside her, putting his arms around her then pulling her over with one arm as he moved to a less steep section of the embankment, where he hauled her on her back into the dirt.

He went back to where they fell in and dove under the water to find her wheelchair. A few moments later, his head emerged above the water, and he swam on his back towards her, with one foot in the air hooked under the wheelchair frame, pulling it along behind him. He reached the dirt and bent his knee up, dragging the chair to where his hands could reach it. Then he turned around and climbed out of the water, tossing her chair on to the ground. Water dripped off of his clothes, hair, and beard as he went back and lifted her up, carrying her back up to a flat area near the trees. He looked down at her, his eyes wide. "Are you ok? I'm so sorry Dee, I'm so sorry." He shook his head, mad at himself for bringing her out there. His heart was pounding. Deihlia's eyes were wide too, and she was soaking wet. She looked at Tony, who was getting more upset by the second as he realized the danger they were just in. Dirt stuck to his knees and the front of his shirt.

171

"Man, you're really dirty," she said, cracking a smile. "Maybe we shouldn't have smoked all that good dope on our way in here."

Tony was still shaking his head, his face white with anger and fear. "I'm gonna get your wheelchair, be right back," he said, pushing his palm towards the ground, as if to say, don't go anywhere.

A moment later he returned, carrying her chair in one hand and setting it on the ground beside her.

"You saved my life man, thank you. I would've drowned if it wasn't for you."

Tony shook his head again, sober and upset. "It was a very bad idea, Deihlia. I should've known better."

She looked at him, then down at herself, running her hands over her wet pants. "I wanted to visit Shangri-La." she said, "I'm the one who said we should go." Then she turned her face back up to him. She was smiling. Tony was visibly upset. Even underneath his brown beard and long hair, she could see that his jaw was tight.

"Yeah, well it was a really bad idea, Deihlia, I never should've agreed to it. What if you'd drowned in there?" he said, brushing the dirt off of his clothes. "We better head back, it's getting late."

Deihlia was silent as she sat on the ground, looking up at Tony, watching the bamboo grove disappear from her view, as if her dream thief had returned and pulled it away from her. She saw how shaken her friend was. Maybe she was a little shaken too, but she wasn't going to let him see it. Then she scooted over, put one hand on her chair, one hand on the ground, and hoisted herself back up into her seat.

Tony got behind her and turned her back towards the woods, back towards the way they came, and bent over and began pushing.

A few moments went by without either one of them saying a word, the silence building as they rolled over one bumpy root and then another.

"You saved my life, Tony. I mean it." Deihlia said.

"That's not how this story goes," Tony replied, angry at himself for being so careless. Deihlia was so capable that he often forgot she couldn't do some things, or he didn't know when it was a liability for her. Though she was in a wheelchair, he thought of her as being just like them. This incident showed him clearly that it was not the case, and that Deihlia was so hell bent on doing things that she took risks she probably shouldn't take. Mostly, he blamed himself.

172

"Did you think that maybe we might fall into that water? Cause I didn't. " He asked, bent low behind her, pushing.

Deihlia was quiet. They passed one, two, three trees before she answered. "I guess I knew it was a possibility when I saw the water."

"And knowing you can't swim, you weren't afraid we might fall in?"

Deihlia's clothes were soaked through. Her chair was wet. But she was alive. "Well, I figured Shangri-La was worth the risk. Besides, death is always a possibility, Tony. We never know when it's coming. I can't spend my life not doing things because something *could* happen. Anything can happen."

That stopped him. He stood up straight, then walked around Deihlia until he was standing in front of her. He squatted down and put his hands on her arms, looking her in the face. "I didn't think about whether or not you could swim, and I don't want you to die, Dee. If it's in my control, I don't want to lose you. We're not gonna do this again. Yeah, anything can happen, but I don't want *that* to happen."

Deihlia looked him in the eyes, searching. His seriousness and level of upset got to her. "I'm sorry Tony, I'm sorry. I didn't really think it was a problem either," she said, holding her hands steady on the wheels. "As far as I'm concerned, you saved my life. You brought me out to Shangri-La and saved me from drowning. You're my hero." She smiled at him, getting her feeling of mischief back as she pictured him with a long green cape, flying out of the water with her in his arms.

Tony shook his head and stood up, getting behind her chair. The way back was harder, and they had a ways to go.

The Lift, Massachusetts, 2006

Donna drove down to pick up Deihlia in Cambridge. She was home from college for Spring break, and had stayed with her friend Sean for a night. Donna, Deihlia, and Kai were heading out in Donna's big black pick-up truck. Kai was in the baby seat in the rear of the cabin. Donna tossed Deihlia's wheelchair into the back of the truck like she'd done thousands of times before. It was a three hour drive back to Vermont from Massachusetts, a trip she made frequently. Donna drove on to Route 2, heading west. Before they even got through Arlington, something started to go wrong with the truck. The engine wheezed and sputtered, and a thin wisp of smoke snaked out of from under the hood. She pulled the truck over on to the shoulder of the road. Cars zoomed by at sixty, seventy miles an hour.

"Ugh," Donna said, shutting off the engine. Deihlia looked at her, and at the smoke coming out of the hood. Donna's cell phone was dead. Traffic continued to whir past them in a blur. Donna looked out at traffic. "We'll have to get out of the truck and get to a phone."

Deihlia shook her head. "Mom, we're on the side of Route 2! How are we gonna get to a phone?"

Donna looked over at her, then at Kai. "The cops will have to give us a ride," she said.

She went to the back of the truck to get Deihlia's chair, and helped to get Deihlia down out of the high truck seat and into her chair. Then she unstrapped Kai from the baby seat, and slammed the truck door. "Let's go," she said, walking ahead of Deihlia with Kai in her arms, staying as close as possible to the outer edge of the road.

Deihlia wheeled along behind her, recalling her forays along Route 140 with her friends. Route 140 was a regular two lane road. Route 2 had three lanes on either side, at least in that section of it, near Arlington and Belmont. Three lanes of traffic whizzed by them like wasps, one after another. They went along like that on the shoulder of the road for five minutes, heading towards the next off ramp. Then a siren screamed urgently behind them, gurgling to a stop.

"What the hell are you doing, lady? Do you know how many calls I got in the last five minutes about a woman with a baby and a kid in a wheelchair walking along Route 2?" The cop asked as he got out from behind the wheel of the police car, slamming his door. He stomped over to Donna and Deihlia in a wide gait, as if he'd been riding a horse all of his life.

"My truck broke down and my cell phone isn't working. I knew if we got out and walked, someone would call," she said.

"I got about a hundred calls!" He reiterated, irritated, his hands on his hips.

"We couldn't just sit there and hope that you'd come along. I have a baby and my daughter in a wheelchair, we couldn't just sit there like sitting ducks." *Isn't his job public safety?*, she thought but didn't say.

The policeman dropped his hands and ushered them over into the police car. His partner looked on from the passenger side as Donna opened the door and held it open for her daughter. Deihlia put her hands on the car seat and lifted her body up and over into the car at an angle, then pulled her legs in behind her. Donna directed the cop in dissembling the wheelchair, popping each wheel off at the hub with the push of a button. The second officer sat there, watching all of them get into the car, his partner placing the pieces of the wheelchair into the trunk. Donna and Malakai got into the car and sat in the backseat with Deihlia. The officer who was driving jumped back into the driver's seat, pulled the door shut, and began to drive. Deihlia saw that the cop sitting ahead of her was staring at her.

As Donna and the officer began talking about calling a tow truck and what to do next, the cop in front turned around, twisting his head to look back at Deihlia. She returned the look directly. She noticed sadness hardened around his face, at the corners of his eyes. "I'm Deihlia," she ventured, "thanks for stopping to pick us up." He averted his eyes for a moment, sliding them sideways, caught, then gazed back towards her.

"Deihlia. I'm Officer Rodriguez." He replied, turning more in his seat so he could speak to her. "Where were you from? Where were you heading?" For someone small she had a big, adult presence, he thought.

She could see that he was looking at her, but also looking to the side of her, a trick people use when they don't want to appear to be staring but very much want to see what her body is like, who she is, how old she might be. "I'm from Franklin originally, and I go to college in North Carolina. I'm home for Spring break, heading back to my Mom's. I was visiting my friend in Cambridge. Where are you from?" she asked, casually making the conversation more personal and less of an interrogation.

Officer Rodriguez proceeded to tell her that he was originally from south central L.A., but came to Boston for the job. Hated it here. Hated it there, too. L.A. was a rough place full of bad memories for him. Didn't like the people in either place. In fact, didn't like people at all, he admitted, looking off out the driver side window.

"I bet it's pretty hard to like people in this job," Deihlia said, "especially if you grew up around so much crime."

He nodded, "Yeah."

"But you get to help people, too, right? That's part of it?" She asked.

He thought for a minute and nodded again, turning his body so that he could speak directly to her now, face to face. She could see him softening a little, becoming rounder and more open. "Yeah, I guess you're right. Maybe half the people we deal with aren't bad, but I still don't trust them. It's just how I feel. People are the worst."

Donna and the other officer were talking. Malakai was on her lap trying to play with something, anything - his Mom's hair, a button on her shirt, something. The car was full of buttons and gadgets that were out of reach, the back seat of the car was empty of everything.

"Aw, that's too bad, man. There's no reason to hate people, we're all here trying to get by and make the best of what we've got, you know? Some people are just messed up. I mean, anyone can change or do better if they want to. Wanting to is the part that matters, don't you think?"

Officer Rodriguez sat there and listened, quiet, pondering, looking over at Deihlia's mother and Kai then back to her.

"You really think so?" He asked.

Deihlia nodded emphatically, a serious look on her face. "Hating doesn't help anyone. It doesn't help you get through your day. It doesn't give you a reason to get up in the morning, does it?" she asked.

He shook his head, "Just the opposite."

"I think we've all got a reason and a purpose for being here. I have one, you have one. Gotta find it, man. Find what makes you wanna keep going. Hate isn't the right kind of fuel. It's only gonna make the ride a miserable one. That's what I do." She placed one hand lightly over her heart to emphasize her point.

Donna and Kai slid out of the car, heading into the local police station with the officer who drove. She made a call for the tow truck and for someone to come and pick them up. She was gone for about ten minutes, then came back. Deihlia and Officer Rodriguez were deep in conversation. He was talking a lot now, about how he was feeling, why he felt that way, listening to her as she advised him on how to tackle his own thinking, how to battle his demons. She enjoyed using what she was learning in her psych classes, and getting behind someone's defenses.

As he talked with her, she became bigger to him. She was funny, wise, and was offering him very personal advice. He wanted to ask her what had happened to her, but he didn't. As he listened, something started to happen; something that had never happened before. He found himself imagining what it would be like to be in her shoes, in her chair, having to wheel everywhere, and to be as positive as she was. Life started to look very different. His own problems shrank and he felt a twinge of embarrassment about the complaints he'd shared.

Donna had the wheelchair set up outside the car and opened the door, trying to get Deihlia out and into her chair. "Deihlia, come on," she said, as Deihlia and Officer Rodriguez continued chatting. He didn't want to let her go, but she slid out of the seat, hopping into her chair. He opened his door and stepped out too.

"Hey, it was nice to meet you, Officer. I hope things look up for you from now on," she said, offering her hand.

He reached down to her, taking her hand in a firm grip. "I think they will, Deihlia. It was really good to meet you," he said, looking her in the eyes and smiling. "Thanks for everything."

Donna watched the exchange, marveling at her daughter who could charm the edge off of anyone.

178

The Lab

Deihlia wheeled into the party at a campus apartment carrying a six pack on her lap. The green bottles were cold from being in her refrigerator. The living room was full of people. It was one of the older, medium-sized apartments and could hold about twenty-five people with a tight fit. Most students were standing. She recognized the lacrosse guys, a couple of basketball players. A tie-dyed Grateful Dead banner hung on the wall. She peered through the crowd to find her friends. The air was pulsing with the cranked up bass from Eminem's party hit *Shake That* rattling the windows. A couple of cheerleaders were already half-drunk. As they moved their hips to the music, beer spilled out of their cups, sloshing onto the people next to them. Deihlia tried to squeeze through the crowd, pulling on people's sleeves for them to move as she made her way to the back of the room.

"Dee!" Mitch said, his hand and face emerging in a tight space between two people's arms and shoulders. At first she didn't recognize the clean-shaven face with the short cropped hair, then she realized who it was. Gone were the long hair and chin strap, the symbols of his freedom to be someone new at college. She thought he looked older and more mature.

Deihlia continued to pat people's arms to get them to move over so she could pass. She was surrounded by butts, backs, and elbows. She wanted to get over to Mitch. Finally she pushed past the loud cluster of guys standing between them. Mitch was sitting with Rickie and Tony on the floor. Rickie leaned against the back of an armchair. "Hey guys, what's going on?"

"You get through them okay?" Mitch asked, furrowing his brows in concern.

Nodding, Deihlia placed the six pack on the floor in front of her. Her chair lurched forward as someone bumped into her from behind. She turned her head to see who was standing behind her.

Mitch stood up and stepped over the six pack to stand next to Deihlia. The crowd behind her was getting louder, shouting over the music. One of the guys behind her pushed another to make a point, laughing. "Why don't you go take that spot over there," Mitch said to her. Rickie and Tony stood up so she could make her way over to the corner, away from the ruckus.

Mitch stood with his legs out, making a barrier between the rowdy boys and his friends. He wasn't a big guy, but he wanted to make sure Deihlia didn't get stomped on, accidentally, or on purpose. He thought of the party they were at last semester. Deihlia was sitting on the rug that night, and one of the basketball players was trying to kick her out, literally. He began by verbally harassing her, then he started to kick her in the legs. Mitch had sprung at him, ready to put him on the ground.

But Deihlia stopped him as he stood inches away from his face. "No, no, no." she said. "I don't want any fighting here tonight. Come on guys. We can all enjoy this party without any violence. Everyone is here for the same thing - to chill and have some fun. No one is trying to step on your toes or start anything. Mitch, it's cool. I'm ok. He's not gonna do it again."

Mitch and the tall muscular basketball player stood looking at each other. Neither one backed down, but neither of them pushed it, either. "Just leave her alone, man." Mitch said as he leaned back slightly, "we're just having some beers and hanging out." He kept his eyes on the guy's freckled face. He'd seen him around campus plenty.

The basketball player looked at Mitch, then down at Deihlia. Why wasn't he punching this guy? Pursing his lips, he turned away, shaking his head as he went.

Mitch hated to see Deihlia get picked on. In the past, when he witnessed some kind of injustice, like someone being harassed or bullied by someone twice their size or strength, he'd get mad but hang back. It bothered him to see it happening, but he didn't feel strong enough in himself to take a stand and say something or do something. Growing up, he'd been really shy, and he'd been beaten up more than a few times by some of the tough guys in high school. Somehow standing up for Deihlia was easier than standing up for himself had been. It came out of nowhere, but it felt right.

As he and Deihlia became friends, he took on the job of being her bodyguard. She didn't know that he had assumed the role, but if they were together in the same place, he was watching out for her. He'd never felt this way before, it surprised and secretly pleased him. He'd gotten in-between her and trouble more than a couple of times, and he stepped in to do the right thing another time when it wasn't Deihlia.

It was a party off-campus, in one of the houses in town. The house was in bad shape, the way old houses are when students have lived in them for decades. Leaning against a wall near a side hallway, he felt uncomfortable as he watched a drunk redheaded girl being led down the hall towards a back room by a guy about his age. She weaved back and forth, her hands pushing against the wall, so out of it she didn't know what was going on. He didn't know her, but she wore a Saint Michaels t-shirt and looked like a freshman. Mitch took one step towards them, then another, inserting himself into the situation quietly. "She's my friend. I was just coming to take her home, she's obviously too drunk to stay here any longer," he said. The dude squinted at him, sizing him up, unsure if he was telling the truth. He pulled her arm, trying to keep the dazed girl moving, so Mitch stuck his shoulder and leg quickly in between them. The girl was a stranger to him, but he could see that she was being put into a situation that she wasn't sober enough to say yes or no to. It made him feel queasy inside, that's how he knew for sure that he should do something. "I'm gonna get you home now," he said. Alcohol and sweet perfume engulfed him. The guy stepped back. He wasn't going to get in a fight over this girl. Mitch put his arm around her shoulder and led her back into the living room, helping her stay upright. Asking around quietly, he found someone else at the party who knew her, and they got her into Mitch's car and brought her back to her dorm together. He saw the girl around campus once after that. She passed him in the hall, not knowing who he was. He liked it better that way.

"Have a beer Mitch," Deihlia grinned, handing him up a bottle from her six-pack.

He bent over and took it from her hand. "Thanks Dee."

"Where were you this afternoon? Came by your place to get a game going but you weren't there." Tony said, looking at Deihlia.

Deihlia took a swig of her beer. "This afternoon? Oh, I was in the lab."

"Oh, the lab." Tony looked around knowingly at Rickie and Mitch, grinning. They smiled back. He knew that each one of them had become one of Deihlia's hypnosis patients. She'd taken a special interest in hypnosis in her psych program, and had recruited them one at a time so she could practice. Though they joked about how Deihlia made them chuckle as she ran through her hypnosis script, saying things like "Maybe the story we're rewriting today has a few

181

metaphors, maybe some meta-fives and meta-sixes…" each of them privately admitted that her sessions worked, once they got past the laughter.

Just two days before, Deihlia had hypnotized Rickie, getting him to retrieve a pivotal moment in his teenage years. He talked about it with her while under, and she helped him come to a new understanding about it. He told Tony about it a couple days later, he felt free from something that had plagued him for years. "Yeah, she's pretty good," Tony admitted.

"Does anyone ever take you into the lab?" He asked, giving Dee a hard time.

"Aw, y'know. I learned from someone, but I'm not gonna say who," Deihlia replied cagily.

Rickie laughed. If Dee didn't want you to know something, you weren't gonna find out. For months she'd been dating someone in town but none of them knew about it. She'd just disappear and no one could find her. A couple months later, Mitch drove past her as she wheeled back to campus from a date. He turned his car around and pulled up beside her. "Dee, what are you doing out here?"

"Just went out for a bit," she said smiling mischievously.

"Come on, get in the car and I'll take you back."

It was only after several beers and bong hits that Deihlia admitted to him where she had been. "Yeah, I've kinda been dating someone who lives in town."

"What?!" Mitch said, coughing on his bong hit.

Deihlia giggled, her body shaking with laughter. She told him the story about the girl she met, and after much pressing, the address. Deihlia had admitted the previous semester that she was interested in dating women. This one she was dating lived with a couple of rough dudes. After that, whenever Dee was missing, Mitch would drive by the house to see if she was there.

Sometimes Rickie went with him. Sometimes they gave her a ride back to campus. *Dee's like a Jedi master, appearing, partying, dispensing wisdom, then disappearing,* Rickie thought, smiling to himself. "I think we should hypnotize you and find out what you're doing when you're not with us," he said.

Deihlia laughed, her eyes sparkling. "Who wants to know?"

The music got louder, the people got louder. Mitch's friends were shouting to each other, but because he was standing up and they were sitting, he couldn't hear any of what they said. Deihlia threw her head back, cackling. It made him smile. As he stood across from her, keeping the rowdy crowd from spilling into their small group, he realized that he wanted to keep helping people, the way he did with Dee. He wasn't sure how to do it - become a counselor, join the army, become an advocate - but he felt like he had some kind of direction now. His fear of confrontation and sometimes crippling shyness had been replaced with a sense of responsibility, an awareness of his need to play a part in the human drama around him.

Deihlia saw that he was far away, not a part of their conversation. "Mitch" She yelled to him, to no avail. Putting her beer down on the floor, she began to wave both arms in the air, like she was flagging down a helicopter. Mitch looked over, and smiled at her. Knowing her had changed him. Yeah, he was a different person than the one he'd been when they met and Deihlia had beat him at Halo a bunch of times. That was just a game, this was real life.

Large Circles, North Carolina, 2007

It was a sunny, warm spring day. Several car loads of family and friends had driven down to North Carolina for Deihlia's graduation. We'd arrived the night before, bedraggled after two days of driving. Guests and family stood around on the grass, waiting for the graduates to arrive. Small children ran around, people chatted, clustered in triangles of shade thrown by the building next to where the outdoor ceremony was being held. "When is it going to start?" someone asked. In the distance, the high pitch drone of bagpipes hit the air. The song cut through the crowd, pulling at strings in me. As a group, we turned towards the sound. The pipe band came closer in their highland dress, snaking a path towards us over the lawn, between trees. As they hit the pavement, they formed two lines so that the graduates could walk in to the ceremony between them.

Something in me split open. The music, Deihlia, the long journey to this moment. I strained, standing on tip-toes to try and see her in the parade of bright blue graduates coming towards us. They moved slowly, coolly, their elation suspended and held by the chant and buzz of the pipes. She was in there somewhere, rolling along in the sea of blue. My heart hurt. She'd come so far. The doctors had said she wouldn't live a week, and here she was, graduating college. I wiped my eyes so that I could see her in the crowd, and there she was, gliding in.

Our whole contingent started whooping and shouting her name like a bunch of rowdy partiers. Deihlia stopped her chair briefly and smiled over at us, beaming, her dreads framing her face under the cap. The bagpipes droned their controlled and artful wail, an extended cry of victory and loss, ending somewhere in the middle. The last note hung in the air, a small platform to step onto, a springboard for moving into the next moment.

First, two students gave their commencement speeches. Humble, funny, and positive, the crowd clapped enthusiastically as each one finished. The school president, a tall slim man, made his speech, focusing on the strengths found in their modest community, on the importance of connecting one on one with others in all pursuits, not just careers or friendships. After his speech, he called each graduate by name, handing them a scroll and shaking their hand. Finally, he called Deihlia's name, and she wheeled over to him, smiling the biggest smile of her life. Once more our section cheered like

Boston sports fans - loudly. Deihlia lifted the scroll high in the air and turned, shaking her diploma towards the crowd. Other people cheered her on too, their whoops and whistles popped out of the crowd here, then over there. Deihlia glowed in the bright sun, moving back into place as another student was called.

Afterwards, the graduates scattered out towards their families. I looked around at the pipe players dotting the post-ceremony crowd. I watched as Deihlia's teachers and friends approached and hugged her, congratulating her, meeting family. Though her first semester was hard, she'd gone from friendless to famous in four years. I thought of my ancestors who left Scotland and France centuries ago. I thought of the ones who crossed the border of Canada and moved to Massachusetts to start new lives. I placed Deihlia among them, going to school 700 miles away from home, with no financial support, no family nearby. She'd done it all on her own. While we all came from hearty peasant stock with a backbone of determination and a strong work ethic, Deihlia clearly came in with much more than that. Not for the first time, I looked at her with awe as she shined in her blue gown, holding court. She was so happy. Her presence was large. I could see that clearly in this context, from this distance. Her spirit extended out and up, a large wide circle. She was so much bigger than us, but she had come to our family, she was our blood. That meant something, too.

I walked over and hugged her, putting my arms around her back. "I'm so damn proud of you," I said.

Deihlia giggled. "Thanks Auntie, me too."

The Test

The bolt on the apartment door made a *swish-click* sound and the door swung open. Deihlia looked up from her laptop briefly as LP entered. "Hey," she said, looking back down at her screen. She'd moved back to Boston from North Carolina two months ago, and lived with LP in a garden level apartment in a brownstone in the South End of the city.

"Hey, what's going on?" He said, dropping his messenger bag on the sofa as he took off his jacket. He knew that Deihlia was busy trying to find a job, but he wanted her to notice the new hairstyle he was sporting after working all day in the salon. His hair was light blonde. Unlike a lot of other people, his hair didn't get darker as he got older.

Deihlia didn't answer, she kept hitting the keys. "Let me just finish this. I've increased my typing words-per-minute by 50% in the past three days."

"Well that's really good," he said half-heartedly, sitting down on the sofa to wait for her to finish. *Bzzt!* The sound of a buzzer going off on Deihlia's computer made him giggle. He watched her read something on her laptop screen, her face a bluish white from the light. Their apartment was garden level and didn't get much sun, and the sun had gone down an hour ago. LP reached over and pulled the switch on a floor lamp behind the sofa. "This might help a little bit, Deihlia," he said.

Deihlia smiled, then looked up at him. "There! I improved by 20 words just today. I'll be ready for that test next week. I only have to improve by another 5 words per minute and I'll meet their requirement. I have to work on spelling, though, because there can't be too many errors."

LP listened, and thought it sounded dreadful, having to take a typing test for a data entry job. How could she do data entry all day and not be completely bored? "I couldn't do it, Deihlia. I like running around the salon, assisting the stylists, sweeping the floor, shampooing. I need a variety of activities. Are you sure you want that job?"

Deihlia could see LP clearly now that he'd turned on the light and she'd closed her laptop screen. "That's a cool haircut," she said. LP's hair was styled into a fauxhawk - a looser, more playful version of a mohawk haircut.

He turned his head, lifting the thin tail at the base of his neck. "This is my favorite part," he said.

"Speaking of tails, I think I heard something rummaging around in the trash today." Deihlia tilted her head towards the trash can that sat next to the structural pole in their open kitchen/living room.

LP wrinkled his nose. "Ugh. Those mouse traps just don't work. I'll take the trash out in a minute." He looked around at their apartment. He'd painted the walls, and they created a projector screen on one wall so that they could watch movies. He'd brought furniture he salvaged from their grandmother when she was getting rid of it, most of it from the 1960's, gold and avocado colored. The curtains they'd put on the windows stayed closed permanently, because their unit was a crack house at one time, and once in a while an old client would show up at their door, ringing the buzzer over and over. LP knew it was hard for Deihlia to live in a unit that was six steps down from the sidewalk. When she was still down in North Carolina the summer after she graduated college, he promised her he'd find them an apartment. Neither one of them had prospects for making a lot of money at this point, so this was the best that he could find. Deihlia moved back two months after he got the apartment. She'd been job hunting most of that time, with no luck until now.

"Yeah, please take care of that. I wish I could work at a salon but I don't really think that's my forte," Deihlia said. "I'm good with people but I'm no stylist."

"Are you nervous about the test and the next interview?"

Deihlia shook her head. "Naw, I've been practicing my typing for 10 days now and I keep getting better. They seemed to like me at the first interview, and invited me back for a second one. They said there are three other people they're considering."

"Three? For a data entry job? Oh my god!"

Deihlia giggled. "Yeah. It's tough out there, LP. There are tons of college grads who work as baristas or in retail and live with their parents. I want to live here in Boston with you. I'm thinking about this job as a foot in the door, y'know? A way to move into other jobs. Gotta start somewhere. I think my Spanish and French could come in handy eventually, too. Any place that deals with the public is gonna need staff who can speak Spanish and French." The organization she was in the interview process with worked with the public defender's office to assign lawyers to people who were facing a criminal charge and couldn't afford a lawyer. She liked the idea of doing work that helped people when they were most vulnerable. Plus, criminal justice was fascinating and tied in with her interest in psychology. She could learn a lot about people and systems working there.

LP nodded, listening. "Are you worried you won't get it? Four potential applicants seems like a lot."

Shaking her head, Deihlia slid her laptop off of her lap onto the sofa. "I just keep imagining myself working at a computer in their office. Like, I visualize it while I'm practicing my typing. I make myself feel what that job is like when I'll have it. Plus, Auntie knows one of the lawyers who used to work there. She's going to put in a good word for me. I think that might help, too. We'll see." She shrugged.

"Maybe I should type with you tonight, to show my support. We can have a typing contest."

"Ha!" Deihlia laughed out loud. "I'd rather you take out the trash," she said, raising her eyebrows.

LP stood up. "Ok, I get the hint. I'll take it out before I do anything else."

The next week, Deihlia sat in a cubicle in the HR office. There was a typing test open on the computer screen, and she had to take it, not once, but three times. It wasn't hard, it wasn't mentally challenging. It was simply a matter of typing what she read as quickly as she could without errors. The HR woman, Mrs. Johanson, had brought her into this cubicle and told her she had ten minutes to complete all three tests. Deihlia looked at the paper in front of her, and began to type. She typed the first document all the way through, then hit enter. She'd done well - 45 words per minute, with only two errors. She took a few deep breaths, and turned her head sideways to look away from the screen. She was in a windowless area with three cubicles side by side, and she was the only one in there. She rested her eyes briefly then returned to the next test.

A few minutes later, Mrs. Johanson stepped in. Deihlia noticed that she wore a button down shirt with slacks and a scarf. She wasn't in a suit. "That's ten minutes, Deihlia. I'm going back to my office for a minute to look at how you did and I'll be right back."

Her score was transmitted to Mrs. Johanson's computer. Deihlia smiled. "Ok, thanks." She didn't feel nervous, or intimidated, or awkward. She was wearing the moss green blazer and some black slacks that her Auntie had bought for her to wear in the interview and if she got the job. Her long dreads were pulled back into a thick ponytail. The dark blue cubicle she was in was empty except for the computer and chair, which she'd pushed out of the way behind her. I hope all the offices aren't like this, she thought to herself. She heard the swishing sound of someone walking, and Mrs. Johanson appeared once more.

"Well Deihlia, you did great. Why don't you come into my office and we'll meet with a couple of other staff members who will want to ask you a few questions."

"Sure," she said, pushing her wheels gently to follow Mrs. Johanson down the hall.

Inside her office, a small round table sat kitty corner to the desk. Three large old windows filled two walls, looking out at brick buildings and, through their windows, into other offices. There were two people sitting at the table, an older African American woman who also had dreads, and a young guy, probably in his early thirties. He wore a button down and tie with khaki's, but no jacket. Deihlia thought the woman with dreads and the more casual tone of the guy were good signs. She didn't want to work in an environment that was too stuffy. They both stood up as she entered.

"Deihlia Nye, let me introduce you to Rich Kingston and Aisha Jones. Aisha is an attorney here, and Rich would be your supervisor. He manages the data systems."

"Nice to meet you," Deihlia said, going over to shake each of their hands.

They sat back down, and Deihlia stayed where she was in the middle of the room, about four feet away from the table and the desk.

"Well Deihlia, it seems that you're qualified for this job and passed the typing test, but why do you want it?" Rich asked.

Deihlia paused for a moment before answering. "I think data is a great way to get to know the work of an organization and the clients. I'm really interested in criminal justice. I was a psychology major in college and I think human behavior is fascinating. Some people might think data entry is dry, but I think if you're collecting the right data, it can be meaningful. I want to work in an environment

189

where people care about what they do, because that's how I am. It seems like this is that kind of place."

Rich nodded, his mouth turned down amiably, considering her answer. "Let's be honest, data entry can be boring. How will you deal with that?"

"Data is only useful if it's correct. I'll make sure the work I'm doing is correct, and if I have time on my hands, I'll offer to take on other tasks. I'd want to help out any way I could."

Rich smiled at her. He liked her answers.

"Deihlia, a big part of this job is people. What would you say your people skills are? A psychology class in college is not the same as the real world." Aisha said to her, with a bit of edge in her voice.

Deihlia smiled a big smile. This woman was trying to make her feel inexperienced. "You know, that's a really good question. When I worked for the folk art pottery business after I graduated college, one of my jobs was to help the artists sell their art at the shows. These were folk artists in the deep South, they lived really different lives from mine, and the shows were full of all kinds of people coming to buy and sell. I decided to hold a little meeting with the artists every morning. I brought them coffee and doughnuts while I asked them how their sales went the day before. I helped them strategize their sales pitches, and for some of them, helped them figure out how to negotiate for the best price. Buyers assumed they were dumb country people and would sell their art cheaply just because they needed money. They did need the money, but their art was one of a kind and very collectible, so they didn't need to sell it cheap. I helped them improve their margins and I made some great friends."

Aisha lifted her eyebrows and pursed her lips. "Folk art in the south? My uncle is a big time folk artist down there. His name is Master Leroy. Did you ever meet him?" She looked pointedly at Deihlia, sitting up straight, her stiff body posture a human question mark, or an accusation.

Deihlia was quiet. She wanted to stretch out this moment before she answered. She turned slightly to look at Mrs. Johanson, then at Rich, then back to Aisha. "Master Leroy? Oh yeah, I heard of him, but never met him. I know he made those animal-spirit jugs that were really popular and at the top of the price range. He was a big deal at the shows."

190

Without moving his head, Rich's eyes went from Deihlia to Aisha. Mrs. Johanson watched quietly too. She was enjoying this interview. The tension in the room had been pulled tight like a rubber band about to snap, and Deihlia seemed to be handling it just fine.

Aisha sat back against her chair and smiled, laughing, letting her shoulders drop. "Yeah, that's my Uncle. He's pretty famous in that circle."

"I tried to get over to his booth so many times, but there was always a huge crowd," Deihlia said, relieved. She'd wanted to say it before but didn't want it to sound like she was brown nosing. She felt that it was important to really hold her own when talking to a lawyer, and she didn't want to appear to be intimidated. And, she wasn't.

"I've got a few of his pieces at home, they're some of my prized possessions," Aisha said, smiling warmly. "Why did you leave that job Deihlia? It sounds so interesting."

"Well, it wasn't steady. Also, I can't drive. I had to rely on my friend to get me around everywhere, and that wasn't really fair to him. I grew up outside of Boston and I used to come into Boston all the time. I'd always known I'd live here, so I came back two months ago."

"Well, this has been very informative, Deihlia." Mrs. Johanson said as she stood up. "We'll be in touch either way by the end of the week. Thank you for coming in."

"Thanks so much for this opportunity. It was nice to meet you, Mr. Kingston and Ms. Jones. I hope that I'll see you again," Deihlia said, moving closer to them so she could shake their hands.

Two weeks later, Deihlia pushed her arms into the same blazer, and wearing some dark plum colored pants, she got ready for her first day of work at the new job.

Mass Ave, 2010

It was winter, Deihlia's worst season. She didn't have to deal with it much when she was down in North Carolina, but she'd been back up North for a couple of years now. Winter was her most vicious adversary and this one was particularly tough. Getting to work and being at work was important to her, but she couldn't always make it in the snow. Today, she did.

She had a second part-time job that she did two nights a week after work and some Saturday mornings, working for an accountant not far from her house. There was no way she could make it into that job today and she'd called him earlier to say so. In the terrible snow, all she wanted to do was go home.

She took the subway home from work and got off at the Mass Ave stop on the Orange Line, going to the elevator. It always smelled like urine and dirty clothes. Deihlia wheeled out of the station, trying to stay on the part of the sidewalk that had a path through the snow. It was hard to push over the icy lumps. Pedestrians coming towards her had to stop and step into the snowbank to let her pass. She found a cut through to the street and went over the curb and pushed out.

Cars were trying to drive around the snow and around other cars parked tail-out in the street because it hadn't been completely cleared. She maneuvered out and waited for a break, then went out into traffic. She moved along behind the line of cars. Another car came up behind her. Cars passed in the opposite lane, spitting slush. There was no other way to get home. She tried to stay close to the side, but the side had become the middle of the street.

The car behind her honked, wanting to pass. Couldn't the driver see that there was nowhere for her to go? Deihlia continued to move along with traffic, her heart beating fast. She just wanted to get home. Near the traffic light, she saw a curb cut to the sidewalk. She looked ahead, across the intersection, peering around the cars in front of her. Someone had shoveled a narrow path through the snow on the other side of the street. She hoped she could get through it.

At the intersection, cars sped through the red light, frustrated with being in slow moving traffic. Deihlia made her way to the sidewalk, squeezing her chair carefully between a car and the snowbank, then through a puddle of deep slush at the half-buried curb cut. She waited at the intersection for the walk light to change. After a few minutes, the white pedestrian walk signal lit up across the street. She put her hands on her wheels and started to move. A car bolted right, ignoring the red light. She stopped quickly, inches from the cab as it sped past her. She looked up the street again to make sure it was clear, and ventured out.

Once across the street, she continued on through the path in the snow. She hoped it would take her all the way to her door, otherwise she'd have to wheel backwards to head back out into the street. After three brownstones, the sidewalk was clearer, with intermittent patches of snow. Her wheels settled on to the brick sidewalk. She was on even ground. She could see her building in the distance. She breathed easier, pushing faster, wanting to get inside.

She reached the steps to the garden level apartment she shared with LP. It was six steps down. After LP had cleared the steps, snow had blown back down off the sidewalk. Deihlia sighed. Someone passed behind her, cursing. The air was wet and biting, powdery snow sparkled in gusts of wind. She sat looking down at the stairs. Winter was such a fight. She felt something creeping up inside her - a wish that she had been born with a normal body. It was a familiar wish, one that had accompanied her all through elementary school - a wish for functioning legs or to be born into a family that could afford her more amenities, like an apartment with an elevator. This place was all she and LP could afford.

She noticed the thoughts. They were old demons. She saw them come in, then pushed them out. They didn't help her with anything. They only made her feel more handicapped, more helpless than she was. Instead, she thought of her friends in wheelchairs who couldn't get out of their chair without help, who needed a motorized chariot, who had to plan every venture, who couldn't be too spontaneous, who could only move their head. She thought of the friends she knew at the hospital and at pre-school who died years ago, never experiencing any real freedom. She carried them with her like totems, like guides. *Yeah, I'm lucky,* she thought. *I can get myself in and out of my chair.* She liked her independence, even though it was really, really hard. It meant more to her than anything, because independence meant experience. Why survive all those surgeries and near misses with death if she couldn't experience things? It was a familiar mantra to her: I want to experience things, I want to have fun.

The six stairs going down weren't very wide. The treads were narrow and the incline was steep. The brownstone she and LP lived in

194

needed some TLC - it hadn't been renovated or modernized in any way in decades, especially their garden level unit. At some point, someone had painted the stairs a light cocoa brown to cover the patched, uneven concrete that went down to their unit from the brick sidewalk. As Deihlia looked down the stairwell, white powder blew upwards, swirling in a cyclone as it made its way up, then dusted her face and jacket as it flew past her. A car in traffic on the road behind her honked, staying on the horn for an extended complaint because it was a green light and traffic wasn't moving. Large amounts of snow created problems for everyone in Boston. Deihlia peered down the sidewalk at the way she came, and saw no one. She turned her head and looked the other way, checking to see if any pedestrians were headed in her direction. Many days she had an audience of random passers-by, or a neighbor, or one of the homeless men and women who frequented this strip of Massachusetts Ave. Their presence didn't stop her, but she did like to know who was nearby because she was vulnerable when she got out of her chair onto the sidewalk.

Her hands were cold and damp under the black gloves, and the metal frame of her chair was freezing as she put her hands on it and steadied herself, then lifted up her torso with her arm strength, pivoting at the shoulders to swing her body forward and out of the chair. Her legs bent up against her as she landed in slush on top of the icy bricks. Putting her hands under her knees, she placed her legs down over the first step. Turning sideways, she reached back and pulled her chair in next to her, pressing the button in the center of the wheel to release it from the frame. The wheels needed constant oiling in the winter because the snow and salt made them stick. Deihlia pulled on the rim of the wheel while she pushed with the other hand against the frame to get it off. Finally, it came free and she dropped it on its side down the stairs. The wheel slid over the steps, bang, bang, bang, bang, until it hit the bottom of the stairwell. Turning the chair on to its side, she released, then tugged at the other wheel until it came off, and sent it skidding down the stairs to meet its match. She made sure the zipper on the small backpack strapped under her seat was zipped, then she moved herself down to the first tread, pulling the frame along beside her. Snow fluttered down, dotting the black gel cushion that was velcroed into the seat of her chair to protect her from getting sores. Flakes landed on her nose, her cheeks, her black gloves. She went down step by step, pushing off with her hands then

195

pulling the battered silver frame down with her until she reached the bottom stair.

Two women walked past on the sidewalk, talking loudly about their workday. Wrapped in their big black down puffer coats, one of the women glanced down the stairs as she went past, the blue of Deihlia's cape a bright swatch of color in the bleak snow. She paused in her step, turning her head to look directly down the stairwell to determine what had caught her eye, but there was nothing that color. Confused, she watched Deihlia at the bottom of the steps, wheelchair pieces splayed in the snow around her. Her friend paused, turning to follow her gaze down the stairwell. They both saw someone putting what looked to be a wheelchair back together. They exchanged glances, then continued on.

Deihlia bent forward and picked up her wheel, pushing the pin in the center of it back into the frame. She had to lean the frame on the stair and push hard against the wheel until it clicked in. Turning the frame over, she reached down and picked up the other wheel and pushed it back into place. She set the chair down on the stairwell floor and dusted off the seat. Even though her pants were already soaking wet from sitting on the sidewalk, she wanted her chair to be as dry as it could be. Tucking the chair sideways against the bottom step, she reached her arm out to the other side of the chair frame and pushed off with her right hand from the stairs. Once seated, she pulled her legs over and set her feet down in the footrest. Removing one glove, she reached underneath into the backpack and pulled out her keys. Deihlia looked back up the stairs to the sidewalk. She wasn't going anywhere tonight.

She unlocked the foyer door, went in, and then shut it behind her before going further down the dark hallway, lit only by a bare bulb sitting uneasily in an old wall sconce. She slipped her key into the bolt lock and turned it hard, opening the apartment door. The light from a table lamp glowed in a circle against the wall. LP sat on the sofa, reading a book. He looked up as she entered. "Hey, why didn't you tell me you were here? I would've come out and helped."

Deihlia shut the door behind her. "I need to get around by myself as much as possible if I'm gonna live here." She tossed her gloves onto the table and rolled towards her bedroom. "I'm a mess, I need to go change." She was glad to be home, out of the elements.

LP watched her go. He felt bad about the **apartment, about** not being able to find something better. He'd been home all afternoon, he would've helped her get down the stairs. He'd wanted for them to live together in Boston ever since he could remember. He'd been a sophomore in high school when she left for college, but with her encouragement, he'd gone to beauty school. Her belief in him was something that had buoyed him through difficult years in high school.

He helped her in and out as much as he could, but Deihlia insisted on doing it herself more often than not. Things were easy between them, but sometimes they took each other for granted, the way people living together can sometimes do.

He paused for a moment, watching her go into her room. Deihlia was the first person he'd come out to when he was twelve, telling her: "I definitely know that I'm gay." And she supported and helped him take steps to come out to others and be comfortable with himself at a young age. She'd been his best friend ever since he could remember. Who would he be without her? He couldn't imagine. He was here chasing after his dreams now in large part because of her. "You're an awesome mess, Deihlia! Love you!" He shouted from the living room.

"You too!" Deihlia shouted back from her bedroom, sighing.

Resurrection

Deihlia sat at the round cocktail table near the tall black-framed windows of the pub. I saw her from outside, framed in the rectangle of window with a long dark bar behind her, and went inside to where she was sitting. "Hey Deihl," I said, bending to give her a hug.

"Hi Auntie," She reached her long arms up and wrapped me in them.

I took off my coat and sat down. "How are you, Bug? What's going on?"

"Not much. Work is pretty busy, and I've been getting out and meeting a lot of new people lately, which I like."

"I'm so glad. I know you've wanted a new group of friends since you moved back."

"Yeah, I'm getting there. How are things with you?"

The waitress came over, a black apron at her hips, covering her jeans. She smiled at us, her freckled round face lit up. "What can I get ya?"

We each ordered a drink and a plate of fried calamari to share. The waitress swung her hips back and forth as she walked away to place the order and get our cocktails.

"Nothing new with me. The job is the same as ever. I'm really working on my spiritual stuff - my meditations, practices, stuff like that. I studied so much the past few years, but I'm really trying to put what I learned into practice on a daily basis. It's a bit hermetic. I'm alone a lot, but I'm really starting to experience life differently."

The pub began to fill up, and clusters of people coming from work came in and sat at the larger tables surrounding the bar. Outside, streetlamps went on as the evening darkened. We were on a small back street, where all the buildings were old brick. We were lucky this pub had a street level entrance, with no stairs. It was only 6:00 p.m. but it was early February, so it felt much later.

"That's cool, Auntie. I know how important your inner life is to you. I'm proud of you for working on that stuff. I've told a couple of my friends about your healing work. I might be sending one of them to you soon."

"Thanks, Deihl. Thanks for saying that. It means a lot."

"So how do you notice a difference? What do you mean?"

"Oh, y'know… like, what's going on inside me - the themes, the symbols - they start appearing in my external reality, that kind of thing. And I just feel lighter and at ease with myself."

The waitress appeared next to the table and dropped off my scotch and Deihlia's IPA. "Your calamari will be out in a few minutes. Is there anything else I can get you?" She asked, holding the empty black tray up above her, spinning it on her hand like she was getting ready to do some sort of magic trick.

Deihlia's eyes went to the tray whirling in the air next to her. "Not for now, thanks."

After she walked away, Deihlia giggled. "It would've been a better trick if she'd done that when our drinks were on the tray."

I laughed too. "What's going on with the family?" I asked.

Deihlia shrugged, sipping out of her pint glass.

"My dad's been on my mind a bit lately. Is he ok? Do you know?" I asked. I hadn't spoken to or seen my father in years. Even when I had, it was circumstantial. I purposely didn't speak to him or see him for the past twenty or so years. I never knew when his geniality was going to turn nasty, and I'd been through it with him so many times that I just decided to keep my distance and leave it at that.

Deihlia furrowed her brows then looked me in the eyes. "I haven't heard anything from Mom about him, but he is getting kind of old, forgetting things and stuff. Have you thought about making amends with him?" she asked.

I looked away from her, out the window. A couple bundled up in winter coats huddled against the cold as they walked briskly past. My father. I'd forgiven his cruel behavior years ago, but I hadn't connected with him to let him know it. I shook my head. "I don't know. I hadn't really been thinking about it, but there he was on my mind. So, maybe?"

"I think you should. Even though my Dad wasn't perfect, I loved him a lot. I wish I'd had him around all these years. Grandpa won't be around forever, you should try and mend things with him now, while you can."

I peered down into my glass, holding it between both hands. The scotch was a reddish caramel color, reflecting the light from the wall sconce behind me. I shook the glass slightly and the liquid sloshed up against the sides. "I just don't want to have a scene if he turns nasty on me, y'know? I'm not putting up with any cruelty these days, and I don't want to invite any in." I said, looking back up at her.

She peered at me through her small framed glasses, her dreads tied in a large tail behind her head. A crystal stud sparkled in the 'monroe' piercing she had above her lip. "I get it, Auntie. I don't think he'll misbehave, but you never know. He can be such a wild card."

She lifted her drink, pausing as the waitress delivered our order of fried calamari. "Thanks," she said to her, smiling.

"I guess I don't want my relationship with him to get in the way of anything else in my life," I said. "I don't want any loose, unresolved family ties hanging out there. And I don't want to have to do this again with him the next time around." I squeezed lemon across the top of the calamari, then we each started nibbling on a tender, fried ring.

"I can come with you if you want company when you go to see him," she said, spearing another piece of the calamari with her fork. "Maybe you can call him first and test the waters."

"That would help a lot, Deihl," I said. "Thank you."

"I know he's difficult, but I bet at this point he'll be so glad you came around that he'll be on his best behavior."

She was realistic and optimistic, a combination I'd sometimes found hard to maintain. "You're probably right."

"I wouldn't want you to get to the end of your life and regret not connecting with him. I know you would regret it, Auntie. But I also know how problematic he can be, so I understand why you haven't."

I took a sip of my scotch. The lights in the pub dimmed significantly, making the candle's glow in the center of each table more pronounced, flickering on the faces of the people sitting around them. All I could see now was the reflection of the flame as two dancing lights on the lenses of Deihlia's glasses. "I think he would appreciate your forgiveness, Auntie."

"You're probably right on all counts, Deihl." I said, piercing another piece of the breaded rings with my fork, then dipping it in the chili sauce.

She nodded. "Let's figure out what we're having for dinner before the waitress comes back."

A few weeks later, I decided that Easter was the perfect day for resurrecting a relationship with my dad that had died decades before. I called him in the evening on Easter Sunday. His wife answered the phone. "Hi, it's Diane. Happy Easter," I said. "Can I talk to my Dad?" She handed the phone to him. "Diane!" He chuckled, "It's so nice to hear from you. What are you up to?" I noticed how childlike he sounded. He'd always had that kind of demeanor too, and I'd forgotten it. As our conversation went on, it was clear that we still didn't have much to say to each other, even after all these years. But I was relieved. I knew it meant something to him. I could hear it in his voice. I told him I'd come down to see him sometime soon.

After I hung up the phone, I looked out the window at the sky turning deep blue, the crescent moon a sharp sliver of light hanging over the tops of the houses on my street. It felt good to get that situation moving on a new track.

One Good Thing

"We need to find you a new apartment," I said to Deihlia. I was sitting on the low gold 1970's era sofa in their basement apartment. It was dark and cold. Deihlia and I were going out for dinner like we often did. She was getting ready before we left.

"I don't know what to do, Auntie. We can't afford a nicer place. They're so much more expensive," she said, her voice coming out of the small windowless bedroom she had under the stairs. The apartment wasn't accessible, and we'd just gotten through another rough winter. I hated her living situation, but I certainly didn't have the money to rent her a place, nor would living with me be any easier. I was in a second floor unit at the top of a hill.

"Why don't you try to get one of the affordable units in one of these new buildings?"

Deihlia poked her head out of her bedroom door. "What do you mean?"

"Boston has an Inclusionary Development Policy. When new residential buildings are built, a certain portion have to be affordable units so that people with a variety of incomes can live there. I think you have to meet the income requirements, and some others, but I'm sure you'd qualify. It's a lottery system."

"How do I find out about it?" she asked, wrapping her scarf around neck.

"Come over this weekend and we'll do some research. I'll help you figure it out."

"Ok," she said, coming towards me. "I know we need to move. I just don't know where we can go that's affordable."

"You need an elevator and a maintenance crew, Deihlia. Something more accessible. We'll figure something out."

She nodded. She'd been in this place for almost two years and it never got easier.

Week after week she filled out applications, researched affordable housing lotteries, scoped out new buildings being built in the South End and downtown, and visited the housing office. Twice they lost her applications. Twice she stopped by after work to drop them off again. She called every other week, checking on the status of her applications.

Seven months later, she received notice that she and LP had been awarded a unit on Albany Street in a brand new building. It had elevators, a maintenance crew, and was closer to the Silver line than where she'd been living. Deihlia was ecstatic.

"Auntie, we got an apartment!" She texted me.

She and LP couldn't wait to move out of the basement apartment, but their new unit wasn't ready on time, so each of them had to find a place to stay for a few weeks in the interim. Deihlia went to stay with Sean, and LP stayed with his boyfriend. He'd met Stefano at the salon and they'd been together for several months. Staying with someone else in a house which required her host to help her get in and out of it, then get her to the subway, reinforced Deihlia's elation at getting an apartment in a building with an elevator.

Three weeks later, she got the key. Opening the door to her new place, Deihlia paused in the doorway. It smelled like fresh paint and plaster dust. There was a large window at the other end of the open living room and kitchen area. To the left was her bedroom, with its own bathroom. To the right was LP's bedroom and bathroom. It was all clean and new, unmarred by previous tenants or neglect. *I'm so ready for this,* she thought to herself, *beyond ready,* and she went in.

Butterfly, Boston

Deihlia was sitting in her wheelchair naked. She'd been feeling bummed lately. She found dating hard. Finding friends was easy, but finding someone who was into her and who wanted to partner with her was more of a challenge. Deihlia went for women - straight, bi, and lesbian who didn't have major physical disabilities. That's just who she was attracted to. It wasn't easy to change who she was attracted to, and why should she? Her friends would go through three relationships while Deihlia was still searching for one. She made a lot of new friends through her dating attempts, and that was good, but she really wanted a girlfriend.

LP wasn't home, so she had the apartment to herself. She rolled over in front of the full length mirror and took a good long look. It was true she didn't always like what she saw. Her body didn't quite match her insides. But it was the only body she had, the one she inherited at birth, with a lot of major adjustments made along the way. She was tired of feeling at odds with her body, of wishing it were different and better, tired of carrying the weight of that discontent around like a backpack full of sorrow and frustration.

After all, there was nothing much she could do about the parts of her body that weren't standard. She'd had all the surgeries she could bear, and many she couldn't. She liked her dreads. They were long and thick, an accomplishment. They represented her. She looked at her face. She liked that. She had a cute little button nose, hooded, clear eyes, and a little bow mouth. She let her eyes go further down again, and sighed. Placing her fingertip on the top of the scar that started at her chest, she traced it down the center of her body. She'd almost died from being septic after that surgery. Other scars criss-crossed her stomach in white lines, meeting the vertical one. She didn't remember the genesis of each one, but went over each of them with her finger. *How many times did I come close to death?* She didn't remember when she was born, but she remembered the times when she hadn't healed properly or had an infection, and there were a few of those. She put her hands on her thighs and looked at her legs. They had no muscle tone, but they were still a part of her. She thought of when she broke her leg skiing. She'd hit ice and her chair flipped over. She'd flown back to college that day, not knowing her leg was broken, but by the time she got back to campus her leg had swelled to three times its size. Michael drove her to the hospital at Duke, where they

204

discovered that she had a blood clot in her leg as well. Then she thought of the time she spent in the rehab hospital in her early teens. Eye surgery. The rods in her back.

My body is a warzone, she thought, shaking her head as she ticked off the list of things she'd been through. *I've been through a war but I'm still here.* She thought of how many times she should've died, and suddenly felt an intense swelling of appreciation for her body. How had it overcome all of those things, and made all the surgeons' workarounds work for her all these years? *It's kind of a big deal what my body endured*, she thought. *What I survived. This body is the house God gave me. It's the one I got.* Deihlia dropped her head slightly, first looking down at herself, then lifted her eyes up to the woman in the mirror. *My body is actually amazing*, she thought. *It's gone through all of that to help me be here.* She thought of Dr. Zee, too, and all she'd done.

Something shifted. A quiet part of her had been wanting to get to this point, to let go of feeling frustrated with her body: a body that had already borne so much. She wheeled back into her room and went over to the low shelf where her clothes sat folded in piles. She pulled out her favorite plum and gold flannel shirt, and her new jeans. She wanted to wear colors that made her feel good, and plum and gold made her feel good. She wanted to dress up and continue to feel this sense of awe at herself.

"Hey, what's going on?" LP said, after he got home from working at the salon.

"Not much," Deihlia said, looking up from her laptop. She still felt different, better. The little face-to-face she'd had with herself was sticking.

"I've been thinking. I need a new look."

"Really? What kind of new look?"

"I don't know. Something that helps people see me better; something more queer looking I think," Deihlia said, surprised by her own words.

"Yeah, I can see that," LP replied, sitting down across from her. "Maybe it's time to get rid of the dreads. Go for something a little more edgy."

Deihlia thought for a moment, reaching up to run her hands over her dreads. She wasn't thinking about cutting them off. "But my dreads give people an in. They make me approachable. They're a conversation starter. I don't know if I wanna give them up."

205

LP shrugged. "Okay. It was just an idea. I guess you want to go shopping then, or put on some makeup. You were pretty good with the makeup if I recall, but I'm not sure that's the look you're going for."

Deihlia rolled her eyes and laughed. "No, I'm not going back to wearing makeup. Those days are over!"

LP giggled too. "Well, when you figure out what you want to do, let me know. I'm happy to help."

The next day, Deihlia woke up knowing it was the right thing to do. After she got herself together, she wheeled out into the kitchen. LP wasn't up yet. It was nine thirty, not too early to wake him up, so she went and knocked on his bedroom door. "You up?" she asked, knowing he wasn't.

LP grumbled.

"Come on, get up. I made up my mind. Let's go get breakfast," Deihlia said.

LP stumbled out of his bedroom, still half asleep. "Made up your mind about what? What are you talking about?"

"About my new look. I think I should cut off my dreads like you said." She smiled up at him, her eyebrows lifted.

LP's eyes opened wide. "Well I'm awake now!" he said. "That was fast. Do you want to do it today?"

Deihlia nodded. "Yeah, I think we should do it before I chicken out and change my mind, after we've had some breakfast."

"Okay, give me a few to get ready," he said as he walked back into his bedroom and shut the door.

Deihlia turned and was facing the full length mirror again. Her dreads draped around her face, framing it like a wild plant. She reached up with two hands and pulled them back so that they disappeared behind her head. She smiled. Yeah, she was ready for something new.

The Fedora

Deihlia felt lighter and more flexible with short hair. She squeezed a little mousse into her left hand and ran her fingers through it, giving it a little attitude at the top. She'd put Miles Davis *Birth of the Cool* CD on, and it played in the background, encouraging her to become even more herself. She'd met some new friends online here and there through Meetup events. Thank goodness for Meetup, an online portal where people posted events publicly so that others could attend. Deihlia had become a member and selected "gaming," "nerds," "music" and "queer" for the event categories she wanted to receive notifications about. The friends she'd made through the events weren't the kind of friendships that she had with her college and Franklin friends. Those were deep, adventurous, and fun. She'd made some queer friends, but they didn't really stick. Everyone seemed to be in some kind of transition or relationship drama that made them go in and out of her life.

She looked at herself in the mirror. *What is this part of me?* She wondered. The part of her that felt like she belonged at Wally's club, just down the block from her old apartment on Mass Ave, located in the basement of a brownstone, hanging out with the cool jazz players. They were tuned into life at a different level, a level that stirred and opened up something inside her. When she was there, she felt the old soul part of her tuning in and coming out. She'd cut her hair. She'd tried different groups, but she needed something to bring it all together. "Help me out here," she said aloud.

She rolled out of the bathroom and into her bedroom. Her collection of hats sat on the low shelf against the wall. The brown Panama hat was her Dad's, and the others she had picked up here and there. She'd been wearing hats since she was ten years old. They allowed her some creativity with her style, matching her moods. The baseball hat she wore backwards when she felt like being a bratty bad boy. The orange and purple knit beanie she wore all through college, she put it on once in a while when she was feeling mellow. When she was in the mood for deep talk at a coffee shop, she put on the copper herringbone newsboy cap. The short brimmed plum fedora was new. She'd purchased it on a whim. Picking it up, she turned it around on her hand, this way and that. It reminded her of some of those jazz guys. The trumpet and sax players.

Her laptop lay on her bed, beckoning. She'd been gaming online in a World of Warcraft guild for a year or so, and she had responsibilities and relationships online with the guild. She'd had some romantic flings through the game, too, but they didn't last. *It's time to get out of that*, she thought. *I spend too much time at home. I'm never going to make new friends if I spend all my time online.* She felt the familiar call of the game, pulling her from the black hole of virtual reality. She knew if she started to play she'd be gone until midnight, or later. It was only 11 a.m. and she wanted to experience the city; get out while the weather was good.

Miles song *Godchild* came on. It was fun and flirty, playful, hinting at something lightly cosmic. Yeah, she wanted to get out and find some trouble to get into. She put on the hat and it felt right. Something fell into place. Her mischievousness rose up, the way it did around women she liked. She was full of music, energy, possibility. She wheeled into the living room. Then it came to her like a bolt of lightning, down from the hat into her heart. *Pork Chop.* That was it!

She removed the hat, holding it upside down in her right hand, looking at the label. What had just happened? She shrugged and placed it back on her head. It made her smile. *Pork Chop.* It was perfect! Her new name. Her new persona. She could see it clearly, like someone had pulled a screen over and a movie appeared. Pork Chop was the life of the party, flirting, doing pranks, taking risks, being bold. Pork Chop was also a musician, hanging out with other musicians at jazz clubs and gigs. Pork Chop was androgynous, queer, and unapologetic. She could see Pork Chop doing things she'd never done as Deihlia. She giggled out loud. Pork Chop was it. But she could also see that Pork Chop didn't play World of Warcraft. That was over. She'd notify the guild later. She put on her jacket and left the apartment.

I picked Deihlia up around two, on a Sunday a few weeks later. "Ready for a family dinner?" I asked, smiling.

"I'm ready. I miss Nan and Pop. I'm gonna tell them about my new name today," Deihlia said as I drove down Albany street in the light afternoon traffic. A siren screeched, flying past us into the emergency area of the hospital a few blocks from Deihlia's apartment.

"So tell me how Pork Chop came about," I replied, stopping my car at a red light at the Mass Ave intersection. I was so glad that she was living in a nice apartment with elevators and maintenance instead of that old Mass Ave place. It was only a few blocks away from the old place, but it was completely different.

Deihlia grinned, looking over at me. "I needed something to help me break the ice with people - a bold persona. I want to start dating more, make new friends. I just wasn't sure how to bridge the divide. Being Pork Chop allows me to take risks and do things that I'm kind of unsure about how to do. Y'know, it's Pork Chop doing it, rather than Deihlia. Pork Chop gives me a persona to work from."

I smiled back at her. "Brilliant, Deihl, but why Pork Chop?"

She slipped on her black Ray-Bans as we drove west into the afternoon sun. "It's my jazz name. I really want to learn how to play the trumpet. I need to live up to the name. It's a personal challenge and a means to getting there."

We moved along in Saturday traffic, the projects on one side of us and empty lots on the other. "Your jazz name, huh. A challenge. You certainly don't take the mainstream road, do you?" The truth was, I was in awe of her again. She was always bolder and more of a risk taker than I was. It wasn't like she didn't have enough challenges in her life already, but this was a mystical one, self-created.

"I've never been on that road in my life," Deihlia replied.

We sat around the kitchen table with Nana and Pop. Nana had made Deihlia one of her 'good square meals' - pot roast, baked potatoes, broccoli, and squash. The meat sat in the middle of the table, sliced on one end.

"Deihl, what's going on? What's new?" Pop asked. He still had a round belly and a beard that went to his chest, but now it had a gray stripe down the middle of it, and his hair had gray sprinkled through it. At 73, he still worked, painting several days a week, but only interiors. He couldn't get up and down ladders for the exterior work like he used to.

Deihlia took a slice of pot roast off the platter and put it on to her plate. "Lots of new things. I've been going to hear a lot of jazz lately. There's a great club in my neighborhood," she said.

Nana sat down, putting her plate on the table. She'd stopped dyeing her hair and let it go to its natural snowy silver. Pop nodded, listening.

"And I have a new name."

Nana looked up, startled. "A new name? What's wrong with your old one?"

209

Cutting her meat, Deihlia kept her eyes on her food. "I wanted something new, something that fits me better. My new name is Pork Chop." She lifted her eyes and looked around the table, first at Nana, then at Pop.

The fork and knife in Nana's hands paused. Pop raised his bushy eyebrows, looking over at Deihlia.

"I think it's fun and creative," I said, lifting a piece of broccoli off my plate. "Lots of people have nicknames."

The table was quiet. Nana looked at Deihlia. Pop looked at Nana. I chewed on my broccoli.

Deihlia turned to Nana and smiled, then to Pop, and went back to her plate, sticking her fork into a piece of broccoli.

Nana lifted her knife into the air, pointing across the table. "Pass the butter, Pork Chop."

The Call

Deihlia tossed strands of Mardi Gras beads out at the crowd lining Boylston Street. She wheeled along beside her mother, who threw out baubles too. Metallic purple, green, and blue strands flew through the air, landing at people's feet. It was First Night in Boston, New Year's Eve, and Donna and Deihlia were marching along with the Hot Tamale Brass Band in the parade. Horns blew, drums pounded. The band's white uniforms were partially hidden under thick winter coats. As she reached into her bag to pull out a handful of beads, she saw something red flitting like a flag in the wind next to her. Her mom's crimson scarf was muffled tight around her neck. It wasn't that, but she distinctly saw some other red fabric blowing behind her mother in the freezing air. *Oh that*, Deihlia smiled to herself. It had been a while since she'd seen her Mom's red cape out of the corner of her eye. It wasn't something she could see by looking directly at it. She remembered seeing it a lot when she was a young kid, when her Mom would sit on the floor and put on her rollerblades then push her in her chair around the Suffolk Universal basement halls. Or when her Mom was with her at the after school sports program, running along beside her. The last time she'd seen it was when she'd moved back to Boston from North Carolina and her mom had helped to move her stuff into the apartment.

Deihlia pulled more trinkets out from the bag on her lap, and aimed them at children lining the street in their puffy coats, mittens, and hats. The parade paused but she didn't notice until she wheeled into one of the horn players at the back of the band. He looked down at her sideways, his trumpet raised in the air. The sound of the trumpet caught her. It was bright and deep at the same time, like what a heart might sound like if it were a horn. She moved back slightly so that her wheel wasn't jammed into his leg, but she stayed near him. The trumpet was calling her. She didn't want to be a cheerleader for the band. She wanted to be in the band.

The song ended with a pound of the drum and the band paused for a short break as another act ahead of them finished their routine. "Hey, Harry. I wanna learn how to play the trumpet," Deihlia said, speaking to the man she'd bumped into. Harry had a goatee, and was bald under his black knit cap. He was stocky and solid, wearing shiny black Doc Marten boots. Deihlia knew he'd been playing trumpet since he was a kid and he was a professional musician. "Can

211

you teach me?" She asked, her breath in the air a puffy cloud. The parade slowly began to move again.

Harry looked down at her. He didn't know her well, but he liked Deihlia. She'd come to a few of their gigs and hung out with them. "I can't teach you but I can get you a trumpet to start with," he said, nodding. Then he lifted the horn to his mouth right on beat and started to blow as the next song started.

Deihlia smiled and nodded at him, making sure he saw her.

A few months later, Deihlia went up to visit Harry in Lowell, where he lived. She'd taken the commuter rail and he picked her up at the station. A week or so prior he'd contacted her to tell her that he had a trumpet for her. She sat in the living room of his big old Victorian house as he went back into one of the rooms down the hall. A white-manteled fireplace took up one wall.

She looked around. Colorful paintings and large plants filled the room. The painting closest to her was tropical, brightly colored, and reminded her of Ecuador. Another painting was a swath of transparent light blue with tiny bubbles rising up out of its depths. A big old fashioned stereo with a turntable and two large speakers took up most of another wall.

"Well, I have two options for you," Harry said, returning with a horn in each hand.

Deihlia looked at one trumpet and then the other. She didn't know what the difference was, other than the size.

"This is the horn I learned on as a kid," Harry said, holding up the coronet in his right hand. "My Dad gave it to me. He was in the Braves Troubadours band back in the day, the official band of the Boston Braves. He taught me how to play on this horn. It was his." He held it out to Deihlia.

She took it gently, placing her fingers in the finger rings and on the valves in the same way he had been holding it. It felt light and friendly in her hands, like it was ready for a new adventure. She turned it this way, then that, looking over its curves and small bell.

"This is another good one. I used to play this one too. It's the first trumpet I bought on my own." He held it up in the air, looking at it, admiring the memories he had with it. "You can take this one too, try 'em both out and then keep the one you like best."

Deihlia was humbled by his generosity. Not one, but two trumpets. She placed the coronet on her lap and took the larger horn from him. "I really appreciate you sharing these with me."

"My pleasure, Deihlia. I'm glad you wanna play, and I can't think of a better use for these old horns. I think they'll work well for you."

She looked up at him. He stood with his hands in his pockets, smiling down at her. "But this horn was from your Dad. It seems really special," she said, putting her fingers lightly on the pipe of the coronet in her lap.

He continued to look down at her, his hands in his pockets. She was a special kid. He had a soft spot for her, getting around to their gigs in her wheelchair, cruising around Boston. She always seemed to be in a good mood and fit right in with the band. He didn't know much about her, but he knew she was really cool. Whenever she hung out with the band, a few of the guys would cluster around her, getting advice and soaking up her stories. She told a good tale. Her advice seemed pretty mature, too.

He didn't have to think twice about the horn. "Deihlia, I want you to have it if it's the trumpet for you. You're right. It is special. That's why I'm giving it to you. My dad bought that trumpet off the wife of one of his jazz mates after he died. Whoever owned that trumpet first was one of the top jazz guys in Boston. It'll bring you good luck."

She smiled at him, lifting each horn in one hand. "Thank you, Harry. This means a lot to me."

"If I lived in Boston I'd teach you myself, but, well, I'm up here." He said.

Nodding, she put both horns down on her lap, their bells facing opposite directions. Something inside her was lit up. She'd been going to Wally's jazz club for several months now. She liked to squeeze into the tiny club and become immersed in the music. It expressed things without words, taking her on emotional journeys she couldn't quite describe. She'd been thinking about playing an instrument for a while, but hadn't been sure which one matched her best. It was only when she bumped into Harry on New Year's Eve that she knew. She wanted to play the trumpet.

A week later, Deihlia was looking on Craigslist for a trumpet teacher. She lived so close to Berklee College of Music and other music schools, there had to be a good trumpet teacher nearby. She'd had the horns a week but hadn't done more than lift them to her lips and finger the valves. She needed a teacher.

Two days later, someone answered the email she'd sent in response to a Craigslist ad. "Yes, I teach trumpet. I have room for another student. I'll come by and we'll see if it's a fit."

A few days later, Charlie buzzed the buzzer outside her apartment building. Deihlia rang the button in reply and he came in and went up the elevator to the third floor. He knocked on her door.

"Come on in, it's open," Deihlia said. As the door opened, Charlie walked tentatively into her apartment. Charlie looked to be in his mid-thirties, with a round, open face and light brown hair. He wore vintage loose-fitting grey trousers, wingtip shoes, and an old Rolling Stones t-shirt that was faded and loose.

Charlie shut the door behind him and looked down at Deihlia. She wasn't quite what he was expecting. He was expecting Pork Chop - a young dude with a Louis Armstrong obsession. He hadn't expected a girl in a wheelchair. She hadn't said that she was a girl, or that she was in a wheelchair. Then he caught himself. Why should she have to? She didn't need to announce anything to strangers. "You must be Pork Chop," he said, reaching out his hand. "I'm Charlie."

"Nice to meet you, Charlie," she said, shaking his strong right hand.

"So you want to learn to play trumpet."

Deihlia put her hands on her wheels and ushered him into the living room. He seemed like a trustworthy guy. "Yeah, I really do."

As he walked behind her the few feet into the open living room area, he saw a light blue shadow on Pork Chop's back. She was wearing a black and grey hoodie. He reached up and rubbed his eyes. *Must be the light in here*, he thought as he sat down on the plum sofa opposite Pork Chop. "What makes you wanna learn this instrument?" he asked, sitting down on the plum colored sofa.

"I've just really been into jazz lately. When I listen to it I go to other places. It seems really expressive. All that New Orleans jazz, Miles Davis, Louis Armstrong, Chet Baker..." She said.

"That's a good reason. A real good reason. Do you have a horn?"

Deihlia reached over to the side table next to her sofa and picked up her trumpet. "Yeah, I have this one."

214

He looked over at it. It was an older, vintage Coronet. It seemed like the right size for her. "That's a nice one. Where did you get it?"

She slipped her fingers into the finger rings. She wanted to do more than just hold it. It itched in her fingers and heart. "This horn player I know from the Hot Tamale Band gave it to me."

Charlie sat up, surprised. "I know the Hot Tamale Band. Who gave it to you? Was it Harry?"

Deihlia smiled. "It was! How do you know Harry?"

"I know him from different gigs and bands I've played in. How do you know him?"

"My mom's friend is in the band and I met him at their gigs. I've gone to a few."

Charlie's smile got bigger. It wasn't often that a new student found him online and had these kinds of connections. It was a good sign. "Do you want to start right now?" He asked.

"I thought you'd never ask," Deihlia said.

Charlie nodded. She was going to be a good student, he could already tell. He could feel a seriousness in her about it. She seemed kind of soulful too. He could sense these things in his students, or the absence of them, which made his job harder.

"Let me see your horn," he said.

Deihlia rolled closer and handed her trumpet to him.

"You'll need a different mouthpiece for this," he said. "I've got one that I think will be the right fit for you. I'll bring it next time I come by, but you can start by blowing on this one." He handed the horn back to her and smiled. He wanted to ask her about the name Pork Chop, but he didn't want to ask her too early. She was confident and mysterious, wearing that fedora and her argyle vest. He got the feeling that she didn't explain herself to too many people. He already had a good feeling about working with her.

"Cool," Deihlia said. This was starting off so well, like someone had set them up on purpose. Yes, the trumpet was the right instrument for her. She knew it in her bones and she hadn't even played a note.

The Streets of New York

Deihlia appeared at Chelsea's side, floating in next to her amongst a group of men dressed as Batman, the Joker, and Robin - all from different periods of the TV shows and movies. Women walked past them wearing a variety of superhero costumes. Xena Warrior Princess, Batgirl, Princess Leia, The Little Mermaid, and a couple of steampunk women in top hats and tweed suits wearing nothing under their suit jackets wandered past them. "This is the best Comic Con ever, so far," Deihlia grinned.

Chelsea smiled. "Why, what happened?"

"I was talking with one of my favorite comic book writers, Richard Starkings. He said he's going to put some kind of character based on me in one of the upcoming *Elephantmen* issues."

Chelsea's eyebrows went up. "Really? Wow, that's so cool."

Ping came running up behind them. "Sorry I'm late! Sorry!" He was out of breath. His short black hair was cut spiky on top, but his hair hadn't been cut in a while, and the rest of it looked like one of the Beatles mop tops. He wore a light pink t-shirt with characters from the old anime TV show "The Mysterious Cities of Gold" on it. Looking at him, Deihlia realized that he looked just like the main character with his hair sprouting and bouncing on top.

"It's ok, Ping. You're not late," Deihlia said, shaking her head. Chelsea turned to look at him.

"I was over at the Star Wars area and I wanted to get a photo with R2D2." Ping's face was flushed. He really did run all the way from the back of the second floor to meet them near the entrance.

"Well let's see the photo then," Deihlia replied, her eyebrows up.

Ping slid his phone out of his jacket pocket and held it out for her to see. "That angle looks like you're trying to kiss him," she smirked. Chelsea bent forward and looked at it, laughing out loud. "It does!"

Ping shook his head. "No, no, I wasn't trying to kiss him. Come on you guys. I don't kiss robots. Not even Star Wars robots, who I love." They laughed some more, and Ping joined in, his face lit up with a smile.

"Let's head back to the hotel and chill for a bit before we go out," Chelsea said.

They went out the front door of the Javitz Center and turned right to get one of the cabs that sat in line out in front of the building. A couple ahead of them got into a yellow cab. They moved further down the sidewalk and approached the next cab in line. Chelsea peered into the cab window. The driver looked past Chelsea to Ping and Deihlia. He shook his head no.

Chelsea frowned at him and moved to the next cab in line, a white car with maroon lettering. She bent over to talk to him. He waved his hand at her to push her away, he wouldn't look at her.

"Unbelievable," Chelsea said, scanning the line of cars.

A plain white minivan further back blinked its front lights once, then twice. The driver leaned out of his window and waved at them to come near. Chelsea went first, with Deihlia and Ping following closely behind her.

"Where ya going?" he asked.

"The Tribeca Mirage Hotel."

"Get in," he said.

Chelsea opened the side door. "Can you get in here Deihl?" she asked. Ping walked around to the other side of the car and got in. Deihlia moved close to the vehicle and lifted her body onto the floor of the back, then scooted back to lift herself up onto the seat next to Ping. Chelsea opened the back door and put the wheelchair inside, noticing that the back was dirty. An empty paper bag and old food wrappers littered the floor. She shut the hatchback then got in and sat next to Deihlia, slamming the door shut behind her. The car rattled.

The driver pulled out of the line and exited the Javitz Center by gunning it into an opening in traffic. A car sped by them from the other direction, honking, just missing them. Deihlia looked at Chelsea as she tried to pull the seatbelt across her torso. It was stuck and wouldn't move. Chelsea's seatbelt didn't seem to exist. She fumbled around looking for it, then gave up. She scanned the car for the taxi information and there wasn't any. No medallion graced the dashboard or the window.

The minivan stopped at a red light. Deihlia looked at the drivers face in the rearview mirror. His eyes were red, hooded. He looked totally wasted. His pale face was unshaven with a day-old shadow. He had dark circles under his eyes. Chelsea was looking at him too. She couldn't see the mirror or his face, but she saw his head drop, like he was falling asleep.

"Hey buddy. We're gonna get out as soon as you can pull over." Chelsea said, speaking loudly to wake him up.

His head jerked up and he shook it, pawing at his face with his left hand. "You said the Mirage Hotel and that's where I'm taking you."

Deihlia looked at Chelsea. She looked back. Ping leaned forward and looked over at both of them, his eyes wide.

The driver continued to move forward, stopping short, cutting in-between cars, angering other drivers as he drove herky-jerky through rush hour traffic.

Deihlia slid her phone out of her pocket and texted Chelsea and Ping in a group text. "This guy is wasted. What are we gonna do?"

Chelsea and Ping took out their phones, turning off the sound. Chelsea looked at the driver then wrote back. "We need to take over the wheel. This guy is gonna get us killed."

Ping and Deihlia read the text. Ping's eyes widened more as he looked over at Chelsea, his mouth open. "I can't drive!" he texted back.

"Shoot!" Chelsea texted.

The car lurched forward, nearly hitting a black Mercedes.

"Where are we?" Deihlia asked, trying to look past Chelsea out the window.

Chelsea turned, rolling down her window to get a better look. They were somewhere along 11th Avenue. Ping looked out of his window. He had no idea where they were.

The light turned red and the driver slammed on his brakes. Deihlia put her hands on the back of the front seat to keep herself from flying forward. Chelsea put one hand on the seat in front of her and the other on Deihlia.

"Let us out here and we'll pay you double," Deihlia shouted, feeling desperate.

The driver lifted his face slightly, looking at her in the rearview mirror.

"Double!" Deihlia said.

The driver tried to see her face in the rearview mirror, but he was struggling to keep his eyes open. His lids drooped, then he jerked his head back up. *They said double*, he thought to himself, the word echoing in his mind. "Double." He said, trying to scan the street in front of them for a place to pull over.

218

Chelsea texted them. "Ping, act like you're looking for money to pay him. Stall so I can get Deihl out of the car."

Ping looked over at her and nodded. He was scared. He'd never lied or tricked anyone before, but he could try to do it. He didn't want Deihlia to get stuck in the car with this guy.

Traffic began to move and the driver went over into the right lane to find a place to let them out. He pulled over in the middle of the block. Cars beeped and cursed as they passed. Before he stopped the car completely, Chelsea opened her door and jumped out. Ping unbuckled his seat belt and opened the door. "How much do we owe you?" he asked.

"Forty bucks." The driver turned around in his seat looking at Deihlia. She'd told him double.

Ping stepped out of the car. His heart was beating fast. "I'm sorry, what did you say we owe you?"

The driver turned and faced out towards Ping. Deihlia slid across the seat and jumped down on to the floor. Chelsea pulled her chair out of the back and put it next to the open door.

"I said forty bucks!" the driver yelled as he opened his car door to get out.

Ping backed up slowly, one step then another, moving towards the back of the car.

A driver stuck in traffic behind them saw an unusual scene. A wasted looking guy getting out of the driver's side of a minivan, lumbering unsteadily towards a young Asian man, who despite clutching his backpack in front of him, looked both strong and scared, a shimmering yellow cape falling from his shoulders. He watched as on the other side of the car, a young woman with long brunette curls pushed wheels into a silver frame faster than he could say the word "wheelchair" then got another person out of the van and into the chair. They too had capes on, blue and purple. *What the heck?* He thought, rubbing his eyes. When he opened them, the brightly colored capes were gone, the people in front of him were in ordinary clothes, the young woman in the wheelchair was speeding away from the van.

Chelsea walked around to stand with Ping. "We're not paying you forty bucks for that crappy ride! You almost killed us!"

The driver stood there in his dirty jeans, his red eyes going from Ping to Chelsea and back again. "You owe me for the ride! It was a twenty dollar ride. You said double."

"And you're not a real cab driver!" Chelsea pulled a ten dollar bill and a few ones out of her jeans pocket. "This is all you're getting. My sister's over there calling the cops right now. You better take this money and run." The bills fluttered in her hand as she reached out to him, stretching her arm as much as she could to keep her distance. He snatched the money quickly and got back into the cab.

Chelsea grabbed Ping and ran to the curb where Deihlia sat watching them.

"What a nightmare," Deihlia said.

Ping shook his head. "I've never had a cab ride like that before."

"That was no cab," Chelsea said. "Come on, let's walk back to the hotel. I don't care how far it is."

After dinner, they decided to go to the Bitter End music club in Greenwich Village to hear some live music. Ping wanted to go to a movie with other friends, so they parted ways. A line of people stood outside, waiting to get inside the small club. Deihlia looked at the crowd. It was a real mix of ages, black, white, people dressed up and people in their everyday clothes. She went to the end of the line.

"I need some cigarettes. Be right back," Chelsea said, walking away.

A couple came along and got in line behind Deihlia. The man was tall, older, and bald, probably in his sixties, wearing a black suit with a crimson tie, and a gray wide-brimmed fedora hat. *He looks like an old mob dude who stepped out of the 1940's*, Deihlia thought as she turned and watched him and his girlfriend pause at the end of the line. The woman completed the picture with her long chestnut colored fur. Her mane of dyed red hair stood out against the brown pelt. Her black high-heeled pumps made her legs look curvy below the fur. They looked vintage but well-maintained, Deihlia thought. The redhead put her arm inside his, then put her other hand on his lapel, looking up at him. He surveyed the long line waiting to get into the club, and frowned. "Can't you get us in there, baby?" the woman asked him.

He looked towards the door of the club, then down at Deihlia, speaking to her. "I'm Joe. This here is Monique. We're celebratin' an anniversary. Your night's on me tonight," he said, putting his arms on Deihlia's shoulders, pushing her around the outside of the crowd, heading towards the door.

220

Chelsea wandered back to the club and saw Deihlia being pushed towards the front door by a guy in a suit with a redhead in a fur. *What the heck?* She wondered, and walked quickly after them.

"Deihl," Chelsea yelled.

The guy in the suit was talking to the bouncer, a big dude wearing a knit cap, leather jacket, and motorcycle boots, sitting on a stool beside the door. He was gesturing towards her sister as he spoke to the bouncer. Deihlia looked back over her shoulder at Chelsea and shrugged. Chelsea walked more quickly and came up behind them. "What's going on?" she asked.

Joe and Monique turned around to look at her.

"This is my sister Chelsea." Deihlia said.

Joe reached out his hand. "Nice to meet you. I'm Joe. I'm taking you and your sister into the club tonight. On me. We're celebrating an anniversary."

Monique smiled a deep red, kitten smile, patting his arm. "This is our special night," she cooed.

Chelsea looked at her, then back at Joe. They looked like they stepped out of an old mafia flick.

The bouncer looked back down at Deihlia and handed her ID back to her. "You sure you're with these two?" he asked.

Deihlia nodded. "Yeah, we're celebrating."

He continued to peer at Deihlia, his eyebrows raised this time, giving her another chance to say no.

"We're good," Deihlia said.

Then the bouncer looked back up at Joe and Monique. "It's fifteen bucks a head. Sixty bucks."

Joe pulled a wad of cash held by a gold clip out of his trouser pocket and peeled off three twenties.

"I'll need to see your ID too," the bouncer said, nodding to Chelsea.

Chelsea pulled her wallet out of her bag and showed him her license.

"Have a good evening folks." He waved them in.

Deihlia went in, followed by Joe, Monique, and then Chelsea. She spotted her favorite table, empty, on the side of the stage. Chelsea got beside her and helped to move some of the chairs out of the way so she could get through. Joe saw her and picked a chair up out of the way, then put it on the other side of the table.

"I knew you'd show us a good time," Joe said, pulling out a seat for Monique at Deihlia's table. "Now what'll you have? Tonight's on me ladies."

"I'll have a Charlie Adams," Deihlia said.

Chelsea sat down next to her sister and looked at her pointedly, raising her eyebrows.

Deihlia shrugged, grinning. "I'm going with the flow. Free drinks and an evening with Joe and Monique sounds good to me."

Chelsea shook her head. "You're never coming to New York without me," she said.

Good Karma

Elsa was at Deihlia's apartment, cleaning. She was happy that Sean and Deihlia, best friends since they were four years old living across from each other on Conlyn Avenue, were sharing an apartment together and were still friends. Sean had moved into Deihlia's apartment when LP moved out to go and work in New York City. She was pleased that both her son Sean and Deihlia had successful jobs and were doing well. It was April in Boston. Elsa knew that neither Sean nor Deihlia would be doing any Spring cleaning, so she decided to help.

She'd washed the floors, done all of their laundry, cleaned the kitchen, and was steam cleaning the sofa when the idea came to her to go out and buy some cupcakes to have waiting for Deihlia when she arrived home from work.

The steam nozzle droned over the surface of the sofa, restoring it to a plusher version of itself. Elsa looked around the apartment. It was neat and clean. She might have time to go out and pick up cupcakes. If only she'd thought to make them before she came. She was looking forward to having some time with Deihlia, to chat like they used to after school. She put the vacuum cleaner away and picked up her purse. A key turned in the lock and Deihlia rolled in, going over to the kitchen table to drop off her messenger bag and remove her jacket. "Hey Elsa," she said.

Elsa put her purse back down on the counter, deciding not to go out after all since Deihlia was already home.

Deihlia went into the living room, hopping out of her chair onto the sofa. She'd been thinking about her game all day and pulled her laptop over. Elsa sat down in the chair across from her, waiting for her to settle in so they could talk.

The open laptop with the 17" screen created a giant wall between Deihlia and Elsa. All Elsa could see was the laptop, Deihlia's legs and feet underneath it, and the crown of Deihlia's head bent over the keyboard. She sat there and looked at Deihlia. Then she looked around at the apartment, admiring her handiwork. Deihlia hadn't seemed to notice that her apartment was now in photo-worthy condition. *Click click click.* Deihlia continued to look down.

Elsa remembered back to when Deihlia was a teenager, when she and Sean were living with Donna and the girls for a while as they moved back from Connecticut to look for a new house. Elsa had cleaned their house that first school day too, and Deihlia came home to a neat house, her laundry piled in a tight stack on her bed. "The same day laundry service is really fantastic Elsa," Deihlia had said, looking up at Elsa with a smile. Elsa enjoyed being complimented for something she did all the time, something her own family simply took for granted. Deihlia was effusive with the praise while Elsa and Sean stayed there, complimenting her cooking, her cleaning, her efficient handling of household matters. The praise and recognition had made Elsa enjoy doing it even more, especially for Deihlia.

Now she sat across from her, watching her type. She didn't feel very appreciated. A few more minutes passed in which the only sound was the clicking of keys. Finally, Deihlia peeked over the top of her laptop.

"Can I get you a magazine or something?" she asked.

Elsa looked at her, not saying anything, taken aback by Deihlia's uncharacteristic rudeness. The silence mounted. A few more keystrokes and then the laptop screen went down slowly as Deihlia raised her face to look at Elsa directly. "I feel like I should be eating Toaster Strudels," she said.

Elsa laughed. "I was going to go out and get cupcakes but you got home before I had a chance," she said.

Deihlia noticed that the pillows had been fluffed and placed in the corners of the sofa, that the magazines on the side table were neatly stacked, and the floor was gleaming. "Thanks for cleaning the place, Elsa. You still have the magic touch!"

Elsa smiled. "How was your day, Deihlia? How is work going?" She knew that Deihlia had gotten another promotion at work, moving to their Haymarket office. She didn't have direct contact with clients anymore, but the work she did still served the greater purpose of helping people with free legal representation.

"It's going well," Deihlia said. "What do you say we bake some cupcakes?"

"Sure," Elsa said, standing up as Deihlia hopped back into her chair, turning it around towards the kitchen. She was glad that Deihlia was having a lot of fun now. Happy that she had a lot of friends, that she was traveling. Elsa had never imagined who Deihlia would become. She hadn't really imagined who her own children would become as adults. Rather than imagining what anyone would be in the future, she had just greeted each day as it came, meeting whatever it brought.

"How did you get home in this miserable weather?" she asked.

Deihlia reached into the cabinet to pull out a box of cake mix. "Well, I called The Ride yesterday to schedule a van. That's the handicapped van service from the MBTA. I knew it was supposed to pour today."

"You really have to check the weather, huh? I guess you can't carry an umbrella if you're hands are on the wheels."

Deihlia opened the refrigerator door and pulled out eggs, milk, and butter, placing them on the counter one at a time. "I don't own an umbrella," she replied, opening another cabinet to pull out a mixing bowl. "And some days I just don't want to be soaked, y'know?"

Elsa nodded. "I bet." She hadn't thought about Deihlia wheeling around the city in rainy weather, waiting for the bus, arriving at work in wet clothes. She knew Deihlia couldn't really clean her apartment, but she hadn't thought about that. There wasn't anything she could do about that. There were more things she couldn't do for Deihlia than things she could, especially now that Deihlia was older. But she had cleaned all day. That was something she could do.

Deihlia turned on the oven and pulled her hand mixer out of a drawer. "I'll make the batter if you line the cupcake tin," she said.

"I'd be happy to," Elsa replied, standing by as Deihlia began pouring the mix into the bowl. Sean certainly didn't attempt to make his mother cupcakes. *Boys are different,* she thought. "This is a real treat, Deihlia."

"It's the least I can do for the food lady," Deihlia said, smiling as she broke an egg into the bowl.

The Kidney Stone

Deihlia texted me to tell me she wasn't feeling well. She was leaving work to go to the hospital. Her colleague Maryellen would accompany her to make sure she got there ok. I'd meet her there as soon as I got out of work. She had a fever and was in a lot of pain. She felt sick to her stomach. I texted her to let her know when I'd arrived. Maryellen left, returning to work or heading home. Deihlia was in the emergency room, in one of the sectioned off beds, shivering as she waited for a doctor, white and scared. "I can't get warm," she said. I pulled the thin blanket up over her and got in the bed behind her, holding her, and pressing myself against her back to try to warm her up a little.

"Thanks Auntie," she said, her teeth chattering.

The attending doctor came in and Deihlia spoke to him, explaining how she felt, and giving him the rundown of symptoms, like a real pro. She knew what to tell him, how to tell him. Even as sick as she felt, she knew exactly what to say. Having had over forty surgeries in her life, she knew the language.

"My post-traumatic stress is also being triggered from being here, doc. I'm having a really hard time right now." Deihlia said. Her body was shaking, and she was extremely anxious; her heart raced. She felt like fear had swelled in her throat, a giant ball that was choking her. She began to wheeze, her breathing squeaked through her mouth.

I didn't know that she suffered from post-traumatic stress from all of the surgeries she'd had. Why wouldn't she? I hugged her tight. I didn't know what else to do.

"I'll order an Ativan right away," he said. The doctor was impressed with her thoroughness, and quickly began to order tests to determine what was going on. After the Ativan, Deihlia calmed down a little. They gave her something for the fever as they conducted tests. I sat in the room with her, waiting. It was a new emergency department, but it felt the same as it always did. Antiseptic limbo. Later, they came in and said that she had a bad infection, brought on by a large kidney stone that pressed against an awkward spot in her kidney.

I called Sean and had him bring in some of her things from home - her phone cord, some clothes, something to read. She was going to be there for a while. I'd meet him outside and bring everything in.

Later that evening, Sean pulled up in his truck and slid open the side door, pulling out a big green army bag. "I brought a bunch of stuff she'll want while she's in here," he said, opening the bag to reveal some games, books, and clothes. "I put a surprise in here for her too," he said, lifting up a shirt inside the bag to reveal a couple of Playboy magazines. I laughed and raised my eyebrows, shaking my head. Sean zipped the bag up and handed it to me, and I carried it into the hospital, up the elevator to her room. "He thought of all the things you might want while you're getting better," I said, dropping the bag on the floor and pulling out the phone cord so we could charge her dead phone. They were pumping antibiotics into her to fight the infection. She wasn't quite ready for the contents of the bag, so I left it there for her while she rested.

Several days later I picked her up, ready to go home. She was feeling much better. The infection was gone, and she was eager to get back to her life, work, and friends. I pulled my car up to the emergency entrance curb and Deihlia wheeled out. I got out of my car and hugged her, then held her chair as she hoisted herself into my passenger seat. The chair went into my trunk, along with the army bag.

"That was a nice surprise Sean put in my bag," she said, smiling, her eyes sparkling. "You should've seen the look on the nurse's faces when they helped me get stuff out of my bag!" We laughed as I pulled out into afternoon traffic, the long summer day still white and bright.

"So what are they going to do about the kidney stone?" I asked.

"They have to blast it and disintegrate it," she said, "I have to come back in a few days so they can do it, but it's just a doctor's visit, y'know, I don't have to stay."

"Ok," I said, weaving back around the subway station to head in the opposite direction down the street. "I'm glad it was something they can take care of pretty easily, kind of a standard procedure."

"Yeah, me too. I was pretty scared when I went in there. I hate hospitals. But the sonic blasting should take care of it," she nodded.

But the sonic blasting didn't work. They tried three times. The kidney stone refused to shatter, it was big and stubborn. Surgery was scheduled to remove it.

"I'm really nervous," Deihlia said, "I hate surgery."

"It's going to be okay, Deihl," I said, trying to think of what I could do to support her, to help make the surgery go well, to help her be less scared. "Kidney stone removals are probably fairly standard procedures, right?"

She nodded, her lips pursed.

By then I'd been using my healing gifts for several years, so I offered to do some work with her in preparation for the operation. I didn't want anything to happen to her during surgery, and neither did she.

"I'm up for it, Auntie," she said. We made plans so I could come over and work on her the night before the surgery, a Thursday, perfect for what I was going to do.

"I wanted to make sure Sean wasn't home," she said, opening the door and letting me in. We went over to the dining room table and had some water, talking once more about the surgery. I wanted to figure out the best outcome for the procedure, so we could work on making that happen in our session that night. "I just want it to go smoothly, I don't want any complications. This thing has been a real pain in the butt so far, I don't want any more problems with it." She said. "It has to come out, so I want it out."

"Yeah, I think that's what I'll work on," I said.

We shut off the lights and she stretched out on the sofa with her back to me so that I could focus directly on the kidney.

"Just close your eyes and relax, Bug," I said. "I'm going to say some prayers and move some things around here. Take some deep breaths and relax."

I did a banishing ritual, to clear the room we were in of any possible obstacles to the healing work we were about to undertake. It cleared mental and psychic clutter, and created a protective shield around us. Things felt instantly cleaner. The apartment was quiet. I closed my eyes and did my thing, pulling out the sludgy energy around the kidney stone, replacing it with the bright blue light of one of the universal forces as I chanted over it. I visualized the kidney stone popping out effortlessly when the surgeon went in after it, ready and willing to leave her kidney, simple and easy, with no need for any additional work to get it out. No digging. The stone lit up for me. I could see it in my mind's eye. This was her kidney after all, an important organ. I continued to pull out the dark matter and put in

228

the blue light, visualizing it in my mind and using my breath at the same time. As I continued, the kidney started to look different. It morphed and looked vibrant, and the energy distilled down to a fine point, then disappeared. I let Deihlia rest for a little bit while I stood close to her.

"How are you doing?" I asked a few minutes later. She rolled over onto her back and lay there, opening her eyes. "I feel really good," she said, "like I had a deep nap. Saw all kinds of colors, too. Some blue."

I smiled and sat down beside her, rubbing her arm. I told her how I visualized the kidney stone popping out easily when the surgeon went in for it, and how he wouldn't have to do anything else to get it out. "That sounds good," she said. It meant a lot to me that she let me work on her. It wasn't the first time, but it still pleased me that she wanted me to do it. It was something I could do, besides being at the hospital, or driving her. "It will go well, Deihl," I said.

"I feel that too."

Her mom brought her into the hospital the next day and I was going to pick her up when she was discharged. The surgery went fine, no problems. Deihlia was eager to get out of the hospital. Once again, I pulled up to the curb at the hospital and she got into my car.

"I'm so glad to be outta there," she said, slamming the car door and fastening her seat belt.

"I'm so glad it went well, Deihl." I smiled at her, and could tell that she was relieved to be on the other side of it.

"So how did the surgery go? Do you know?" I asked as I drove away from the hospital, out of its maze of small one way streets.

"Oh, I made a point to ask the surgeon how it went - for you, Auntie." She shook her head, nodding, slipping her sunglasses on even though it was starting to get dark. "And you know what? He used the exact words that you used to describe what you did. No lie. He said that the kidney stone just popped right out and he didn't have to do anything else to get it out. It came out easy, and he was really pleased with how it went."

"Really?" I asked.

"Really, Auntie," she said. She was so thorough. I was proud of her for about a hundred different reasons, like I always was, and I was proud of us. We smiled at each other as we drove the familiar way back to her apartment.

"What would you like for dinner?" I asked.

"We can pick up something in my neighborhood," she replied.

I turned up the radio when a good song came on by Robyn, her poppy *Stars 4ever*. We were in bumper to bumper traffic, and dusk pierced the sky with slashes of pink and dark blue. Old brick buildings, the Emerson Theater, the shiny new W hotel, pedestrians darting between cars. Red light, green light, blue light. Tremont Street, the bicycle shop where she got her wheels fixed, the Boston Center for the Arts, dogs on leashes, the ice-cream shop, cyclists whizzing by, weaving in and out of traffic. Everything felt like home; like new.

Public Transit

"Let's go back to my place and invite a bunch of people over," Deihlia said, wheeling along the sidewalk in Harvard Square.

"Ok, sounds good," Tom replied. He walked beside her in a t-shirt and jeans, his short crew-cut hair a requirement for his job in the coast guard.

Harvard Square was bustling like it always is on a late Saturday afternoon. Old brick buildings stood sentry next to gray concrete buildings built in the 1970's. They passed a café, a bookstore, a bank. Students and tourists crowded the streets, going into shops, carrying coffee and shopping bags. Deihlia maneuvered around them at a leisurely pace. Tom ambled along beside her. "You wanna take the #1 bus back to the South End?" he asked as they neared the T station.

Deihlia nodded, continuing to wheel past the Harvard subway station. The bus was more direct than the subway, and they could catch it on a curb next to Harvard Yard, rather than riding the escalators that brought people down several levels to the inbound train.

They crossed Mass. Ave and stood by the bus sign. That side of Harvard Yard still had the old houses that had been part of the original campus. They joked, talking about a game they played a few nights before. Other people came and stood near them - an old Chinese woman in a light yellow raincoat, students listening to iPods and looking at their phones. Down the street, an older guy in a wheelchair started coming towards them. He raised his hand and waved at them, using his fingers to wave like he was squeezing a bird in his palm.

Tom looked around, ignoring him. Deihlia acted like she hadn't seen him. They continued talking.

A few minutes later, the guy in the wheelchair pulled up next to them, pushing the students out of the way with his hand as he made his way through them. "Hey cutie. Is this your boyfriend? I saw you from down the street. Looks like we're going in the same direction."

Deihlia turned towards Tom. "So anyway, when I got there no one else was there yet…"

The man got closer, using his feet to pull the chair along. Grinning, he angled his chair so that it blocked the sidewalk and no one could pass by him. Deihlia and Tom were on one side, the others were on the other side of him.

Tom bristled, and looked the guy over. He was probably in his forties, he hadn't shaved in a while and he looked pretty robust.

"I asked you if this is your boyfriend."

"What's it to you?" Tom asked.

"I think we have something in common, little girl," he said, focusing on Deihlia, staring at her face, ignoring Tom.

Deihlia looked back at him, silently sizing him up. After 30 seconds or so, she said "What we have in common is that we're both con artists. But the difference is that I need this wheelchair, and you don't."

The man continued to smile at her. "Where are you going tonight? I think we could have a good time together."

Deihlia sat in her chair, her hands on her lap. Tom stood next to her, folding his arms across his chest.

"You're not coming anywhere near us, buddy. Fuck off and get out of that wheelchair you asshole."

Tom raised his eyebrows. He didn't want to look too surprised for this guy. Deihlia could handle herself, but he was right there in case the guy did anything else.

The bus pulled up next to the curb, then reversed and lowered the back ramp down so that two wheelchairs could get in.

"After you," the man said.

"You first, dickhead," Deihlia said.

The man pulled his chair over to the ramp. The bus driver stood nearby, making sure he was on the ramp correctly then pressing the button to raise it.

"We'll catch the next bus," Deihlia said to the driver, wheeling her chair back, away from the curb. Tom watched as the guy turned around to face them as the door closed. He began waving at Deihlia again, only the top half of his fingers moving. He continued to smile and wave at her as the bus wheezed back into gear.

"What a creep," Tom said.

Deihlia nodded, watching as the bus pulled away.

Tom stood near her, putting his hands back in his jeans pockets. *What would happen to her if she was alone*, he wondered. He knew she was smart and fast and confident, but she was still in a wheelchair. He didn't like to think about it, but he did think about it. She was one

232

of his best friends. He'd only had a friend or two since he moved to Boston from Maine a year ago for his coast guard assignment. He wanted to make friends outside of the coast guard, and keep his personal life private and separate from his work life. He had one male buddy he met through a gamer group, and that's who made the introduction to Deihlia, when he brought Tom over to her apartment one day. They'd just walked in. The door had been unlocked. All Tom saw that day was someone huddled underneath a bunch of blankets, only the tip of a nose and glasses poked out from under them. "Who's this dude?" Deihlia asked their mutual friend, Richard.

"My buddy Tom. I wanted to introduce you guys. Thought he could play some games with us sometime."

Deihlia nodded, reaching her hand out through the maze of blankets. "Nice to meet you, man," she said. Tom noticed the wheelchair sitting empty next to the sofa as he reached out his hand to meet hers. Her hand was really cold. Richard hadn't mentioned anything about Pork Chop being in a wheelchair. "You gotta meet my friend Pork Chop. She's the bomb, and a killer player," he'd said.

"I'm sorry guys, but I'm sick. I want to play with you but I'm not feeling too well."

Richard nodded. "Is there something I can get for you, Pork?"

Deihlia shook her head no, and Richard and Tom turned around and left.

It was a few weeks later when he'd run into her again at a Meetup event. A girl in a fedora came up next to him. "Hey Tom, how are you doing?"

Tom looked down at her and recognized the wheelchair. "You must be Pork Chop," he said smiling.

Deihlia giggled. "Must've been hard to see me underneath all those blankets."

"Looks like you're doing better now," he said.

"Wanna ditch this lameness and do something fun?" she asked.

Tom looked around at the people. So far, Deihlia was the only person who talked to him, and he'd been there for almost an hour. The people seemed cliquey, they barely said hello. Why post an event on Meetup and make it open to the public if you were only going to talk to the people you always hang out with already? That didn't make sense to him. He looked back down at Pork Chop. "Yeah, sure."

They left the apartment together. Tom held the door open for her and they walked out to the sidewalk. He wanted to know how she got the name Pork Chop, but it was too early to ask.

"Do me a favor. Let me see your phone." Pork Chop said.

Tom pulled his phone out of his pocket.

"I'm gonna call this number. When the person answers, just tell her 'Nine o'clock at PC's crib. Bring beer and Cheetos.' Ok?"

Tom wasn't sure what he was getting into, but he shook his head. Deihlia dialed a number using his phone, then handed it back to him.

"Hello?" he heard a woman's voice on the other end of the phone.

"Nine o'clock at PC's crib. Bring beer and Cheetos." Tom said, wondering who was on the other end.

"What?! Nine o'clock at PC's crib? Who is this?" the voice replied.

Then, after a few seconds, he heard laughing. "Oh! Pork Chop's crib! I'll be there! See you then."

Tom slipped his phone back into his pocket.

Deihlia grinned up at him. "Let's get back to the South End. We're gonna have our own party tonight."

They continued walking towards the subway station. She seems pretty cool, he thought to himself. When they approached, Tom pulled out his subway card, and Deihlia pulled out hers. He slipped it over the pad on the turnstile, then walked through. Deihlia had wheeled over to the gate, flashing her card at the person who sat inside the glass box. The gate buzzed open and Deihlia started to pass through. The subway attendant stepped out of the door. "Miss, there's no elevator on this level. You have to go outside and get the elevator on the left side of the building."

Deihlia pushed herself through the gate. "I know. My buddy's gonna help me get down, no worries." She said, wheeling quickly past her and heading towards the escalator going down. Tom followed.

"Just get on the escalator and turn around to face me. I'm gonna wheel on right behind you. Just help hold my chair on the step," she said, her chair poised near the top of the escalator.

Tom looked around and saw the subway attendant watching them. *I can do this*, he thought to himself. "Ok," was all he said, getting on the escalator then turning around quickly to face Deihlia, who wheeled her chair on, two steps above him. He climbed up a step and held on to her wheels, holding them in place. Her hands were on the rails. She smiled down at him, watching the platform below get closer over his shoulder.

Tom held on to her wheels, looking back over his shoulder to see how close they were getting to the bottom. As they approached, he turned around and hopped off, then turned back towards her. Her wheels hit the platform and she pushed off, landing next to him.

The train screeched into the station, speeding by them. *Who is this Pork Chop? How did she get to be like this?* Tom wondered.

"Now you're gonna meet some cool people," Deihlia said as she pulled her chair into the doorway, holding on to the pole with one hand.

The subway car was almost empty, but Tom didn't want to sit down in the seat next to her. If she wasn't in the seats, he wasn't going to be either.

Deihlia liked how quickly Tom jumped into her world.

"I'm looking forward to it," Tom said, putting his hand on the pole above Deihlia's. The train began to move. They were on their way.

In the Club

Deihlia, Avery, and Melissa were sitting at the Trident Café having lunch, thumbing through comic books they'd picked up next door at Newbury Comics. Avery sat in her chair, her long blonde hair fell down over the latest X-Men comic she was reading as she took a bite out of her chicken wrap. Melissa had picked up a used copy of *Birds of Prey*. They both liked the strong women characters in the books. One of the character's outfits made Melissa think about dancing. "Let's go to the Gilded Cage tonight. I'm in the mood for clubbing," she said. The Gilded Cage was the largest nightclub in Boston, with two floors, private booths, a huge stage, and a teddy bear mascot that came out on the dance floor sometimes. Avery and Melissa liked to go dancing every few weeks, and hadn't been in a while. With Melissa's jet black hair, she and Avery often dressed to appear like twins, one blonde and one brunette, kind of like Betty and Veronica in the Archie comics.

Deihlia was a big Alan Moore fan. She'd finally found a copy of *Promethea Book 5*, which she'd been hunting for. The artwork was incredible, and the mystical content made her think. She'd loved Alan Moore since V for Vendetta and wore the Anonymous mask to many events. She began to unfold the poster that was enclosed in the back of the book, but thought better of it. She looked up from the book, glancing at Avery, then at Melissa. Clubbing. She liked to dance, but she wasn't sure about going to the biggest club in Boston. Would she be able to get on the dance floor, or up to the third floor where the club was? She reached over and picked up her glass to have a sip of water.

"Yeah, let's go clubbing. I feel like getting sexy on the dancefloor," Avery replied. She looked up at Deihlia. "You comin' Pork?"

Deihlia wanted to hang out with her friends, and she was in the mood for an adventure and some dancing. "If I can get in, yeah, I'm coming."

Avery thought for a moment. "I know they have an elevator. Let's meet by the Chinatown stop around 11 and go in together, k?"

That evening, Deihlia put on her darkest pants, a silvery-grey button down shirt, and a vest. She put some mousse in her hair and styled it into a look with long boy-band bangs. She rolled into the living room to grab her jacket. She was kind of tired. Part of her wanted to just hang out on the sofa playing video games. She'd been going out almost every night for the last few months to parties, meetups, game nights, dinners, trumpet lessons, live music and last week she'd gone to New York for Comic Con with Chelsea.

As she passed the bulletin board near the door, she noticed the Marvel Comics vintage calendar was still on September, and stopped to put it on the right month. I could just stay home and rest, she thought, her hand on the top of the calendar. She looked at the small even squares that marked each day of the month. There were only a few left and then it would be November. Something inside her wouldn't let her rest. It felt too much like being stuck in a hospital bed while life went on outside the hospital walls.

It was almost November, and then the holidays and her birthday would be coming up. Twenty eight. "I'm gonna be twenty eight," she said out loud. She thought of all the years she'd spent at Suffolk Universal and all the times she couldn't do things because her body was too fragile. It was a long time ago, but it wasn't that far away.

She lifted the calendar page again, looking at November, then flipped past that into December. There were only so many squares a month, and only so many months a year. Everything was finite.

She let the pages drop and turned away from the wall. Pulling out her phone, she texted her friend Melissa. "See you at Chinatown in 40 minutes."

After looking at their ID's, the bouncer directed them through a back hall to the elevator. Deihlia and her friends got in, pressing the third floor button. "This is the cleanest elevator I've been in in a while," Deihlia said, pushing her bangs into place as she looked at herself in the steel door. "You look smokin' in that dress, Avery," she said, smiling at her friend's reflection. Avery's coat was open. Her long blonde hair came down over her breasts, which were showcased in the deep V-neck sequin top she wore. Her short black skirt clung to her thighs.

Avery hit Deihlia lightly on the back with her clutch. "Pork, you're such a flirt."

Deihlia grinned, shrugging. "A girl's gotta try."

Avery rolled her eyes and Melissa looked on, pulling her wool coat tight around her. She was still cold from standing in line outside.

After they paid admission and checked their coats, they went to the bar and ordered drinks. A beer, a rum and coke, and a margarita. Deihlia grabbed the beer from Avery and they clicked their drinks. The club was starting to fill up, people clustered around the bar. Two other women walked up to them. "Hey! Thought that was you, Pork!"

Deihlia raised her cup in the air. "What's going on, Andrea? You're here to buy us drinks, right?"

Andrea laughed. "Maybe next round. I'm here to shake my bootay!" She shimmied, lifting her short skirt to reveal fringed panties underneath.

"Let me play with your fringe!" Deihlia laughed, reaching for her friend's skirt.

The club darkened, and multi-colored lights started to spin around them, skidding across the floor, their clothes, and up the walls. Orange, blue, red. Orange, blue, red. The music got louder, the beat deeper, vibrating in the air around them. They sipped their drinks then moved closer to the dance floor. Andrea started dancing in place, unable to resist the beat. Deihlia finished her beer and started dancing in her chair, her arms in the air. The other three girls joined in a few songs later. After a few songs, two of them left and went to get more drinks.

In addition to the stage, there were four pedestals in four corners of the large room. Each pedestal was round and about five feet tall. The club dancers emerged out of the crowd, and climbed on to the pedestals. Each dancer had on a different skimpy outfit with a gold eye mask. One began to dance and spin on an aerial bar above the dance floor. Deihlia watched as she twirled around the bar in gold lame shorts and bra top, her long ponytail flying a few inches above the tallest person's head. Bodies crammed in, the crowd grew. The bass kept beating in their bones. *Boom Boom Boom.* Andrea kept dancing, her eyes closed. Deihlia paused to sip on her beer. She felt someone behind her, pushing against her. She jammed her elbow back, trying to signal that it was too close. Her chair lurched forward, her knees went into Andrea's calves. Andrea stopped dancing, falling forward on to Deihlia.

"Pork!" She put her arms on Deihlia's shoulders, trying to catch herself from falling completely onto her.

Deihlia reached up to catch her. Andrea steadied herself and stood back up. She saw a guy laughing right behind Deihlia, smirking with his friend. Deihlia saw the look on Andrea's face and turned her chair around. He was tall, blonde, and probably in his early twenties. He looked down at her, a grin on his face.

"Watch it next time, buddy," Deihlia said.

He lifted his beer cup to his mouth and took a long drink, keeping his eyes on her while he emptied it.

Deihlia turned around to Andrea. "You ok?"

Andrea nodded. "Yeah. Some people are just jerks. Let's move away from them."

"No. Let's stay here. I'm sick of people like that always trying to push me around."

Andrea looked down at Pork Chop. She was surprised. She'd never heard Pork say anything like that before. She was usually the peacemaker. Pork Chop looked up at her. Andrea could tell she wasn't going to budge.

"Okay, whatever you wanna do, Pork."

Their friends returned with another round of drinks. Deihlia sipped on her beer. Andrea started to dance again, and so did Melissa. Deihlia drank a few more sips then placed her cup down on the edge of the table next to them. She put her hands in the air again and started to get into Rihanna's *Right Now*. She closed her eyes and moved her torso, grooving with the beat as Rihanna sang.

Suddenly her chair pushed forward again, banging into Melissa this time. "Man, I'm sorry!" she shouted over the beat.

Melissa stepped back a little and looked behind Deihlia. A blonde guy was standing there laughing at them.

Deihlia turned her chair around. "Come on man! You're not even dancing! Stop bumping into me like that!"

The blonde laughed. He didn't apologize. He didn't move. He stood there looking down at Deihlia. She got the sense that he had done it on purpose, just to mess with her.

"What's your problem, dude?" she asked.

He shook his head. "I don't have any problems. My only problem tonight is you."

Melissa and Andrea moved closer to Deihlia, standing on either side of her chair. How could this guy be such an asshole? Why was he picking on Pork?

"I've really had it this time," Deihlia said, pulling her arm back and curling her fingers together. Before she could think about it, her fist landed on his abdomen. She'd never hit anyone before, but every guy who had kicked her at college parties or stood in the way on purpose when she said excuse me and tried to get through a crowd was there at the end of her punch. He raised his arm to hit her back, and one of his friends stepped in between them. "You're gonna get us thrown out of here," his friend said.

"She just hit me!"

"You deserved it, you jerk!" Andrea spit at him.

His friends pulled him away, off into the crowd.

"Was he actually going to hit a girl in a wheelchair?" Melissa asked, shaking her head.

Avery stood by, watching the guys disappear into the crowd. "Pork, are you ok?" she shouted into the loud music.

Deihlia nodded. She was a little shaken. A little surprised. Mad. But she also felt really alive. As she put her hands on her wheels to turn around, she saw the blonde coming back towards them through the crowd. "Uh oh," she said.

Avery looked up in the direction that Deihlia was looking in, and Melissa did too. "Come on, let's get out of here," Melissa said.

Deihlia sat where she was, watching him get closer. "I'm not going anywhere. We have every right to dance where we want and we weren't bothering anyone."

Melissa and Avery exchanged glances. "I'm getting a bouncer," Avery said, walking quickly in the direction of the front door.

Melissa stood close to Pork. "Let's just go with Avery," she said, gently pleading. She was starting to become afraid. She wasn't going to leave Pork all by herself to face the bully alone, but she didn't see any reason why they should court danger and wait for him. A guy who would pick a fight with a person in a wheelchair had to have a few screws loose, and that was dangerous.

He came straight towards them, and bent over and threw a punch at Deihlia's stomach. Her chair flew backwards. He walked towards her, and Melissa went after him and began to hit him, pulling at his shirt. Reaching over, he tried to push her away. People began to clear the area where they were. Melissa started screaming "He hit my friend! Stop him!" But no one moved. Deihlia was bent over in her chair, holding her stomach.

Avery ran through the crowd, and a burly dude dressed all in black walked quickly behind her. Then she saw them. She ran in front of Pork, putting herself between Deihlia and the bully. Melissa was still pulling on his shirt, kicking him in the back of the legs. The bouncer stepped in, pulling Melissa off of him. Other club staff appeared out of the crowd and grabbed the blonde, who stood with a grimace on his face in the center.

"Pork!" Avery said, squatting to sit next to her friend. "Are you ok? Do you need to go to the hospital?"

Deihlia shook her head no. "I don't think I need to, my chair took most of the punch" she said, but she was still reeling. She thought they'd have a few more words before any punches were thrown, but she hadn't thought past that point. Looking up, she saw the faces of people standing nearby, watching her and Avery. "Is Melissa ok?" Deihlia asked.

One of the bouncers was talking to Melissa, getting her side of the story. Then he walked over to Deihlia. "Are you ok, Miss? What happened here? I want to hear your version of the story."

Deihlia looked up at him. "We were dancing. He kept pushing my chair. He was trying to pick a fight with me."

Looking down at her, the bouncer put his hands on his hips and sighed. He'd seen guys like that a lot. Not every weekend, but more than enough. "Booze and bullies are not a good mix," he said. "Come on, let's take you back to the security office. I want to get your information. Make sure you're okay."

Deihlia looked up at her friends, who stood next to her in their sexy club outfits. She'd been having fun dancing with them. The music was good and the atmosphere was too. She hated that their night was destroyed. She hadn't thought of that either. "Guys, I'm really sorry you're night was ruined."

Avery and Melissa shook their heads, watching the blonde guy disappear with the security guards through the crowd. The people around them began to turn back to their friends and the dance floor. The night was still young.

Later, as they walked along the sidewalk looking for a cab, Avery looked down at Pork Chop. "You really didn't want to press charges against that guy, huh?" she asked.

Deihlia moved along beside them. She was lost in thought, hoping that the punch she'd taken hadn't done any damage. She couldn't feel anything below her chest, so she had no way of knowing.

"Pork?" Avery asked.

Deihlia looked up. "Oh, yeah. They kicked him out of the club for good. That's enough for me. I don't want to have to deal with the police or court or anything. I do that enough during the day."

Avery and Melissa exchanged glances.

"I've never ever been hit by a guy in my life, or hit one, for that matter." Avery said. "I still can't believe he did that."

Melissa sighed. "I wish it had never happened. We should've just left the first time he started bothering us."

Deihlia looked over at Melissa. "Maybe you're right, but I get tired of always moving out of the way for people who don't wanna share the space. We had every right to be there, all of us. I'm sorry I got you into it, though."

Melissa put her hand on Deihlia's shoulder. "It's ok, Pork. I'm just glad that you're okay. Look, here comes a cab."

Deihlia stopped in place while Melissa and Avery, in their coats and short skirts, ran to the curb and flagged down the cab. She hung back so that the cab driver wouldn't know he was picking up a person in a wheelchair, because usually they wouldn't stop if they knew. After a cab pulled over and Melissa slid into the back seat, Deihlia moved quickly over to them. Avery stood outside the cab to get her chair, dismantle it, and put it in the trunk after Deihlia got into the cab.

"Thanks, Avery. Let's get out of here," Deihlia said, getting into the car.

In Black and White

In late December 2011, I got a very clear message. One night, before sleep, I asked to be shown something that was coming into my life in the coming year; something I had no idea about. I like to be prepared. Two days later, I woke up with a start. I'd had a dream in which the word 'Cancer' was spelled out in black letters on a white background, "Big C" Cancer and "little c" cancer, rows of the word spelled out over and over. I opened my eyes, the image lingering. "Oh no," I said aloud, grabbing my dream notebook and writing the dream down. Black and white, it didn't get much clearer than that. I didn't want it to be true, but I knew that it was.

It was a dreary winter and Pop had been sick with pneumonia at Christmas. He'd come to Donna's for the family Christmas Eve party. He was friendly but wasn't quite himself. Three weeks later, he still wasn't feeling well. The antibiotics weren't working. Nana brought him into the doctor and they did x-rays. When the doctor put the x-rays up on the light board, Nana gasped quietly to herself. It didn't look like pneumonia. It wasn't. It was stage four lung cancer. With further x-rays and tests, they discovered that the cancer was everywhere. All they could do was some chemotherapy to give him a little bit more time. He'd been admitted to the hospital by then to see if there was anything they could do to help him. Nana, as a geriatric nurse, knew the trajectory of the disease, the options, the time left, but this was her husband. It was heartbreaking.

Each of us made our way to the hospital to see him, to let him know that we were there to lend our support and comfort. When I first arrived, Pop sat in the bed, alone in the room, looking out the window at the dark blue Boston evening. It was so quiet. This was a lot to take in, to process, to come to terms with. The TV wasn't on. It was usually on in any room where Pop was sitting. His kids had been in and left. Nana had been in and left. I walked in, quietly entering the room. "Hey, Darrel," I said, going over to the bed. He looked surprised to see me. I was surprised that he was surprised, but I went over and gave him a hug. It was hard to know what to say, so I asked "How are you feeling tonight?" I could tell he was in shock, that his world was turned upside down and part of him was spinning untethered in a different space.

Then Deihlia rolled into the room, wrapped in her many winter layers. She came in close and pulled off her gloves. "Hey, Pop," she said. He looked even more surprised to see her there. It wasn't that we'd interrupted his solitude and contemplation, it was something else. Like he couldn't really believe that we'd each trekked in to see him in the hospital.

"Deihl," he said, looking at her, seeing her. Something in him changed and he became lighter, more present. "Listen, Deihl, do you remember that twenty bucks you owe me? Am I gonna see it before I die?" He asked, smiling, breaking the ice. It was an old family joke.

"Yeah, here's my first payment," she said, pulling a plastic bag out of the backpack that hung under her chair and handing it to him. He opened it and started grinning. The bag was full of large size Kit Kats, Snickers, and Hershey bars. He had a sweet tooth.

He was in the hospital for a couple of weeks, and Deihlia went in most nights after work to visit him, taking the bus from downtown to Longwood, navigating through the slushy Boston streets. I met her there.

Another hospital setting, but not her this time.

Like most people, we'd all been going along, taking each other for granted, but when the Bus Driver paid a visit to the family again, making it clear he would be returning with a passenger at the end of the ride, we woke up quickly and rallied. Pop was given five or six months to live, and at first he chose the chemo to have a little more time. After a couple of treatments he felt so awful, he decided less time was ok. More time feeling horrible didn't feel like the best decision. He knew what he wanted and he made the decision without drama.

Six months passed quickly, too quickly, with so much visiting to celebrate Pop's last Easter, last birthday, last Father's Day. The diagnosis occurred in January, and it was June. Darrel was tenacious, and despite the pain and the meds he was on to control it, he had a strong will and still went out to watch the Memorial Day parade. He decided he wanted some fried oysters, one of his favorite foods. Off they went, carrying the oxygen tank with them.

I saw him the day before he died. I knew that he was afraid. Facing one's death frightens most people. "Would you like me to rub your back?" I asked.

He nodded.

I closed my eyes and put my hand on his back. Shimmers appeared in a circle around him. Certain people came into view, people I knew, others I didn't. They came to help him on his passage, to accompany him on the bus ride home. His transition was near, soon. He slumped against me, relaxing as I held his shoulder and touched his back, silently telling him it was okay, everything was okay, there was nothing to be afraid of, that his friends were here to help him on his way.

His funeral service was held at their church. I delivered the eulogy to a full house of 250 mourners. I'd never delivered a eulogy before. I had practiced a bit but still felt nervous trying to deliver both serious and funny lines so that people were free to laugh and cry. Deihlia brought her trumpet with her to the service, wanting to play *When the Saints go Marching In* for Pop at his funeral, but it wasn't part of the program. She hadn't discussed it with Nana, who wasn't really open to surprises at her husband's funeral service. Deihlia was hurt and disappointed.

Later, as people gathered after the marine burial to have lunch together in a room at the church, Deihlia took out her trumpet. Everyone was eating, talking, so no one saw her pull it out. She sat in the doorway, lifting the horn to the air. Sputtering through, she played the song. The horn blared loudly, cutting through chatter. People stopped talking, and listened. Deihlia was nervous, breaking into lunch like that, but she wanted to give Pop a musical send off, a special gift just from her. If Nana wasn't going to let her be part of the service, she'd be part of the after-party.

Out of the corner of my eye I saw him standing near her, smiling. Now he was a shimmer too.

I walked up to her after everyone clapped. "Pop appreciated the song," I said, whispering to her.

Deihlia looked up at me. "I'm glad. This is the only funeral he's gonna have, right?"

Flying, Hawaii, 2012

"I really wanna come to your wedding," Deihlia said, "but I think it's a long trip from Boston just for a weekend." She hadn't seen her hippie college buddy Eric in a while and was intent on being there for his wedding. She was almost twenty nine. Hawaii had been on her bucket list ever since she and Eric had become friends and he'd told her all about it during their nights hanging out on campus.

"For sure, Dee, for sure. Just come for the week and have the whole Hawaii experience. We'll take good care of you and hook you up." He said on the other end of the phone.

Deihlia didn't need to think twice. "Really? Ok! I want the whole Hawaii experience."

"Awesome!" Eric said. "Just tell me what you're up for and we'll make it happen."

A few months later, Deihlia boarded a plane bound for Los Angeles, where she'd get a connecting flight to Hawaii.

"Here you go," the flight attendant said, pulling up next to her with a blue wheelchair. The big, sturdy kind that they use in airports to transport people. Another attendant stood next to her.

"Thanks, just give me a minute," Deihlia replied, reaching under her own seat to unstrap the small backpack that she kept suspended there. After a few moments, she put the small backpack, red with black skulls on it, into the larger satchel on her lap. She placed it on the floor.

The attendant watched curiously as Deihlia moved a bit forward in her seat, then stretched her arm out over across the blue wheelchair while her other hand held her own chair steady. Then she lifted her body out of it and dropped down into the airport issued chariot. "Okay," Deihlia said, picking up her satchel.

"I'll check this for you," the second attendant said, maneuvering Deihlia's wheels away. Deihlia nodded, watching out of the corner of her eye as her custom built wheelchair disappeared. Even though she'd done it many times, it was still a little unnerving to be without it and have to rely solely on the flight attendants if she wanted to get out of her seat on the plane and use the bathroom. She couldn't see the flight attendant standing behind her, and it's not like they introduced themselves or anything. Whenever possible, she liked to take hers on the plane and disassemble it just prior to boarding,

246

storing it in the cabin. But this was a booked flight, and she had to check it.

The attendant wheeled her onto the plane ahead of all the passengers standing around impatiently by the gate door, watching her go in. What did they see as they stared at her? Did they even see her, or did they just see some young person in a black and grey striped hoodie, grey jeans, and vans sitting in a wheelchair? Did they even see that? She was used to being stared at, watched, looked down on, spoken down to, and seen through. Into the plane she went, across the threshold, down the aisle.

She couldn't be in an aisle or middle seat because she couldn't get up and out every time someone in the row needed to get up. That meant the window, which made it much harder for the attendants to help her. When she needed them, she'd have to scoot over until she got back to the aisle. Then the attendants had to bring the wheelchair over to her, and it disrupted the flow of the flight and everyone around her. She hated it but what could she do? She couldn't sit in the emergency exit row, even though that would have been easier, because she couldn't physically handle the emergency door if the need arose. It was going to be a long flight from Boston to California, then another one to Hawaii.

"Here we are, Ms. Nye," the attendant said, stopping at row twenty three. Deihlia tossed her bag onto the floor in her row, then hoisted herself into the first seat. "Is there anything else you need right now?" the attendant asked.

Deihlia shook her head, looking up at the attendant. "No, thank you, I don't think so," she said, sliding over into her own spot. The plane was still empty as she pulled her bag over and shoved it under the seat in front of her. People started boarding, filling up first class. In thirteen hours, she'd be in Hawaii.

Every three hours she had to call the flight attendant to bring her to the bathroom. She couldn't feel when her bladder was full, so she had to be diligent and empty it every few hours. She wasn't tall enough to reach the button on the ceiling to call them, either. "Sorry to bug you, but can you press the button for the flight attendant again please?" She asked her neighbor. He was a young guy, wearing a yellow Lakers t-shirt. He nodded in a serious way and reached up and pressed the button. A few minutes later a male flight attendant came to the aisle. Since this was the second request, he knew what she wanted. "I'll be right back with the wheelchair," he said.

"Thanks," Deihlia said to the Lakers fan.

"Sure, no problem."

We'll be landing in an hour, Deihlia thought, *but I better not risk it. I better do this now.* The flight attendant returned with the chair, and her row mates stood up and stood in the aisle as Deihlia slid across their seats, lifting the arm rests so she could get by. The flight attendant pushed the chair next to the last seat and Deihlia got herself into it. She was pulled backwards to the back of the plane and then turned to face the bathroom door. Deihlia turned the lever to open the bathroom door. There were no bars in the bathroom. She had to hoist herself in and sit on the toilet in her pants and take care of herself from that position. It was a tight squeeze, and she had to lean back against the wall as she sat there. The flight attendant waited outside. As long as the plane didn't hit any turbulence, she was ok. Precarious, but ok.

Thirteen hours after she'd left Boston, she arrived in Honolulu.

"Dee, I'm so happy you're here," Eric said, bending over to hug her and grab her bags. "How were your flights?" he asked with a grimace.

"They were fine. How are you and Zoe holding up before the big day?" she replied, moving along beside him.

"Not too bad. Everything's going pretty good here. Glad we're gonna have some time to hang out and show you the island. Your kayak vest arrived a couple of days ago so we're good to go for the water sports!"

"Awesome," Deihlia said, grinning. She noticed that Eric's unruly red Mohawk was gone, and he was looking more settled in himself. He had less nervous energy, walking patiently next to her, not jumping out of his shoes like he had all through college. It was still hard to believe he was getting married. She wanted to witness this ritual of his maturing, and toast him into his new life. She knew his fiancée Zoe, too. Eric met her when he lived in Albany and went to massage school after college. Deihlia had visited them a few times and they'd come to Boston to see her, too. "You look older already," she said.

Eric ran his hands through his hair. "Yeah, I think the haircut helped with that."

A few days later they were standing around as Deihlia tightened the straps on her kayak vest.

"You sure you wanna do this?" Eric asked. "It's a big drop. Anything can happen when you hit the water."

"I'm all buckled up and you're asking me that now?" Deihlia shot back at him, smiling under her Ray-Bans. "I'm so positive I want to do this. What's the worst that can happen? I become more crippled?"

They all laughed, standing around in their swim trunks and bikinis. Deihlia was in pants, a t-shirt, and her kayaking life vest. "So who's gonna be the lucky guy?" she asked.

Mike spoke up. He was the tallest, strongest guy of their group. His blonde hair was white in spots from the sun. "Me. I'm the lucky guy," he pointed at his chest, raising his other arm to show off his bicep. "I've got you covered, Dee."

"Cool. I've been dreaming about this for months. What are we waiting around for?" she said, moving her chair back and forth, impatient. She handed her sunglasses to Sheila.

They all looked around at each other and nodded. "Ok, let's do this." Eric said. "Joe and Lisa are down there in their boat, they'll bring us back in."

Deihlia nodded, beaming a big smile. Mike bent down and picked her up, and she wrapped her arms around his neck as well as she could with the life vest on. "When I say "go," we're gonna let go of each other. We've gotta do it high enough up so that we don't land on top of each other," he said.

"Got it," she replied, trying to see past his shoulder as they got nearer to the cliff. "I just wanna look down there before we jump," she said.

Mike carried her closer to the edge and turned his back to the water, trying to turn her body so that she could see better around him. Eric stood nearby, ready to jump with them. He looked out at the sea and waved to his friends in the boat further offshore.

Deihlia peered over Mike's shoulder down at the water, twenty five feet below, like jumping from a roof two and half stories up. "This is fricking awesome," she said. "Let's do it!"

Mike turned back to face the water, standing at the very edge of the cliff. "I'm jumping," he said, and he bent his knees and sprang off, trying to get as far out as he could. A few seconds later he said "Go!" and let go of her, raising his arms in the air as they continued to fall.

Deihlia was smiling, her arms up, rushing through the air for what felt like a split second, then landing with a smack in the water, her legs pushed up towards her body by the force of it. Then she went under, under. She let the water take her down for a little bit, then began paddling her arms to return to the surface, her life vest pulling her up to the air.

Eric and Mike swam over to her. "How was that?" Eric asked.

She blinked the sea out of her eyes. "I think I hurt myself," she said.

Eric's face fell. "What? Where?"

Deihlia grinned. "I'm fine, man! Did you see me fly through the air? I loved it!"

Eric pushed his hand through the water, splashing her. "You're a shit! Just for that we're not gonna do it again."

Deihlia shook her head. "Oh, we're doing it again. And again."

Eric looked over at Mike, who treaded water next to him. "You up for some more, man?"

Mike nodded. "I sure am. Let's get her into the boat," he said, waving to their friends as the boat drew nearer.

Deihlia bobbed in place. "This is so awesome. Thanks for making this happen."

Eric smiled, his face glistening wet.

They rode back to the beach, where the rest of their crew waited. They were well organized and knew what they needed to do to get Deihlia back up the cliff, and they did it several more times.

After the fourth jump, Eric suggested that she have a ride behind the boat. She couldn't water ski, but she could do a tethered tube ride.

"I'd love to," Deihlia said, and they proceeded to get the tube out of the boat and put her in it, laying her legs over the top and leaning her back against it. "We'll go out a little deeper so you can see the area from a distance," he said, then climbed into the boat.

They went out into the deep and Deihlia looked around. The sea surrounded her. It sloshed and rippled around her in little waves after the boat cut through. It was fun gliding along like that, even if it wasn't going that fast. They picked up a little speed and the waves got bigger, smacking against the tube. The sun shone in her eyes. They took her around so she could see the shoreline, the trees, the beaches. She'd never seen land from this vantage point before, or been out in the ocean that deep. It felt freeing and a little mesmerizing, too. She wanted to feel every part of it.

Deihlia closed her eyes for a few minutes, feeling the water against the tube, floating buoyant and easy where sun and sky met.

"Dee!" she heard Eric call her name. She opened her eyes and looked up at the boat. Eric was gesturing with his hands in a frantic, circular motion. Deihlia squinted, trying to understand what he was doing.

Eric put his hands around his mouth and shouted: "Fins! Fins! We're gonna turn around, there are sharks in the water!"

Deihlia pushed against the tube, trying to sit up a little more so she could see better. She looked at the surface of the water on one side and didn't see anything. Then she looked over to the other side and saw a couple of fins rising and falling below the waterline.

"Hang on, Dee!" Eric said as the boat began to turn, steered in the opposite direction of the fins. There wasn't too much of her body in the water in the middle of the tube, but she was still starting to get a little nervous. Sharks. What are you supposed to do with sharks? Would they really be interested in a person in a tube? Not one, but two fins. She craned her neck to watch them, and they started to swim in her direction.

"We're gonna go faster, Dee. Hold on," Eric yelled.

Deihlia held on more tightly to the sides of the tube, careful to keep her hands high.

Whoosh! Something leapt out of the water, sailing over her. Another followed - a grey flash against the sky.

Dolphins!

Eric saw them and slowed the boat down again. The dolphins swam around the tube, then back out, hurling themselves into the air, arcing over her once more. Small drops of water rained down on her as they flew in the air above, their silvery bodies like great wingless birds glistening in the sunlight. They cavorted and played, swimming around her and showing off, putting their heads above water and chattering to her as if they knew her. Deihlia smiled. She couldn't

251

believe it. She called out to them, "Hey!" and giggled, watching them look at her and talk to her. She wished she knew what they were saying. She knew it was something good, the way they both turned their noses toward her and squawked. "You guys are funny," she said, "I don't know what you're saying."

The boat slowly made its way back to shore. Fins and snouts bobbed up and down in the waves. The dolphins swam on each side of the tube; sea envoys accompanying her as she returned to land.

Paint it Blue

Deihlia peered out the window of the cubicle space she shared with Emma at work. Their "office" was a partition in the hallway between the Director's office and a larger, open area where several people had spaces sectioned off with half-walls. Deihlia and Emma's windows overlooked the roofs of shorter buildings clustered behind them in downtown crossing. They were lucky: they could see sky. As Deihlia typed up an email to her colleagues in the Atlantic Avenue office regarding the next training meeting, she thought of her friend Avery, one of her comic and gaming friends she'd met in the past couple of years at a gaming event. Avery was twenty six, and painted beautiful, brightly colored canvases of birds and women, tropical and woodland scenes. She also worked two part time jobs, waitressing a few nights a week and working in an office the other three days. She struggled with her bi-polar disorder, and had called Deihlia that morning as Deihlia was arriving at work. She sounded terrible. Deihlia couldn't talk at 9:00 a.m. because she had a meeting to get to, but she tried to call her back at lunch and got her voicemail. Deihlia looked out at the blue sky, wishing her friend felt better, and that there was something she could do. Though the streets of downtown Boston were eight floors below, everything was quiet this far up. The vibrant blue sky reminded her of Avery's painting. Suddenly, a sea gull flew past the window, a fast gliding blur of white wings and grey. Deihlia was startled, moving back slightly in surprise at the bird so close to the window, but she took it as a good sign.

Once she got home that evening, she called Avery back to check on her. "I'm glad you picked up. How are you feeling? Did you get your meds?" Deihlia was sitting in her apartment on the old plum colored sofa that used to be in the Franklin house years before. She leaned back against the pillows.

"Yeah, I got them. But I don't know, Pork... I just don't think they'll help." She sighed.

"What's going on?"

"It's not just that I struggle with my mental disorder, I've had it for a long time. I know that if I don't take my meds I have bouts of super energy and restlessness, and then bouts of utter despair. It's more than that. Everything has been so hard lately. I lost my office job, and haven't been able to find a new one yet and I need it for the health insurance. My Mom moved down south with her boyfriend, and no matter how hard I try to move ahead with selling my art, it never happens. Something always comes up that gets in the way. I need to move out of my apartment because the landlord is turning it into condos. I don't have any money. I keep trying to push forward, but I feel so overwhelmed and kinda lost." She began to weep quietly on the other end of the phone. "Things just aren't working out for me."

"Avery, you definitely have a lot going on. With your art, things take time. You'll get there if you don't give up. The important thing is to keep going and just take small steps each day. Try to focus on one thing at a time."

"I don't know if I can, anymore," she said quietly.

"What do you mean? I know it takes a few weeks for your meds to start kicking in, but once they do you'll feel more stable and able to handle things, right?"

"It's not even worth it. I don't really wanna keep trying, Pork. I just wanna die. I don't wanna try." She whispered.

Deihlia listened, taking in her friend's delicate state. Her heart hurt knowing that her friend was so low that she wanted to die, and it really bothered her. "Avery, I gotta tell you something. I don't share this with too many people. I almost died a bunch of times when I was a kid, for real. Complications from surgeries, stuff like that. Death is nothing to be afraid of, but it's the kind of thing that ideally should happen to you after a life well lived, y'know?"

Avery sniffed on the other end of the phone. "You did? I didn't know that, Pork."

"Yeah, I did. I had so many surgeries, I should've died. Having one after another, and having no say in what was happening to me was really hard sometimes. Talk about being overwhelmed. Try being in surgery for 15 hours and then in a coma for a couple weeks. I never wanted to go through another operation and spend any more time recovering in the hospital, away from home and my friends. I felt really helpless and hopeless sometimes, too. I mean, I basically spent the first five years of my life in the hospital."

Avery sat up in her bed, leaning back against the wall. She'd been in bed for several days, and her long blonde hair was tangled and dirty. Her shades were down and the room was almost dark, because the sun was going down. "That sounds pretty hard, Pork. I had no idea you'd gone through all that."

"It was, but looking back, I had to go through all that to get to this point, to get here. I knew I wanted to do things in life, even as a kid. I held on to that, even when I had to surrender to my doctor's plans, which happened all the time. It took me a lot of years to get to the point where I felt like things in my life happened for a reason."

"What do you mean? What reason? It sounds terrible. How could there be a reason for all that you went through?" Avery asked, shaking her head, imagining what it would have been like to be Pork as a child, putting herself in her position.

Deihlia paused before answering. "I'm here, aren't I? I'm doing things I wanted to do. I have fantastic friends, I'm having a ton of fun, and doing work I really care about. College at Saint Michaels was one of the best things ever! Travel. Learning new stuff. Playing trumpet. I just think that I'm here for a purpose, Avery, maybe a few different ones. Plus, I'm friends with you. Those are pretty awesome reasons."

"But it sounds like you had such an awful childhood. All those surgeries and almost dying! No one should have to go through all that." Avery said angrily, upset about what her friend had gone through.

"I wouldn't wish it on anyone, that's for sure," Deihlia said. "But every time I went home from the hospital after another surgery, I felt lucky. I was at home with my sister and Mom, with my friends, with my video games, my dog and cats. Everyone I loved. Some kids died in the hospital, right next to me. I could've been one of them. Over time, I just started to trust that things were working out, that God had something else in store for me here, because I kept not dying. I kept getting stronger. Believe me, I could've and should've died a few times," she said. Deihlia could feel Avery taking her words in through the phone line, letting them settle inside her. She didn't share this part of her life casually, but when a friend was going through a rough time, she knew it would help. It had helped several other friends to share this part of her with them.

"Pork? I never knew any of this about you. It's kind of amazing. I feel like such a dumbass, talking about giving up on my art and my life."

Deihlia smiled to herself. *Mission almost accomplished.* "It's okay, Avery. Don't give up on your life, just stop worrying about why things aren't happening now and trust that things are gonna work out for you. Other opportunities are gonna come along, but you have to have your head up where you can see them. That's why I want you to just do what you need to do to get stable, take your meds, then start looking around for new things. Life is gonna keep coming at you. Don't you want to see what it has in store for you next?"

Avery listened, trying to follow the optimistic line that Deihlia's words were inserting into an unwritten future she could not yet see. Was it really there? The past few months had been one disappointment after another piling up on her.

"I want you to just trust me. Just listen to me and see what the future holds. Don't paint it black before it even gets here," Deihlia said, aware of how her friend's mind worked, that she was weighing a certain past against an uncertain future. "Cause if you do, it's definitely gonna meet your expectations."

There was silence on the phone for several minutes. Deihlia sat with it, letting her friend wrestle with her own thoughts. She gazed out the window. It had a view of the back of the building next door. A diffuse, milky sunlight came in through the glass that her hibiscus plant stretched towards hungrily, its spindly twigs clustered near the window. *I should water that plant*, Deihlia thought to herself.

"Ok, I'm gonna take your advice and try to get back on track. Stop moping about the past. See what happens next," Avery said.

"I know it's been a rough time, but things change. Maybe you can get some support. There have to be peer groups around you could join so you don't have to worry about the cost. And I'm here if you need me. Just reach out. I'm gonna keep in touch with you, too."

Avery brightened and smiled for the first time in over a week. "I'll paint the future blue instead! Like in one of my paintings!"

Deihlia laughed. "Yeah, sky blue! Great idea."

"I love that color. I can see that canvas already. Hey, are you going to Melissa's party tomorrow night?" Avery asked.

"I wouldn't miss it. Are you?"

"Yeah, I want to go. Her fancy dress up cocktail parties are always fun, something to look forward to."

"Right. We'll talk tomorrow night and plan some other stuff to look forward to." Deihlia smiled.

"Thanks, Pork. Thanks for telling me that stuff about your life. It's kind of a big deal, isn't it?"

"What is?"

"How much you went through to be alive. It's kind of a miracle, really."

Deihlia laughed. "Yeah, I guess it is. Like I said, I'm here for a reason. So are you. I'll see you tomorrow night, Avery," she said, and hung up the phone.

Raising the Bar, Boston, 2012

Deihlia added a new photo to her profile on the online dating site, and answered a couple more questions. She'd been emailing different women on the site for several weeks, but hadn't had more than an email here or there. She added a few more activities to her profile, like impromptu cocktail parties, and playing trumpet. She didn't want to put "copious amounts of time spent gaming" even though it was true. Well, maybe she should.

A few days later, she got an email from a woman named Jessie. Jessie had a blue-black fade faux-hawk, worked as an EMT, and lived south of Boston, in a suburb near the ocean. Deihlia wasn't too picky about geographic hurdles. She really wanted to find the right person for her. She answered Jessie's email, and they went back and forth a few times, then talked on the phone and agreed to meet up at a bar in downtown Boston a few days later.

Jessie arrived at the bar first, and she was a little nervous, so she sat down and quickly ordered a beer. The bartender popped the cap off of the bottle, setting it down in front of her next to the pint glass. "Thanks," Jessie said, looking around at the Petite Pub. It was a narrow bar tucked in an alley between two old historic brick buildings. The bar had ten stools, and enough space for three small tables against a wall. It had a tabletop jukebox down one end, and a bust of Elvis adorned with Christmas lights at the other. The mirror behind the bar looked old, with veins and dark spots that gave it a spooky quality. The bartender had a thick Boston accent, and seemed to be a fixture of the place. What a cool, weird little bar to pick for a first date, Jessie thought, looking around at the two other customers. One was a guy in a gas company uniform, huddled over his scotch like it held deep knowledge at the bottom of the rocks glass. The other was a young man in a suit who stood at the bar with one leg up on the footrest of the stool next to him. He put down his empty pilsner glass and said "One more please" before it hit the bar. The song *Good Vibrations* by Marky Mark and the Funky Bunch was playing on the jukebox. Jessie felt like she'd stepped back in time as she sipped her beer, watching the bartender wipe the glasses before placing them on the shelf.

"Jessie," she heard her name called. She looked in the mirror and didn't see anyone, but the guy in the suit had turned his head in the direction of the door. Jessie turned around, swiveling on the stool.

She looked down. A woman in a wheelchair wearing a fedora hat smiled up at her, and came over.

"Deihlia?" Jessie asked, looking down.

"Yeah, hey Jessie," Deihlia said, stopping in her chair, removing the fingerless glove off of her right hand, then extending it.

Jessie was surprised. She didn't know Deihlia needed a wheelchair. Somehow that hadn't come up in their emails or on Deihlia's profile.

"Why don't I help you get up here?" Jessie asked. She was a big butch who was used to lifting people.

"Sure," Deihlia said, reaching under her seat to pull her wallet out of the backpack underneath.

Jessie got off her stool and bent her knees, crouching down and wrapping Deihlia in her arms, then placed her on the stool next to her.

"Would you mind just pushing my chair out of the way?" Deihlia asked.

"Not at all," Jessie said, already moving it over into the corner. Both of these gestures meant something to Deihlia. She looked at Jessie, smiling mischievously.

"What are you having?" Jessie asked.

The bartender came over and repeated the question.

"I'll have a Blue Moon," Deihlia said.

"Nice choice. So tell me about this bar. Why did you pick this place, Deihlia?"

Deihlia liked the way Jessie just jumped into conversation without pausing to look at her body or formulate a way to ask her why she was in a wheelchair. She liked that Jessie knew that she needed help getting into the tall stool, but didn't make a big deal out of it or get awkward. She had earned a few fast points, but the night was still young. "Aw, I come here after work sometimes with my co-workers. It's just a funky, off the beaten path kind of place, right in the middle of everything. It's not too fancy or hipster, but it is kinda quirky," Deihlia said, picking up her glass and raising it. "Here's to something new," she said, holding the glass up to Jessie. Jessie picked up her bottle and clinked it against Deihlia's glass.

She took a sip out of her bottle then turned back to her date. Deihlia was pulling off her other fingerless black glove, and loosening her scarf. "Deihlia's an interesting name," Jessie ventured, guessing that maybe Deihlia had other names she went by too.

Deihlia laughed. "My friends call me Pork Chop," she said, her eyes glittering mysteriously.

Jessie didn't say anything, she seemed to be chewing on it, or had something on her mind. "I think I'd like to call you Dee, is that ok with you?" she asked.

Deihlia was taken aback but didn't show it, lowering her eyes to her glass of beer, focusing on the foam still floating on the top. She nodded. "Yeah, that's ok."

She paused and then looked Jessie in the eyes. "My college friends call me Dee," she said, searching in Jessie's eyes for something, but she didn't know what.

The bar grew darker as the angle of sunlight that came in the front door shrank into a sliver, then disappeared. The bartender kept his distance, giving them privacy, attending to the other customers and cleaning up behind the bar as he went. He could tell they were on a first date, and he didn't want to hang around them, invading the small bit of privacy they had. He recognized Deihlia. She'd come in a few times with a bunch of other people after work, and she was always the center of the crowd, holding court and making the others laugh. She was a nice kid, always joking. Even though she was smaller than everyone else, she seemed bigger. He never carded her, never thought to. He wondered what caused her to be in a wheelchair, then a new guest came in and sat down, ordering two shots of scotch, straight up, and his attention went back to the other side of the bar.

Deihlia and Jessie were laughing, Deihlia's hand was on Jessie's arm, gripping it lightly as she made a point, rolling her eyes and shaking her head.

Jessie laughed so hard she spit her beer all over the bar in front of them. "Oh shit, look what you made me do," she said, grabbing a napkin and wiping the bar in front of her.

"I'm sure this old bar has seen worse," Deihlia replied.

"You ladies okay over here, or do you need a bib to go with your beers?" the bartender joked, handing Jessie another napkin.

Deihlia giggled. "Don't make me fall off my stool, now. I don't think you wanna have to pick me up off the floor tonight, at least not this early in the evening."

The bartender liked funny banter, it made his night. He liked this little handicapped woman, too. "Just cause you cleaned up my bar with your last beer, the next ones are on me," he said, tossing another napkin at them. It was the most basic white square napkin. It half fluttered as he threw it towards them, sliding onto the bar like an empty envelope.

Deihlia put her hand on Jessie's thigh, sliding the napkin over in front of her. "Tell me a secret," she said, pushing the napkin closer to Jessie, smiling up at her.

They were inseparable all through the spring, summer, and fall. Deihlia was happy to have a girlfriend, someone to share herself with, someone to dote on, someone to love in the easy, warm months when Boston sparkled. It felt sweet, carrying a whole watermelon home under her hoodie one day after work when Jessie wasn't feeling well. She liked doing things for her, and knew Jessie loved fresh watermelon, so she put it under her hoodie on her lap so it wouldn't drop as she wheeled herself home. Mostly, Jessie stayed at Deihlia's apartment, rather than asking her to travel all the way to the South Shore without a ride. But something happened in the late fall. Jessie was growing restless. She wanted something different, even though she wasn't sure what. She was indecisive. Deihlia didn't like her indecisiveness. She had put a lot of energy and emotion into their relationship, so she made the decision herself, and broke it off.

Good Times

"Meet me at work. We're hanging with my work crew tonight," Deihlia texted Tom.

He showed up at 4:45 at the office where Deihlia worked, stopping at the reception desk.

"Yes, send him up," she said to the receptionist.

Tom stepped off the elevator and made his way to Deihlia's cubicle. He'd been there twice before, he knew his way. Walking along the hall with the ivory walls, he counted one, two, three doors until he was in the large open office area, where he took a right to get to her space.

A small group of people approached Deihlia's desk at the same time that Tom arrived. "You ready to go, Deihlia? We're gonna start the party at 5," her colleague Rachel said, looking curiously at Tom.

Deihlia nodded. "Yeah, me and Tom are definitely coming."

Rachel, a young attorney wearing thick black framed glasses, looked at him. "Oh, you must be Tom. Do I know you?"

Deihlia feigned a look of surprise. "You don't know Tom? He works over at the Atlantic Ave office."

"Oh, I - no. I've never met you before, Tom," Rachel said, feeling a little awkward as she extended her hand. "Nice to meet you."

"It's cool. Nice to meet you too," he replied, playing along with Deihlia's ruse.

Deihlia grinned, her eyes glittering behind her glasses.

Two hours later they were feeling no pain as they sat in a bar on the sixth floor of a building that overlooked the Boston Common. There was a lot of talk about The Wire, a crime drama TV series set in Baltimore they all watched, and banter about who did the craziest antics at the last after-work outing. Tom didn't mind being an outsider, chatting with people as the opportunity came up. He stood near Deihlia, sipping his beer. She cracked jokes and told some funny stories, but he noticed that she didn't share any of her wild escapades.

"Want another beer, Pork?" he asked.

Deihlia heard him, and ignored his question. She smiled at Rachel.

Tom realized what he'd done. "Deihlia! Want another beer?"

She looked up at him. "Sure, one more, then we're all going to Silvertones to have something to eat."

Tom grinned to himself. He had to play the part of a colleague while Deihlia kept Pork Chop hidden. Friday nights were his favorite night of the week. They always started with a bang when he was with Pork.

Saturday morning landed in Deihlia's apartment with an extended sigh. Tom turned over on the sofa. The window in her living room faced north so there was no way to tell what time it was. He reached over and slid his phone off of the side table. 10:30. He sat up, rubbing his eyes.

Pork's bedroom door swung open and she came out. "Hey. I'm gonna make some coffee, want some?"

Tom nodded. He could feel last night's bar hop in his head, a fuzzy headache right between the eyes.

Deihlia went into the kitchen, banging around as she tried to fill the pitcher with water. The sink was at eye level. Luckily, she had long arms. "All I have for breakfast is cupcakes," she said.

"Ugh. Let's just go to the diner and get something. That way you don't have to make coffee either."

Deihlia paused the water. "Works for me." They walked the five blocks to Mike's City Diner on Washington Street.

Eggs, bacon, and pancakes made for a good hangover remedy. Deihlia looked down at her plate. Mike's always served huge portions. "Morning Tom!" she giggled. "Weren't we going to have an event tonight?"

Tom gingerly speared scrambled eggs with his fork. "Are you really talking about tonight already? I haven't recovered from last night yet."

"Well, if we're gonna do it, we should post it soon."

The diner was full. Every table was taken. Deihlia and Tom had squeezed her chair into a corner spot. He sat against the wall, looking into the dining room. Everyone was talking. He could smell bacon, eggs, maple syrup, pancakes, coffee. He heard snatches of conversation, like they were coming down a tunnel. "I can't think about tonight yet, Pork. I need to eat."

"We can always go to that party that Branwen posted."

Tom chewed on his eggs, trying to focus on his own plate.

"Sometimes she has a good crowd," Deihlia continued. "Yeah, why don't we just do that."

Tom looked up at her. "That's fine with me Pork. I need to eat, and then maybe take a nap."

Deihlia picked up a slice of bacon and took a bite, holding it up in her hand. "That's cool. You can crash at my place. I was hoping we might play some Tekken today."

Shaking his head, Tom cut into his pancake. He didn't know where Pork got all her energy from. She put away a few the night before too. He vaguely recalled stumbling along beside her as they walked home from the T stop. Bits and pieces of their evening came back to him in flashes. He remembered that they'd gone to some bar with a dance floor, and Pork had gone out there when an old Wu Tang Clan song came on. They were one of her favorites. He could also swear that he saw that blue cape on her again last night while she was out on the dance floor. It was the strangest thing. He only saw it when he was pretty buzzed. And whenever he saw it, it was floating around behind her, never underneath her wheels. If he turned his head, it would disappear like it did last night. He had looked away. When he turned back to her, Pork had her hand on some woman's butt, and the next thing he saw was the woman sitting in Pork's lap, making out with her. No cape. "Did you get that woman's number last night?" he asked, furrowing his brows.

"Which one?" Deihlia asked, taking a bite of her pancake.

A young waitress with a blonde ponytail stopped at their table. "How are you guys doing over here?"

Tom looked up from his plate. "We're good. Can I get a to-go box? No way I'm gonna finish all this."

Deihlia looked at him. He was pale and had dark circles under his eyes. He still looked like he'd just unstuck his face from a long night sleeping against a leather seat. "Yeah, you need to pass out for a while longer," she said.

That night, they arrived at Branwen's at 8:30, fashionably late. It was a good crowd this time. People were talking in small clusters while music videos played on the TV screen. Katy Perry's *California Girls* blew Technicolor kisses. Tom grabbed a bottle of water and drank half of it down. Deihlia went over to a redhead with a short bob and black vintage cat-eye glasses on. A tattoo of a panther poised on a jungle tree ran down her right arm.

"I like your pussycat," Deihlia said, smiling up at her.

The redhead turned her head towards Deihlia "I bet you do."

"I'm Pork Chop. What's your name?"

"Marcie. How's your night going? Are you having a good time?"

Deihlia looked her in the eyes. "Anytime is a good time," she reached up and tipped her hat back slightly, off of her face. "Don't you think?"

"Anytime?" Marcie asked, turning to face Pork directly.

Giggling, Deihlia shook her head yes. "Anytime is a good time for something. Just depends on what it is."

Tom stood on the sidelines, watching Pork. Whatever she was saying to the redhead was making her laugh. Pork was the most confident person he'd ever met. Though she was small in stature, she was big in presence. He looked around the room, searching for a cute girl he could approach. When he first moved to Boston, he was much shyer, holding back and waiting for others to approach him, but he'd learned from Pork how to take risks, break the ice, and connect with strangers. She was a pro. Whenever she entered a room, something happened. Things got funnier, wilder, and people would end up clustered around her. She was like no one he'd ever known before.

A pretty girl with long, wavy, light brown hair streaked with pink stood in the corner with a friend. Yeah, Tom thought, she's cute. He looked over at Pork, doing her thing, her arm around the redhead's waist. He had his own style of approach now, one he'd cultivated in their adventures out. First he'd say hello, break the ice. If that went well, he'd bring her over to meet Pork. With his loose plan in place, he walked towards the corner, smiling at the brunette as he approached.

Missing Pieces, December 2012

I'd been working at a restaurant for a year, my shifts adding up to about 25 hours a week. It was a lot on top of my full time job consulting, but I really liked being at the restaurant. I liked being part of the team, and flirting with the kitchen staff. It meant that I was tired a lot, and had very little time for a social life, especially with all the family stuff that went on that year.

Even when I'm tired, I dream, but sometime around November, my dreams dried up. I can have a week or two here or there where I don't dream much, or all I get is fragments of my day, regurgitated, but those times are rare.

It had been several weeks, and my nights were a grey, unpopulated canvas. Unexplored. I'd wake up and wonder where my dreams went, or worse, where I had gone in my sleep. Somewhere I couldn't remember, off gallivanting in the cosmos without a passport. I still did my meditations. They helped me stay connected to my higher self, to clear my mind of unnecessary clutter and stay centered. One night I was laying on my bed, resting in the lovely, clear energy present after my meditation. My eyes were closed. Figures began to appear around me - my aunt, my uncle, my grandmother. People who had passed on, some I recognized and some I didn't. They encircled me, not in a claustrophobic way, but gently, just standing there. I was very relaxed, floating in a dream-like state, but their presence made me take notice. Did I just happen upon an ancestral gathering, crashing the party in another realm that I hadn't tried to get to? Or did they come to me for a reason? It made me worry. Was something happening, or were they just providing support for the rough year I was going through with all the family stuff?

The days progressed towards Thanksgiving, then into December. I started growing uneasy, just at the edge of my consciousness. My dreams were gone, missing. I didn't feel right, waking up without them to inform me, guide and inspire me. They were such an integral part of my experience. I prayed every night before I went to bed: "Dreams - come back." I put mugwort oil, associated with the moon and dreams, on my forehead and the back of my neck, but night after night the screen was dark.

Deihlia's birthday came up fast, too. She'd celebrated turning twenty nine with a bunch of her friends all weekend long. By the time I saw her, she was mellow and partied out.

"Let's just get pizza and stuff and hang out at my place, but please don't say anything about the mess in my apartment," she said.

"Whatever you want," I replied, calling and ordering ahead so that it would be delivered when I arrived. We sat at her table like we had so many times, catching up and eating. Her apartment was cluttered with detritus from months of parties - empty beer bottles in cases, snacks in containers, shoes, stuff in boxes all over the place. I pretended not to notice and didn't say anything. I was just glad to see her. "How about a tarot reading?" I asked.

"Yeah, I'd like one for my birthday!" I pulled out the deck I use when I read for others - the original Rider Waite deck. I liked to use it for readings because the images on the cards made it easy for others to enter the story and connect it to their own life. Deihlia shuffled the cards and pulled them out one at a time, thoughtfully selecting each one from the row spread face down on the table. There were a lot of pentacles, and The World card sat prominently over the entire spread, Venus's arms outstretched with a wand in each hand as she danced in the center of a wreath. This card signified completion, success, the end of one cycle and the beginning of another, Saturn Return. We looked at the cards together, and she made connections to what was going on in her own life. Together, we read them as being very positive. I knew she wanted a girlfriend, a relationship, something awesome. We didn't see that in the cards, and it remained unspoken, a kind of ghost at the table, or a ghost wish.

"I read this as pretty positive, Auntie," she said, scanning the cards one last time.

I looked at the World card one more time, and glanced over at Deihlia. She was twenty-nine. She'd been my superhero for so long that I sometimes forgot everything she'd gone through to get here. She was warm, funny, insightful, and compassionate. While she was discerning about people, she was also incredibly accepting and kind to most everyone - qualities she came in with. She knew how to have fun, connect with people on a personal and vulnerable level, and not take herself so seriously. She was also really comfortable with herself. She was confident and unafraid of being different. I wanted to be more like her, but she was way ahead of me. Her cape hung over the back of her chair, and no matter how far it was dragged along the streets of Boston, it remained untattered and clean. Like her, it had unusual staying power. I remembered the texts we'd sent just a few weeks before, in which she said: "We've come a long way, but it was worth it." Our relationship was the main foundation in my life. I became who I am by loving and knowing her.

"Happy birthday, Deihl," I said. "I'm so proud of you. You've accomplished just about everything you set out to do."

She smiled. "Almost everything. I'm feeling pretty good about my life."

Christmas Eve, 2012

I pulled my car up to the curb in front of Deihlia's apartment. The street was quiet. It was Christmas Eve and people were gone. Metered spots sat empty, the flower market was closed, a slight chill wind turned a piece of trash in a cinematic arc and twist before landing on the sidewalk against a building. I turned on the seat warmers in my car so she'd be comfortable for the ride. She wheeled out of the glass doorway with a bag of Christmas gifts on her lap.

"Hey, Auntie," she said. I took the bag and placed it in the back seat, then held on to her chair so she could launch herself out of it into the passenger seat, pulling her legs in after her. Then I took the wheels off and placed each one in the trunk of my car, followed by the aluminum frame, like I do every time I pick her up for a holiday, a trek, funerals, or just for fun, whatever. It was good having her so close by, a 12 minute drive door to door I made frequently.

Eminem's *Going Through Changes* from the *Recovery* album was playing. "How are you, Bug?" I asked, turning down the music.

"Doing ok, practicing my trumpet a lot," she said. "How about you?"

There wasn't a lot of traffic, it was late afternoon, we were going to see *The Hobbit* before heading to Donna's for the Christmas Eve party she held each year. She always had a full house with lots of food, kids running around, music on too loud, cats jumping on the counters, and a tree loaded with gifts for the kids. But we wanted to see *The Hobbit* first and ease into the Christmas festivities.

It was nearing dusk, the red tail lights of cars stood out against the fading afternoon light. Deihlia sat in the seat next to me, wearing multiple layers of clothing and a scarf. It was winter, we were both always cold. We started to get into one of our conversations about life, about choices, about trying to take care of ourselves in a dysfunctional world. What led us down that path was sharing our concern about someone else. Traffic moved easily, almost lazily along Columbus Ave. The light turned green and I floated through it.

"I thank God I had you, Auntie," she said, half turning her face towards me, leaning over casually. "You showed me that life is supposed to be fun."

"I did?" I asked, incredulous, feeling anything but fun.

"Oh yeah," she nodded, like it was no big deal, continuing with her train of thought while I sat stunned in the driver's seat, taking it in. She was the most fun and adventurous person I'd ever known.

Her statement settled in me, a spontaneous gift.

Perhaps it seemed like the comment went unnoticed, because the conversation went along its trajectory, traffic light by traffic light, as we wound our way through the neighborhoods. Perhaps it seemed like just another moment in one of our fortifying talks, just another piece of kindling we tossed into the fire to keep our bones warm through another dark night. But it wasn't. I took her words in and let them resonate. They meant something coming from her. My heart burst and I felt suddenly whole. Her words put the nesting dolls of my many selves back together, one inside the other, as if they'd lived apart for years. "Thank you, Deihl. That means a lot coming from you. I love you so much."

We'd been through a lot that year - Pop's cancer diagnosis and then his death, my own father's strokes shortly afterwards, his decline and move to a nursing home, trying to help my mother recover afterwards, and all of the emotions that came with all of those things. I was personally wrung out from all of it, and Christmas felt like another horn calling from the distance, trumpeting the weary soldiers back to the battlefield after not enough sleep. Going with Deihlia made it bearable. What she said to me changed my frequency deeply. I hadn't known I needed it, but there it was, returning some essential part of me back into the fold. Deihlia was emotionally generous, an understated gift.

I parked the car on the street as we stopped to pick up a friend. The afternoon dark as midnight, the early dusk still a surprise. A single orange candle glowed in each window of a neighboring house, a big red bow graced the front door. A few leaves clung to mostly bare trees, fluttering in the breeze. The night felt rich and opened up, a little bit of spring hinted at in the lush winter darkness.

By the Station

Deihlia was waiting outside of the Davis Square T stop. It was six o'clock on a January night. People blew through the doors of the station like bees let out of a jar. Where is Johnnie? She wondered. They'd become friends at a concert, while waiting in line. She'd gotten him and his friend front row seats in the handicapped section. Johnnie was never late. She pulled her phone out of her jacket pocket, looking at the time. No text. She'd wait another five minutes before she gave up on him.

"Pork," she heard him say behind her.

Deihlia turned her chair around. "Hey, I was just about to give up on you!" Johnnie's face was pale under his dark brown hair and thick glasses. His blue pea coat didn't look warm enough for the night they were having.

Johnnie looked her in the eyes. "Sorry I'm late. Almost didn't make it."

He didn't look like himself, Deihlia thought. "Are you ok?"

Johnnie shrugged and looked down at the pavement. There was no use trying to pretend. "I just found out an old friend of mine died in a car accident yesterday."

Deihlia's smile fell. "I'm so sorry. It feels so wrong when you lose someone."

Johnnie nodded.

"Do you want to talk about it?"

Johnnie looked over at Pork Chop. Even though he didn't usually notice her wheelchair, he was aware of it. He knew that Deihlia had problems of her own that she never talked about. If he could talk to anyone about how he felt, it was her. "Yeah, ok." People navigated around them going into and coming out of the subway station. He began to walk slowly past the entrance, where light fell on them in large rectangles. Deihlia turned the wheels of her chair gently to keep pace with her friend.

"We were best friends growing up. We spent so much time together after school, we'd go into town together all the time. Played video games constantly. We used to sneak away from our parents to eat junk food because they were so strict. He used to call it 'eating chili fries until we popped!' " He smiled briefly.

"It's really hard to lose an old friend like that. They're such a huge part of you."

271

Johnnie nodded, and continued. "He was kind of like the brother I never had. We were the same age and everything, but we'd known each other since we were in preschool."

They made their way along Elm Street, passing the small shops and restaurants. They approached The Alley Tavern, their destination. "We don't have to go in if you'd rather do something else, or go home, or whatever," Deihlia said.

Johnnie stopped and lifted his head. He looked at the street stretching ahead of them, then at the black painted door to the restaurant. He didn't know what he wanted. "Let's go in, Pork."

He held the door open for her and they went in. The Tavern was darkly lit, with wooden booths along the wall that had small amber-shade table lamps, giving each table a warm glow. They sat at a table in the middle of the room. Johnnie was still a little bit far away as they opened their menus. Deihlia noticed that they had chili fries on the menu - an unusual coincidence. She peered over her menu at Johnnie to see if it registered with him. He was still scanning it. Then he looked up at her sharply. "They have chili fries," he said.

Deihlia nodded and smiled. "Let's order some!"

Johnnie smiled a little. It seemed perfect to eat chili fries in honor of his friend's passing. "Ok."

Twenty minutes later the waitress appeared at their table with a large plate of French fries, dripping with chili and cheddar cheese. "Thank you," Deihlia said.

Johnnie took a sip of beer. He did feel a little better sitting in the dark dining room with Pork, talking about Mike. He looked at the mound of fries.

"You should have the first one," Deihlia said.

Johnnie reached over and pulled a long, crispy fry off of the plate. Melted cheese stretched in a gooey string. "This one's for you, Mike," he said, then took a bite.

Deihlia smiled at him, reaching over to get one for herself. "To Mike," she said. Tables started to fill up around them.

"These are pretty good," Johnnie replied, taking another.

They continued to eat their way through a third of the plate as Johnnie regaled Deihlia with stories of how he and Mike would sneak out of the house through his basement window. "We had this one neighbor on my street who was super mean. We had to cut through his yard to get away and we were always afraid he was going to catch us and rat us out."

"I had a neighbor like that too."

Johnnie finished his beer. The waitress picked up the bottle. "I'll have another one," he said.

The waitress walked away. "You've gotta eat all these fries for Mike's sake," Deihlia said.

Johnnie laughed, shaking his head no.

"Go on, have some more," she said, pushing the plate in his direction.

I can do it for Mike, he thought. *He's gone now. I'll never share chili fries with him again.* He pulled two more fries from the pile and ate them one at a time.

Deihlia sipped her beer.

Johnnie took several more fries and bit off the ends all at once, then made his way along them until he finished. A second beer bottle was dropped in front of him. He took a long swig.

"Have some more!" Deihlia encouraged.

Johnnie was starting to get into the spirit of their evening, and continued to eat fry after fry, sipping his beer between every few bites.

"I lost a few friends myself," Deihlia said. "Some when I was a kid, and a high school friend a couple years ago."

Johnnie listened, not saying anything.

"Plus my Dad. He died when I was 10."

Johnnie knew she'd be able to relate, but he didn't know why. Losing your Dad as a kid is a terrible blow. He tried to imagine what it would've been like to lose his Dad when he was ten. His heart dropped. "Man, I'm sorry Pork. That's rough."

"I'm sorry about Mike, Johnnie. Death is just a part of life, but it hurts like hell when we lose someone."

Johnnie's stomach felt painfully full. He put his beer bottle down on the table. The waitress saw him and came over. Suddenly his stomach turned and he spit up, vomiting on the waitress's shoe and the floor around her.

"Oh dear, are you alright? Let me get something to clean this up." She bent down and wiped off her shoe, then walked away, careful not to step in it.

"Oh my god!" Johnnie sputtered, his face red.

"It's ok, they'll get it cleaned up. Don't worry." Deihlia said.

273

Johnnie took his napkin and wiped his face. The waitress returned with a mop and bucket. Other diners looked on, grimacing. The waitress cleaned it up quickly. "Thank you. We're sorry. We should probably get the check when you have a chance," Deihlia said to her.

Johnnie pulled his wallet out of his jacket pocket and took out two twenty dollar bills. The waitress returned and gave the check to Deihlia. She put it down on the table and reached for her wallet. He threw his money down on top of it. "Let's get out of here," he said.

Deihlia added more cash to the pile on the table and they went towards the door. Johnnie was mortified. He'd never done anything like that in his life. He and Deihlia opened the door and went out, the cold fresh air reviving them as they began to move back along Elm Street.

"I think you popped!" Deihlia said, looking up at him, trying to ease his embarrassment.

Suddenly, the waitress ran up behind them with a doggie bag. "You forgot your fries!" She said. Johnnie hung his head. Deihlia reached up and took the bag. "Thank you!" she said.

Johnnie started to laugh, he couldn't help it. Then tears filled his eyes. How could he be laughing and crying at the same time?

They continued to go towards the subway station, giggling their way along the sidewalk. "I've never been so embarrassed in my life," Johnnie said.

"I have," Deihlia nodded, "many times!"

The thought of Pork Chop spewing on someone's shoes made him laugh and cry even harder. As they stood outside the subway station getting ready to say goodbye, Johnnie started to feel sadness wash over him again. Deihlia could see it happening. She reached her arms out, indicating that she was going to hug him. They didn't usually hug goodbye, but he needed it tonight. He bent over, putting his arms around her shoulders.

"Just go with the flow and take care of yourself. It hurts the most now, but it'll get a little easier with time." Deihlia said into his jacket as he stood up. "And Johnnie - I'm really sorry about Mike."

He nodded. He didn't want to say goodbye, but he couldn't really keep it together. "I felt like Mike was with us tonight," he said. He'd felt it in the restaurant while he was stuffing himself and Pork was laughing.

Deihlia shrugged. "Who knows, maybe he was."

"Night, Pork," Johnnie said and turned around. Deihlia watched him disappear down the street, then went into the station. She pressed the elevator button, waiting for it to come up from below. *Death is always nearby,* she thought. The bell rang and the elevator groaned, coming to a stop. The silver doors slid sideways, disappearing into the wall, and she went in.

Birthday Gifts, January 2013

The restaurant was empty. It was the last NFL game of the season before the Super Bowl. No one was out that evening except for me and my friends, celebrating my birthday. The restaurant, Lucky's, was situated in the basement of an old brick building on Congress Street. It had been an Irish mob hangout for decades. There was supposed to be a live band playing Sinatra music that night, but the set was cancelled due to the game. We were squished into a booth not far from the door.

It was a mix of some of my oldest and newer friends, a small intimate group. We ordered dinner and drinks. Our gallows humor started early. We were the only customers in the entire place. Even the bartender and wait staff stood watching the game on TV. We could be as loud as we wanted.

The door opened and a gust of cold air and leaves blew in. We all shuddered, looking at the door. A tall guy in a black coat put his hand up at us, as if to say: "Hold on." We turned back to our conversation. Another group of people came towards us.

"Hey, Auntie!" Deihlia said.

"Deihl! What are you doing here?" I asked, confused. I didn't recall telling her about my birthday dinner. I was celebrating with her and some other friends the following weekend.

"We're celebrating John's birthday. We're over at PAX East, at the Convention Center."

"Wow. Ok. Happy to see you!"

"Hi, everyone," she said, nodding to each of my guests. "Angelina - I'm really happy to see you."

"Hey, Dee," Angelina said.

Deihlia's friends slid into the orange 1970's-era booth behind us. The waitress came over and handed them menus.

"It's weird that Dee and her friends showed up here," Angelina said, looking at me. She and Deihlia had a little history from when Angelina dated Sean a couple years back. Deihlia adored her, and had a huge heart-on-her-sleeve crush on her. She hit on Angelina every time she saw her. Angelina was beautiful, with big blue eyes, a bright white smile, and chestnut hair that fell in waves. She was sweet, kind, and baked cakes that people begged for.

"I know, it is," I replied.

Our dinners were delivered and we began to eat.

276

"What's good here, Auntie?" Deihlia yelled from the booth behind us. Each of us told her what we ordered, and she and her friends placed theirs.

A few minutes later, Deihlia appeared at the end of the table. "Excuse me, can I get in there?" she asked my friend Sheila. Sheila got up and Deihlia got into the booth, sliding over next to Angelina. When seated next to her, Deihlia only came up to Angelina's shoulder, but it didn't stop her from flirting. Angelina was squashed up against the wall with Deihlia leaning hard against her.

"Pork! Your beer is here," Tom shouted from the booth behind us.

"Pork? Who's Pork?" My friend Mel, an Irish butch, asked. Her blue eyes crinkled and glittered as she leaned back against the booth, adjusting her bow tie, and asked the question to the table. Deihlia took her eyes away from Angelina for a second and glanced at Mel. "That's me."

"You know her as Deihlia, but her other name is Pork Chop," I said to clarify.

Mel laughed. "Love it!"

Deihlia began to hit on Angelina, putting her hand on Angelina's thigh under the table. Angelina pushed it away.

"Dee, stop," Angelina said.

Deihlia spoke low so only Angelina could hear, her face turned towards her, grinning. My friends watched, trying not to look too surprised, but unable to keep their eyes off of the scene. I was aware of Deihlia's friends sitting behind us, that Deihlia was Pork Chop to them, and Pork Chop was a player. This went on for twenty minutes. My friends and I had snippets of conversation around Deihlia's heavy flirting.

The waitress began to deliver food to the table behind us. "I better get back to my friends," Deihlia said. Sheila stood up to let her out of the booth. "By the way, happy birthday Auntie."

"Thanks, Deihl," I said. I was secretly pleased that I got to witness Pork Chop in action, and that Deihlia didn't think twice about tempering her antics in front of me and my friends. She seemed to be having a great time. She and her friends ate quickly, wanting to get back to the convention.

"Bye now," they said as they walked out. "Bye, Auntie. I'll see you next weekend. Angelina, it's always good to see you," Deihlia said as she went to the door.

I watched them leave. I still found it very curious that Deihlia ended up in the same restaurant as us, there were plenty of other restaurants and pubs nearby.

The following weekend, Chelsea came down for my next birthday event. It was a milestone birthday for me, so I was celebrating it a few ways. We were going clubbing at the Gilded Cage, and Deihlia, Angelina and some others were coming with us. "Whatever you want to do, Auntie," Chelsea had said.

On Saturday afternoon, Deihlia texted me. "I'm not feeling great. I think I'm gonna skip the Gilded Cage."

"Okay, Bug. Are you sick? What is it?"

"Just not feeling myself. Not up for a club."

I told Chelsea. She texted Deihlia and told her to come to my neighborhood so we could have dinner together. It was a plan. We met her at the subway stop down the street from my apartment and walked together the five blocks to a local restaurant.

It was a rare occasion for me to have the two of them alone together, just the three of us. Very rare. Usually there were other family members around, or friends. I couldn't remember the last time I'd been alone with "my kids." It meant a lot. Being their aunt was the most gratifying part of my life. Once Deihlia and Chelsea were born, I decided not to have children of my own. With all that the girls were dealing with - Deihlia's medical precariousness, the loss of their dad, the financial stress of being in a single parent household - I felt that devoting my energy towards them was the best thing that I could do. If I'd had children of my own, it would have taken me away from them. I also couldn't imagine any child of my own being more perfect for me than Deihlia and Chelsea.

Sometimes it was hard because my sister and I didn't see eye to eye on some things. We were in sync about a lot when it came to the girls, but there were times when she didn't want my opinion and didn't tell me about the decisions she'd made and things she'd done until they were finished. She didn't have to. I was just her sister, after all, but since I was the one who was there, those decisions inevitably impacted me as well. It was a precarious position, being an aunt and not a parent, but being involved like a parent. Deihlia would call me when she was frustrated with what she felt were injustices taking place in the household. "Auntie, can you weigh in here?" She'd ask. I tried to be diplomatic and consider everyone's point of view, but what usually happened is that I ended up making promises to do something or buy something to help keep things even. I was happy to do what I could. It was an honor to be the one that was called; the one that could help balance the scales.

I felt that love swelling up in me as we walked together, and felt it coming back at me, surrounding me, simply by virtue of them being there, making the effort to spend time with me for my birthday. We went into the restaurant, a casual neighborhood place a few blocks from my house, and sat down. As we ate, I brought up our evening at Lucky's the weekend before. "Did I tell you that I was going there?" I asked.

Deihlia shook her head no, still wearing her knit hat, in multiple layers of jackets and fleece, her scarf tied tight around her neck. "I didn't know you were gonna be there, Auntie. Jo had picked that place for John's birthday dinner. I was surprised to see you there, too."

"Kind of crazy, right?" I said, marveling again at the workings of the universe.

She and Chelsea made a lot of jokes as usual. Our bawdy humor was the best kind of dinner conversation. When the bill arrived, Chelsea reached over and grabbed Deihlia's wallet off of the table and pulled out her bank card. "You and I are buying Auntie a birthday dinner," she said.

I snapped a picture of Chelsea holding up the card in mock surprise as Deihlia got a squirrely grin on her face, caught. "All right," she said, grinning. I felt like the Queen sitting there, having the two of them all to myself.

We left the restaurant, crossing the street. Chelsea and I walked Deihlia to the bus stop, waiting in the cold darkness under the streetlamp with her until a bus came along. "You guys don't have to wait with me, I'll be fine." She said.

"We're waiting with you, just shut up." Chelsea replied, her cigarette tip glowing orange.

Winter wind blew down the street, through the leafless trees. Trash sputtered in spots, half stuck to the pavement. The three of us waited, huddled in our winter coats, our hands jammed in our pockets, our shoulders curled against the cold into a hunch. Chelsea held her cigarette, and we all stood around quietly, the way family does sometimes when everything is clear, and nothing more needs to be said.

Headlights with a bar of text overhead appeared down the street, heading in our direction. "Thanks for coming out, Deihl," I said. "Love you." And I bent down to hug her. She hugged me back and said "Happy Birthday, Auntie." The bus pulled up to the curb and started to lower the back door handicap ramp down with a mechanical grind and a *huffff* as the bus adjusted and lowered to reach the curb. "Bye Chels," she said.

"Love you," Chelsea replied.

Deihlia rolled over to the ramp and we kept watching her. She waved at us, a wave of dismissal - go on, get out of here, stop looking at me. But we stood there, wanting to make sure she got on. As the ramp lifted, Deihlia turned to face us and smiled. Her cape spilled onto the ramp around her wheels; her pool of blue. Time seemed to stop for a few seconds as she sat on the rising ramp, framed in the light of the bus door, grinning back at us. We didn't turn around and walk back to my apartment until the bus wheezed and pulled away from the curb.

"I worry about her," Chelsea said, watching as the bus turned the corner and zoomed on to the next stop. As we began to walk, something fluttered up behind us like a sail, snapping against our backs and ruffling our hair. Out of the corner of my eye I saw Chelsea's purple cape being tossed about by the wind, and my own pink one bobbing along with it.

Wolf Moon

Bling-Bling. Bling-bling. Deihlia heard her phone going off inside the bag under her chair. She was at work, back at the office near Downtown Crossing, where she'd returned after becoming the training coordinator. She wasn't going to answer texts while she was at her desk. On her lunch break, she went outside and sat on the sidewalk, checking her phone in the winter air, her fingers cold. She had thirty-three texts. She usually got about 10 every morning, and several more in the afternoon, but thirty-three was a lot.

There was a text from Michael, asking if she was free to talk. Two texts from Tom. A text from Melissa. Three texts from Sean. One from Eric. Three from Jessie. Two from Hana. One from Auntie. Two from Chelsea. One from Charlie, her trumpet teacher. One from her Mom. A bunch more from the Boston Social Nerds group members. She scrolled through them to see if any were an immediate priority. Only the text from Avery, saying "I really need your opinion right now" seemed urgent.

"What's going on?" Deihlia asked over the phone.

"Ugh. Thanks for calling me back. I'm worried about Melissa. We kind of had a fight last week and I said something pretty hurtful in the moment. I apologized a dozen times but she still hasn't responded at all. It's not like her. You know how we can argue."

Deihlia thought for a moment. Avery and Melissa were like sisters, including the squabbles and arguments and sharing clothes. Melissa was easygoing, though, and usually let things go once they were finished arguing. Deihlia had seen it in action a few times. "I haven't heard from Melissa in a while, but you're right, it's not like her. Do you think she lost her phone, or what?" People walked by her, hurrying to get where they were going and back into somewhere warm.

"I don't know. I haven't seen her on social media at all either, which is weird."

"Maybe she's sick? Have you gone to her apartment to check on her? She lives in that tiny studio, if she's sick no one would even know."

"I guess I could do that. Not sure how I'd get into the building, but maybe if I knock on a neighbor's door they'll let me into the hall so I can knock on her door."

"It's worth a try. Now you've got me worried about her."

"Not like her."

"Let me know what you find out. I'll try to call her too and see if I can reach her." After she hung up with Avery, she called Melissa and got her voicemail. She was concerned. She looked at her phone - lunch hour was running out. She went down the street to try to find some lunch, wheeling along in the crowd. Downtown Boston was bustling at lunch hour, lines of people popped out of café doors and went down the block. Men and women in business clothes, urban youth, shoppers, and tourists walked briskly along the brick sidewalks. Old churches that still had full crypts from the 1600s lining the cellar sat politely between tall new buildings, trying to retain their historic face amongst a changing landscape.

Deihlia got into line at the sandwich shop. Her phone began to ring. She reached into her pocket and pulled it out.

"Michael, how are you man?"

"Hey, thanks for all the trumpet messages on my voicemail," he said.

Deihlia laughed. "I'll be leaving you more."

"Y'know, I'm doing okay, just having a rough one. My girlfriend is so mean and miserable, it's out of control."

"You can't put up with that shit. Get her some help or get her out. That's not cool." She felt very protective of Michael. They'd been really close all through college, and afterwards, when she'd lived with him and his family for several months. He was like a brother to her. The sandwich line moved a little, so Deihlia pushed forward.

"But how do I get her help if she doesn't think she needs help?"

"Tell her it's too much for you to handle and she needs professional help or she needs to make some choices about her life."

Michael thought for a moment. "Good idea, Deihlia. The truth is, I can't handle it. Nothing I can do."

"Take care of yourself. Let me know how it goes."

Deihlia looked up at the sky. What the heck was going on? Was it a full moon? Her Auntie always said that things intensified at the full moon. Maybe she was right. She liked to stay in touch with all of her friends: her great friends from college, her new nerd friends, even her friends from high school and the hood, like Julia and LP. She liked to feel connected to them, to know what was going on in their lives. Especially now.

It was winter. She wasn't feeling right. She didn't feel sick necessarily, but she didn't feel herself, either. She didn't want to go to the hospital and go through a series of tests. Being in the hospital caused severe anxiety and post-traumatic stress. Her heart beat wildly anytime she thought of going in.

"You coming out tonight?" Sean texted.

Deihlia was bummed for a moment. "No. Not feeling great. Could you come over with one of the dogs?" Sean had a dog training and day/night care business and always had dogs with him. Deihlia was particularly fond of Westie, a white West Highland Terrier.

"Oh. Yeah, sure. Tomorrow night."

Being around dogs always made her feel better. She wished she knew what the problem was so she could solve it. She felt sad, like she was losing something she couldn't grasp. She was just trying to hold on until something changed, hopefully for the better.

That evening, as she lay on the sofa in her apartment playing a video game, Avery texted her. "Melissa was in the hospital with a bad bout of pneumonia! She's home now. Heading over to bring her some soup."

"Wow, glad you found her. Give her some soup for me," Deihlia texted back. *Things feel kind of weird right now*, she thought to herself, then turned her attention to her game.

The Sprint, February 2013

It was a Friday morning, and Deihlia wasn't feeling well. She called me, and I went back and forth to her apartment bringing her medication, then brought her to the emergency room at Suffolk Universal around 10:30. She was in a lot of pain. She thought it was an intestinal blockage, and so did the emergency room doctor, Dr. Fine. He was young, calm, and confident, perhaps in his mid-thirties, with dark hair and chiseled good looks. There were three other patients in the emergency room that day with blockages. After giving her something for the pain, Dr. Fine put a plan into action. It was the same emergency room we'd been in when we came in for her kidney stone, antiseptic and familiar. I sat with her as she went in and out of consciousness, moaning in pain. I thought we were in the right place for her to get the right care, we'd been going to Suffolk Universal since the day she was born. I called my sister to let her know that I'd brought Deihlia into the hospital, and that I was there with her. I called Chelsea and Nana to let them know, too.

The room was light blue and grey, the curtain was pulled closed at my back. It was private, quiet, and still. I sat in that chair for twelve hours, watching Deihlia sleep and occasionally wake in a fit of pain. I spoke to the other doctor who came in to check on her. I didn't know what to do for Deihlia in that moment except pray that the doctors knew what they were doing and that what they'd done would work. I was tense and jagged. My phone was running out of power, I was tired, and Deihlia was asleep. It was late, almost eleven. I needed to go home.

"I think I'm going to go home now, Bug," I said quietly. "Is that ok?"

Deihlia opened her eyes, groggy and out of it. "What's going on?"

"The doctor is going to move you up to the eighth floor. He thinks you should be feeling better. That the tube should be relieving pressure soon."

"I don't want them to open me up."

"I know. You told them that when we came in. Dr. Fine doesn't think they have to do that."

"Ok, Auntie."

"Your mom will be in tomorrow morning, and I'll be back in the afternoon, okay?"

284

"Okay."

I stood next to her bed and touched her arm. "I love you."

"Love you too," she said as I started to walk away. I turned around to look at her and she lifted her hand off the bed, waving to me. I opened the door and walked out, leaving her there like I'd left her there countless other times.

It was late on a cold February night. After sitting in the small room all day, the air outside was refreshing, the darkness a relief. Exiting the hospital, I walked around the corner to the parking garage. I stopped to pick up my keys, and took the elevator up to the third floor. Then I made my way along the row of cars in the chilled concrete building. Winter wind blew in over the half-walls, biting my face. I got into my car and put the key in the ignition. The engine hiccupped then gasped as it started. I was worried about Deihlia but felt that she was in the right place to get the right care. My breath made small clouds as I shivered, waiting for the car to warm up.

As I reached down for the gear shift, I felt something flutter next to me. I turned my head to look back, but my car was empty. An umbrella was lying on the back seat. It couldn't be a bug in the dead of winter. My arm began to prickle and a voice appeared, crystal clear in my right ear. "You were always better for her than I was," Linc said, as if he were sitting beside me in the passenger seat. The girl's Dad came in every once in a while to say something when I least expected it. We never really liked each other when he was alive, so I didn't really want to talk to him when he was dead, either. What did he want? Was this his way of saying thank you? I was tired and wired. Lifting my hand, I shooed him away and backed out of the parking spot. Linc. Weird.

My sister's call at five a.m. rang like a fire alarm and made my heart beat wildly. The hospital had called her. "What?" I said, sitting up, turning on my light, wide awake.

"They don't think she's going to make it!" She said, her voice rising into hysteria.

"I'll go in now. Call Mom and have her come in with you. I'll meet you there, ok?" I hung up and got dressed, pulling on the clothes I'd taken off a few hours before. I splashed my face with water. It felt like the middle of the night. My hair was a mess. I went back to my bedroom to put on some socks and do a quick blessing ritual that I did every morning before I left the house.

I began to say the prayer, but I just started crying. "No, not Deihlia, no!" I said, sobbing, my room a blur. "Not Deihlia, please," I begged, but everything felt wrong, and real, and true.

I took the first subway train in at 5:45 a.m. The station was empty, I was the only person waiting on the platform. The inky blue morning sped by the windows. When I switched trains at Downtown Crossing, I looked across the tracks at the outgoing side. A wheelchair sat empty and abandoned on the other platform. My heart sank, and I began to cry.

I went up to the eighth floor. Dr. Fine came out and told me that they'd had to open up her up, and when they did, they discovered that things were in very bad shape. Her kidneys were failing. She was on every form of life support while they tried to do what they could. I sat down, dumbfounded. The lights in the hall weren't on yet. I sat in a single chair against the wall. The waiting room behind me was dark and full of people sleeping on chairs under their winter coats. Donna and Nana arrived, then later, Chelsea. The doctor's prognosis went up and down. The lights brightened, nurses changed shifts, the hospital started to wake up. We were moved into a private conference room. Windowless, bland, and corporate. We sat in a circle, crying. How could this be real? Deihlia had escaped death so many times.

I was worried about her. Where was she? Had she already left her body? I closed my eyes, trying to connect with her, going into the stillness of my meditation point. "How are you, Bug?" I asked mentally. I heard her voice in my head. Plaintive, sad. "I want you to let me go," she said. I cried, wiping my tears on my sleeve. "I want you to let me go. Please let me go."

I looked up at my sister, who sat across from me on a metal chair. "Deihlia said she wants us to let her go," I told her quietly. She looked at me then left the room. She returned a few minutes later, shaking her head, her face deep red from crying. "Yeah, I think you're right."

The day went on. Doctor Fine told us that there was nothing more they could do. "Even if she did survive this, I don't know how she would recover. I don't think she could. I'm afraid she isn't going to make it."

They let us go into the room with her. A thin white blanket covered her swollen body. I grasped her hand. Smudges of blood marked the floor. She was unconscious, her half-open eyes lubricated

286

under the tape that covered them. "I love you so much," I said. Each of us said it, tears streaming down our faces. We shook our heads. It was so hard to believe. We each told her what she meant to us. How amazing she was, how much a part of us she was. How she helped to make us who we were. What a miracle her life was; her incredibleness. Everything looked blurry, I was crying so hard. The rhythmic whoosh of the machine that kept her lungs going was mechanical and unreal. We hated seeing her like that. Deihlia was the one who was always cracking jokes, easing the tension, elevating the absurd, the center of the circle.

It hurt to know she was there but not there. Somewhere in-between. I tried not to focus on the condition of her face and arms, while also registering it. I tried to be present for her as best I could, loving her strong and hard like I'd done so many times before. She could've been gone already and watching us from outside of her body, or from inside, or from some other vantage point that I knew nothing about.

After a while, we went back into the conference room. Sean, then Julia arrived. LP was on his way, driving from New York City. They went in to see her together. LP arrived and I went in with him. It wasn't fair to have him go in by himself. It was traumatic, seeing Deihlia like that. In a hospital, things are very real - the starkness of the rooms, the technology that works but is foreign to visitors, the flimsiness of the curtains, the staff who move around quietly in the background. Even if you want to deny something is happening, you can't. It's not anything like real life; there are no pretty things to delude you. Hospitals may as well be decorated in black and white.

Hours later, Sean said his last goodbye and left. Shortly after he walked out, his mother Elsa walked in. "Sean didn't want me to come in with him, he wanted to do this alone, but I wanted to be here. I wanted to be with Deihlia myself. I hope it's ok," she said. We were all still in shock, our outer selves unzipped and dropped on the floor like clothing we'd worn through a terrible storm. It felt like only our inner selves were present - love, sorrow, and tears. Elsa went in with Donna to say goodbye.

A little while later Doctor Fine came in and sat down with us, joining our circle in the one empty chair by the door. He looked around at us. "Well, things have progressed to that point. The point I was talking to you about earlier. This is that time. I have to ask you to

287

agree that we can take her off of the life support machines. When we do, there isn't any chance that she is going to survive. She's being kept alive by several different things at this point, because everything stopped working." He looked at us gently, sitting calmly amongst us. We turned to each other - Donna, me, Nana, and Chelsea - looking in each other's eyes, searching. We didn't want to say yes, we didn't want her life to end. We wanted Deihlia here with us, like she had been. We held our gazes and agreed silently, nodding our heads at the doctor while our hearts said *no, no, no.*

"Ok," he said, getting up slowly, looking at each of us, one by one. "I need to do a couple of things, but then I'll come and get you, if you want to be in the room with her when we do this."

There was no way to stop the tears. There was no reason to try, and every reason to let them go. There was nothing to say. Our circle of chairs was complete but for the one vacant chair, so we sat and cried some more. Dr. Fine opened the door a little while later. "You can come in now, if you'd like," he said, waiting for us.

Once again, we looked at each other - Donna, me, Nana, and Chelsea. Each of us was wrung out, emptied, and completely full of sorrow. We'd been through so much in the last twenty hours. I didn't know if we could go through anymore, if we had any strength left. But I thought of Deihlia in that room alone. If the machines were turning off and she was stepping out of her mortal suit, I was going to be there. Little star. I looked at my sister. "I'm going in," I said, standing up to follow the doctor. Everyone else stood up too, and we walked single file to her room, silent and somber, holding on to nothing but ourselves.

Donna stood near her feet with Nana and Elsa. Chelsea and I stood opposite each other on either side of Deihlia. As we stood there, I saw a glimmer behind Chelsea, a spark that grew and opened up, something emerging in its center. The Bus Driver stepped in, joining our group, filling in the space between Deihlia and the machines. I didn't want to look at him this time. I wanted to keep my eyes on Deihlia, because I would never see her again. The breathing machine stopped. The monitors went blank. The room became still and silent.

Deihlia left in a blaze of pink light. The Bus Driver was ready, giant wings sprouted out of his back so that he could carry her across the threshold. Deihlia knew why he was there and pushed his arms away, she wouldn't let him carry her. She wanted to take off on her own, running the tunnel through the realms between the Earth world and the infinite one. So she took off, glancing back at her mom, sister, Auntie, Nana, and Elsa crying around her body in the hospital room. Then she ran and ran, thrilled to have her legs back. It was as if she had reserves of fuel from all of her twenty-nine years of not being able to run propelling her forward now, she was using it all in her sprint back to the source. Her blue cape streamed behind her. She knew where she was going, the terrain was familiar. Death flew next to her; an aerial guard. Things became clearer as she went. She saw herself as a newborn with a lower body cast in the NICU with wires and tubes, her sister as a little girl reaching up to get something for her that she couldn't reach, her mother holding her tight and crying as the surgeon reached over to take her, her Auntie and Nana next to her hospital bed, her father pushing her in the stroller at Disney World, she and LP playing in the front yard in their wizard costumes, Dr. Zee working on her in the operating room, she and her friends running around the neighborhood, at school, in the hospital. She saw back and forward through time to memories she'd forgotten. They came at her like a movie as she continued to run through it. She felt every feeling of every member of her family going through her like a river, but they weren't just pictures, they were people she loved. At first it was a surprise that she could feel them all, and then it wasn't, their feelings became hers. She ran until she saw people on the horizon, and then she ran some more. In the distance, friends and family stood waiting. Not the ones she'd left behind, but others who had gone before her. She could see her dad, children, other adults she didn't recognize but knew were family. She saw a couple of high school and college friends, then their dog Spike and cat Mugsy. She saw their old friend Angie who'd died of cancer twenty years ago stretch out her arms, ready to catch and embrace her as she plunged into the vast web of the after-life.

From Fire to Fire

Donna, Elsa, and I sat in the small funeral home office. We were there because they were handling her cremation. Chris Donley was a handsome Boston Irish guy. The suit, tie and excellent manners couldn't hide the mischievous gleam in his blue eyes. He was good at his job, listening attentively as we told him a bit about Deihlia, about some of her antics and adventures, justifying our decision to hold her service in a venue more appropriate to who she was, the Boston Center for the Arts Cyclorama. A funeral home or church would not have felt right. He laughed out loud, shaking his head. "Pork Chop, huh? I think I like her already. I'm sorry I didn't get to meet her when she was alive."

We talked some more about the logistics of the cremation, the timeline, the container for her remains, intermittently laughing and crying, red-faced. It was hard to think about her mortal suit lying in the hospital morgue, the same hospital where she'd spent what probably added up to several years of her life, recovering from surgery and escaping death. I liked to think she was glad to be free of that suit, free of the pain she experienced constantly in the upper half of her body. Free of the body that didn't match her energy and spirit, but that housed it nonetheless. I didn't think she wanted to die, but I knew that death had been a driving force in her life. So, when it came time to make the leap, she didn't hesitate. Like the cliffs in Hawaii, the trip to Ecuador, the bouncers at the VIP parties, the stairs, escalators, ski slopes and hills she said yes to over and over, I knew that when death opened its door, she looked through quickly, and jumped. I thought a lot about her body as we sat there, planning for it to be cremated. It had been through so much. Donna wiped her eyes as she signed papers.

"Can we get her rods back after the cremation?" I asked, more to Donna than to Mr. Donley. They both turned their heads to look at me. "I'd like to have those rods if I could," I said, choking on my words. To me, the rods were emblematic of Deihlia's resilience and free will. I didn't want them to be tossed in a pile somewhere by a stranger.

Glassy-eyed, my sister nodded at me across a wide river of sorrow. I looked at Mr. Donley. "Please make sure they return her titanium rods with her ashes," I said. He turned back to the form and started to write.

"They were in her back," I said softly, to clarify. He diligently made notes for the crematorium. "Return the metal rods," he said out loud as he scribbled.

Donna looked at me, processing things in her mind, perhaps thinking of Deihlia and all she'd survived. The loss of her was hard to fathom and accept. I'm sure both of us still looked shocked. We were. The small office seemed to shrink as the immensity of Deihlia's removal from this world struck us again, a hole in each of our hearts that grew, filling the room. Elsa reached for us, offering us a line to help bring us back. "I can come with you to pick up her ashes if you'd like," she said.

A week later, Donna went alone to pick up the ashes. I went to her house the next night so we could do some more planning for the service. I asked about Deihlia's ashes, and if they'd returned the rods.

"I got them," she said, lifting a rolled up plastic shopping bag and handing it to me. I began to unravel it, and she turned to me, angry. "They look like medieval torture devices! We never should have let them do that to her," she sobbed.

I stopped opening the bag. "Donna, she chose that surgery herself. She wouldn't have made it to twenty-nine if she hadn't had them put in. You know that," I said gently, trying to remind her of where we were ten years ago. "She would have died at twenty or twenty-one, not twenty-nine." I said. "She wanted to experience life. It really wasn't an option." My sister stood there, anguished, and I felt helpless to comfort her.

I continued to open the bag, reaching my hand in to pull out the metal pieces. In my mind, I'd pictured titanium rods that were silvery and refined, like her wheelchair frame. What I pulled out were rough-hewn, and blackened by fire. The first thing I noticed were the nuts, bolts, and screws that went horizontally through the long center piece that served as her spine support. They were so common looking, every day fasteners used in homes, machines, and vehicles around the world. Then I saw the hooks on the crossbar - two u-shaped hooks, one at each shoulder. The whole thing formed a cross. I was astonished at how unsophisticated it looked, how rough, something a teenager would put together in her father's basement tool shop. I held it in my hands, unable to see clearly how it had worked inside her, and it hurt too much to go any further in imagining. Donna

291

stood nearby, holding a wooden box. Made of cherry wood, it looked like it could hold a magnum of champagne. "I told you," was all she said.

"Her ashes?" I asked, tenderly wrapping the black titanium pieces back inside the bag and placing it on the table.

"Mm-hmm," she said, holding it in her arms like she held Deihlia as a baby, on one hip. "Feel this." I took the box from her. It was much heavier than I expected. Why do we think ashes will be light like dust when they come from bone?

"She got heavy, that kid," she said, opening the latch and using two hands to pull the plastic bag of ashes up to indicate that they were the heaviest part of the box, not the wooden container. I had no words. I just nodded. I knew she was just trying to get through a really, really hard moment. We both were. I held the box as she let the bag slide back inside. The ashes were Deihlia's but they weren't Deihlia. Though I hated that she was gone, I was relieved that the cremation was completed, and that her warrior's body had been returned to something essential and universal.

In fire all things are made new.

Under the Dome

We needed a couple of weeks to pull together a service for Deihlia, a celebration of her life at the Cyclorama. "The Cyclo", as it was referred to, was an old dome-shaped building built in 1870 to house a painting of the battle of Gettysburg. In its time, the painting hung on the walls, forming a circular panorama, kind of a museum or amusement park where visitors could relive the battle. In its current incarnation it served as an art and event space, the antique brick heart of an arts block that had theaters, artist studios, and restaurants. It took me a week to write her eulogy. I knew that her most recent friends and colleagues had no idea what Deihlia had gone through when she was younger - what a miracle her life was. Deihlia didn't explain herself to anyone. She didn't need to, but I was still struggling with grief, shock, and loss. How was I going to get up and comfort everyone when I was a total wreck?

Two nights before the service, I had a dream. It was a dream in comic book style with all the colors and the cartoonish images. I was in it but I could also step outside of it and watch it like a movie, back and forth. In the dream, a superhero infant was born, and it was my job to protect her. The problem? I was no superhero. I was just me, ordinary and faulty. How does an average person protect a superhero? I didn't have time to figure it out. Creatures started flying in, attacking, shooting at the baby, their giant wings flapping black against a grey-blue sky. They swarmed, circling and shooting. I turned around, away from the infant to face the creatures as they zoomed in closer. I pulled out a sword with one hand, swishing it awkwardly in the air. Then I saw and felt a zigzag of energy going from the baby into me, coming in through my back. I was getting my courage from her. She was giving it to me. I held my sword more confidently, fighting the attackers, then woke up. I knew then that I could do it, I still had Deihlia's strength with me.

The day of the service, we arrived at the Cyclorama early to set up, and started in, draping plum table cloths over the folding tables. One table was on the left of the entrance, and another on the right. Chelsea placed collages of photos from Deihlia's life on the table to the right. The table on the left held the box of ashes, Deihlia's trumpet, a giant framed photo of her face that Chelsea had taken at Comic Con. Some flowers. Chelsea set it up, sliding a large cardboard box on the floor, nearer to the table.

"Let's put these on this table. Will you help?" she asked Kai, opening the box.

"What's in there?" I asked.

"Deihl's collection of Simpsons figures. We're going to put them out and ask people to take one as a memento," she said, reaching into the box and pulling out a bright blue and yellow Homer Simpson, placing it on the table.

Kai looked on, dubious, curious, undecided, standing there in his off-white suit and vans, his thick mop of hair. He shrugged his shoulders. "Okay," he said, digging into the box and pulling out a handful of Barts and Lisas, setting them up one by one. We all pitched in for a few minutes, grabbing handfuls of Simpsons characters and placing them gently on the table. I thought of Deihlia as a kid wheeling along Route 140 with LP, Chelsea, and Julia, heading to Reeves to buy another figure and some more Magic cards. I breathed deep, trying not to cry, and saw everyone else doing the same, one plastic figure at a time.

The room filled. The Hot Tamale Brass Band played a few songs, her trumpet teacher Charlie and Harry blew a couple of horn solos for her. I delivered the eulogy. People got up one by one to share their own Deihlia story, her friend in a wheelchair approached the stage and I held the microphone down so he could share his thoughts. Other people clambered up. We were all laughing and crying. I could feel her in the room with us, and then I saw her sitting next to her mother in the front row, smiling, bigger than life. I was so happy to see her! At the end of all the stories, Mitch came to the front of the room in his full Highland dress. Choking back tears, he played Amazing Grace. The bagpipes ripped open what was left of everyone's composure.

Afterwards, we all went to J.J. Foley's, Deihlia's favorite neighborhood joint, a dark Irish pub where locals and cops went after work for a few beers. "She was my soulmate," another one of her friends said to me. It was the ninth time I'd heard it that day. "She was my best friend," "we were soulmates," "knowing her made me who I am today" and "she changed my life" were recurring refrains. I heard it from so many friends from every part of Deihlia's life, her childhood, the Hospital School, teenage years, college, Boston, Albany Street, her job. In every case, it was true.

In the Collections

My sister's way of dealing with Deihlia's death was to clean out her apartment and try to get rid of everything as quickly as possible. She had been in an anti-materialism phase, a period in which she got rid of furniture, bric-a-brac, family heirlooms, and other goods. For the most part, she didn't want to add more to her material plate, plus having the contents of Deihlia's apartment piled up in a spare room at her house was overwhelming. I'd meet her at Deihlia's apartment and we'd go through her things, trying to figure out who we could give things to.

Deihlia had kept everything she'd ever owned - all of her collections: every piece of jewelry someone gave her even if she never wore it, every comic book, her collection of Nike sneakers, the hoodies she wore in college, her cut-off dreads, books she'd read as a teenager, her dad's favorite hat, the body pillow he'd given her one year as a kid, the bird skull she picked up somewhere, her hand bike, her badges from anime, gaming, and comic conventions, her goth make-up, all the jewelry her mom had given her, her college graduation cap, her first laptop with the broken screen that I'd given her, her hand blown glass pipes, the tie-dyed silk skirt I'd worn in my mid-twenties then passed on to her and Chels, her Star Wars cards, her Ganesh tapestry from college, the blouse she wore on her job interview, every piece of art pottery, the racing bike, antique fruit crates, the Star Wars bank I'd given her, my great-grandmother's silver hand mirror, the piece of art from the street artist I'd given her when she was ten, bandanas, signed comic art, t-shirts she'd worn as a teenager, Magic cards, movies, video games, bird's nests.

I was in her room, opening the cigar box I'd given her when she was a kid. I couldn't believe she still had it, but she did. Inside was a magpie assortment of jewelry and little mementos, including the ring I gave her one Christmas. She didn't really wear rings because her hands were always on the wheels and the rings would catch, so it was like new. A little silver band with small crosses encircling it. Deihlia. I slipped it on my finger, wanting to go back in time for a moment, back to the Franklin days.

Donna looked over at me as she went through another box. "She kept everything. Everything! I found a pair of handcuffs under her bed the other day," she said, rolling her eyes, trying to lighten the mood. It was really hard for her, going through her daughter's things -

295

a daughter who had beaten death so many times - but she was doing it, one box at a time. I smiled wanly, unwilling to return from the past, turning the ring on my finger, seeing her and Chelsea at Halloween one year, pre-teens in their black and white costumes. Deihlia was her favorite fantasy character, The Crow, and Chelsea a spooky skunk.

I was in Deihlia's bathroom one of those days, scrubbing it, trying to help clean the place so someone else could move in. It was kind of dirty. Though new, the bathroom had no window and was a bit of a cave. The grout in the floor was grungy. Not terrible, but in need of cleaning. I got down on my hands and knees, scrubbing the floor. I wanted to do it. I cried a little as I pushed the brush across the shower floor, wiping tears on my t-shirt sleeve as I cleaned.

"Thanks, Auntie," I heard her say, as if she was sitting next to me, her wheel at my elbow. I lifted my head, turning to see if I could see her. I know it's a common occurrence after someone dies for people to think they see and hear the deceased. I didn't know if it was her, or just my grief speaking to me. But I wasn't taking any chances. "I love you, Deihl," I said, then turned back and continued scrubbing.

Opening the Gates

Grief is a river, wide and deep. I sought refuge in my meditative practices, where I cleared away the mental clutter so I could just let my feelings be. I sat in the dark each night, remembering things I hadn't thought about in years. Sometimes, the darkness was clear and light, and I was grateful. Not having Deihlia in the world hurt, but the victory of her life gave me comfort, reinforcement.

One night, not long after her death, she appeared in my room.

"I want you to stop crying," she said. "I'm doing great. Better than ever. Look at me!" She stood up out of her chair, changing form from her Pork Chop self, the way she looked when she died, into a tall, long-limbed version of her younger self. Her dreads were back. Her face glowed. Her chair disappeared. I couldn't believe my eyes. Deihlia walked around my bedroom. "This is real life over here, Auntie. Down there, where you are, that's the hard place."

"How can I be sure it's you?" I asked.

"Come on, we always had a strong connection, we could talk about anything."

That was true, but I wanted confirmation. "Sorry, Deihl, but can I have some proof? I'm kind of a mess right now."

She shook her head, then got serious. "You think Chels is doing okay, but she isn't. Stay close to her. I'm worried about her."

Deihlia was right about a few things. She and I could talk about anything. Our conversations were easy and real. There was also so much between us that was understood, without needing to be said.

She was right about Chelsea, too. When I called her and told her what Deihlia told me, she said "She knows me really, really well."

Her visits became more frequent. At first, I thought it was just my grief making them up. I questioned myself. I read back over my journals, where I recorded as many of my experiences with the invisible worlds as I could. Why shouldn't I trust Deihlia, one of the people I loved most? Her comments were never wrong.

"I miss you so much. I hate that you aren't here," I said.

"But I am here. Not the same way, but I can be with everyone at the same time now."

I stayed in touch with some of Deihlia's friends. They too reported having experiences of Deihlia in the afterlife.

"She visited me in a dream last night. She kinda kicked me in the ass and told me that it's time to grow up, let these old hurts go, and get on with my life." Michael said.

LP told me: "I talked to her this morning. She was mad when I went to the psychic to try and connect with her. 'Why did you do that?' she asked, 'We don't need a medium to talk. Come on! It's us.' "

"We lost a dog in the woods. They don't usually survive in there overnight with the coyotes and everything. We went back the next day and asked Deihlia to help us find the dog. Right after that, a group of hawks - yes, hawks who are lone birds - went flying overhead. We followed them into the woods. They landed in some trees and under those trees was the dog, perfectly fine. I know that Deihlia helped."

"I've been missing her real bad. I was happy to see her in my dream but then she chewed me out. Told me I needed to stop messing around and get to it."

Over dinner one evening, Angelina told me that she'd had a dream about Deihlia the night she died. Deihlia wheeled up to her, popping in to say goodbye. Angelina knew immediately what it meant when she saw her and started to cry, bending over to give her a hug and a farewell kiss on the cheek. As Angelina leaned in and got close, Deihlia moved her face, turning it up so that Angelina's kiss landed squarely on her lips. Deihlia! Even in death she was up to her usual tricks, not letting the conditions stop her from going after the experience she wanted.

"Did you really do that?" I asked her when she came to me next.

"I always loved Angelina," she smirked.

"I don't want any of us here to keep you from doing what you need to do," I said. I was worried that she wasn't moving on.

Deihlia shook her head. "Auntie, it's ok. I'm doing what I need to do here, but I can still be with all of you, too. It's my choice. I crossed over just fine. See?" She held out her arms to show me her healed self, her tall self, her spirit body.

"Did you see Pop? Your dad?"

Deihlia nodded somberly. "Oh yeah, I did. And I've met all the family I didn't know. Love my Grandpa! What a guy."

"You're not lonely, then?"

"Nah. Don't worry about that. I had friends waiting for me, too. Friends from when I was little, and a couple others."

Tears sprang to my eyes. She'd lost several friends before she was ten. She'd been through so much, so fast. "The last time I saw you, you were in pain. You were dying and I didn't know it." I began to sob. My bedroom was a blur.

"Auntie that was just my death. It was my time to go. I'd gotten a few extra rounds, remember? But even those run out eventually. You weren't supposed to know. Please stop crying about it. I'm not in pain anymore."

Her death was still so close. It was hard not to cry. "I know it was your death," I choked out. "But it's still hard. I miss you so much. It feels like I'm going to miss you forever. If the situation were reversed, I think you'd be over here crying too."

She looked at me. "Of course I would. But we all die. It's not death that's hard, it's only the dying. You're gonna die too, Auntie. You'll be over here with me soon enough. That's why I want you to stop crying and go out and have some fun! Do what you want to do."

I agreed with her about the shortness of life, and about having fun. But I had something else in mind that I wanted to do, something important. It had been floating around me like a star in the immaterial, sparkling just out of my reach. I wanted to grab it and bring it into this world, it was meant to be here. "I want to write a book about you; about your life. I want the world to know how incredible you are - you and your story."

The room was still. Had she heard me?

Deihlia began to laugh, smiling. "I know you do, Auntie. Don't worry. I'm gonna help you with it."

Afterword

I can't imagine my life without Deihlia. Yet here I am, two years after her death, conversing with her in the afterlife and completing this book. When she passed over, I had to do something with my love for her, and with my immense grief. This book started out as a tribute and testament to Deihlia, but as I wrote it, I realized that our family and her friends were equally important to her story. We were all key players in her adventure. Without her family and friends, Deihlia's mischief and accomplishments would not have been what they were. Though she was the big superhero, in capturing the stories I came to understand that everyone in her life was also a superhero. Being with her brought out our best and most daring qualities, the parts of ourselves we only shared with sacred friends, the parts we weren't always comfortable with, and those we may not have known yet. Somehow, she saw them in us and encouraged their articulation. There was just something about Deihlia that made you drop your guard and step into other parts of yourself, often some of the best parts.

Just as her life story needed all of the players who were part of it, mine very much needed her. For me, meeting Deihlia in the neonatal intensive care unit the day after her birth was the day that I emerged out of a post-traumatic protective haze. I was three weeks shy of turning twenty one. Her life jolted me out of my own suffering and the defenses I'd erected to handle what I'd gone through in my family. Meeting and knowing Deihlia as an infant forced me to face things head on so that I could be stronger for her. It wasn't that I was looking for a reason to break free; when I met her it was simply there. I wanted her to live and thrive, to experience the full expression of being Deihlia. In order to be of any use to her, I had to recover and blossom more myself. I didn't think any of these things consciously at the time, but I felt them, and they became my navigation, along with Deihlia and then Chelsea, my two North Stars.

As Deihlia grew up, she struggled with shyness and being an outsider in elementary and middle school because of her disability. Outside of school, she was the coolest kid in the neighborhood and the center of the Conlyn Avenue gang of kids. She was the goalie in street hockey, the mastermind to mischief, the hub of a playful wheel. She made up for her frustrations by having well-concealed secret lives which her friends were party to, but family wasn't. We'd learn of some of her adventures and escapades when a guilty-feeling friend might let slip that Deihlia almost fell over the side of a cliff, almost drowned in a high tide, or almost got in a fight. Like the best-trained spies, Deihlia's friends hid her secrets in plain sight.

She got over her shyness and got into more trouble in college, becoming the key player in her friend's parties, road trips, skiing weekends, and gaming marathons. If Deihlia was on board for something, then the rest of the gang would follow, so she was always the first person recruited. Back in Boston, she made so many new friends and started a whole new phase of daring. Pork Chop was born, and Deihlia managed her several lives deftly and playfully - work, Boston Social Nerds, her jazz life, family, love life, and others that I don't know about. I was glad to have her back in Boston, and saw her frequently.

I can't imagine how I would've grown up without Deihlia's unconditional love and her deep knowing of me. One of Deihlia's most beautiful qualities was the power of her attention. When we talked, she was fully present, and gave 100% of her listening, her wisdom, and her seeing. Talking to her, I got the feeling you get when you know you're special to someone, that you are someone dear, and deeply known. The truth of it is I was those things to her, but so were all of the other people she called family and friend. We had a special bond, but she had a special bond with many others, too. She made me feel that I was the only one, as she did with everyone else. Deihlia had a capacity for connecting with people that felt expansive and endless. No one was shut out of her club. Everyone was welcome. She forgave easily, too. She didn't try to be that way. She was just like that.

Though her physical disabilities restricted what she could do with her body, Deihlia was the most unlimited person I've ever known. She was aware of what she couldn't do, but those things were like the floor, or the wall, or a table in the middle of the room. She saw them but she saw her destination more acutely. She trained her eyes on where she wanted to go and what she wanted to do, how she got there was the adventure of it. She'd capitalize on serendipity and reel in her friends, her cousin or her sister, me, her mom, or someone else she met along the way. Together, we had the fun of figuring things out and making them happen as we got caught up in the next trajectory.

More than anything, I learned from Deihlia that our connections with other people are the most important part of our journey. Who we love and how we love is our real legacy, it's what we leave behind and what we take with us. Experience, growth, and love – that's why we're here. It would have taken me several lifetimes to grow and learn as much as I did in the past thirty years with Deihlia. Even though we talk all the time, I still miss her terribly. I probably always will. That she still loves and is present for me while doing her thing on the other side is proof I can't deny. She came into this world for a reason, for many reasons. Showing me how it's done is only one of them.

Acknowledgements

Deihlia's superhero friends continue to be a great inspiration. The depth of their love and commitment to Deihlia is extraordinary and beautiful. Their stories became important pieces in this book. Deihlia's life experience and this book would not have become what they are without these people: Mary Beth Collins, Richard D'Arata, Heidi Donaghy, LP Giardino, Zack Grant, Chalkey Horenstein, Beth Kelly, Brian Kelly, Jenn Kyett, Adriana Marcelli, James Melton, Phil Riccardi, Tannya Rivadeneira, Mathew Stucke, Hana Vered, and Reverend Doctor Kenneth Walker. Deihlia had so many great friends and impacted so many lives. While many of her friends are not included in this book, it doesn't mean they weren't important to her adventures – they were! I simply couldn't include everyone and every story here. I included the stories of friends that were shared with me personally by them and by Deihlia.

I have so much appreciation for my writing partners Margaret Cronin and Ronni Olitsky, whose comradery, writing, and support helped to keep me inspired and connected while I wrote this book.

I cannot thank the following people enough, whose generous review, insight, and care helped to shape this story: Margaret Cronin, Elizabeth Gentry, LP Giardino, Thea Hillman, Natalie E. Illum, Laurie Kutchins, Lesa Lessard Pearson, and Hana Vered.

I'm grateful for Paul Gould and his beautiful illustrations, which arose out of our shared vision but which he took to the next level.

Thank you to my editor Mark Stavish for pushing me to give every character their due.

Chelsea Nye is by far the baddest graphic designer, photographer, and photo editor out there. Her talent & heart made the book cover vibrate with energy and love.

I wish to thank Carol Farwell Kelly for dispensing love along with everything else when Deihlia was her student at Baylies preschool at the Massachusetts Hospital School. Carol made a real difference in so many lives.

Thank you too to Artie Barbato and Sam Dechenne for helping Deihlia get more into her jazz life.

I also couldn't have done this without my cosmic team: Deihlia Nye, Nancy Donald, Jenae Nicholson, God/the Universe, and my family and friends on the other side.

Most of all, I have a deep love and appreciation for my family, who supported this book and lived the story: Malackai Cameron, the Cameron's, Chelsea Nye, Deihlia Nye, Donna Nye, Robert (Linc) Nye, Annette & Darrel Hamlet, the Hamlet clan, Blair Easter, Adele & Gary Fraser, LP Giardino, and Sandy and Paul Giardino. Together we've had a profound adventure, I'm glad we've been in it together.

Lastly, I wish to acknowledge Deihlia's surgeon Dr. Zee, her team, and the doctors and nurses at Suffolk Universal Hospital who cared for Deihlia as a child and teen. Without their skill and care, this story would not have happened.

Guide to Illustrations

About the Author

Diane Fraser is a writer and cosmic consultant. She's been writing her whole life, and has been on a spiritual quest just as long. She won several writing prizes in college, was a Stadler Semester for Young Poets fellow at Bucknell University, and was a founding member of a small writing group, *Erograph*, who wrote and did readings together for 12 years. She also studied with three esoteric teachers in the shamanic and hermetic arts, and provides healing services and cosmic insight to clients. This is her first book. She lives in Boston, Massachusetts.

To learn more and connect visit growingupsuperheroes.com.

CPSIA information can be obtained at www.ICGtesting.com
Printed in the USA
BVOW06s1327140715

408749BV00010B/50/P